ONE STRIDE AHEAD

ONE STRIDE AHEAD

An Expert's Guide to Cross-Country Skiing

MARTY HALL

with *Pam Penfold*

Winchester Press

TULSA, OKLAHOMA

Printed in the United States of America

Winchester Press
1421 South Sheridan
P.O. Box 1260
Tulsa, Oklahoma 74101

Library of Congress Cataloging in Publication Data

Hall, Marty.
    One stride ahead.

    Includes bibliographical references and index.
    1. Cross-country skiing. I. Penfold, Pam,
joint author. II. Title.
GV855.3.H34   796.93   80-25129
ISBN 0-87691-331-1

Book design: Susan Trail

1 2 3 4 5   85 84 83 82 81

My greatest inspiration in this and every other project has been my wife, **Kathy.** She has always supported my efforts, encouraged me during any difficulty, and exhibited patient understanding during all the long trips I've had to make over the years. There is no way to thank Kathy adequately for her support, interest, and enthusiasm.

CONTENTS

ACKNOWLEDGMENTS

Much of the information in this book is based on the knowledge I was able to acquire while working with the U.S. team (1969–1978). I had the chance to observe and participate in all the changes on a first-hand basis; I had access to information and knowledgeable people throughout the world. Friends in North America and Europe shared ideas, philosophies, and theories about skiing. Through the years the staff and members of the U.S. team and I could experiment with various theories, test new techniques and equipment, and compare our program with those of other nations. Ideas and information from all over the world were used in developing a viable and successful U.S. program, and I certainly appreciate the longevity as coach I was granted by U.S. team officials.

Many people have been extremely helpful in writing this book. My coauthor, Pam Penfold, deserves a great deal of credit, not only for taking the vast majority of photos for the book but also for taking the often rambling array of information I dictated into a tape recorder, writing it up, and reworking it with me into a readable and organized presentation of cross-country skiing for the expert.

Among the other people who assisted me in writing this book are Chuck Dillman and his assistants on the U.S. team's sports medicine council who were willing to share their information with me. Tony Wise and Tom Kelly at Telemark, Dick Taylor at Devil's Thumb, and the officials at Mont Ste. Anne were very cooperative in letting us use their ski areas in taking many of the photos in the book. Two-time Olympian Doug Peterson contributed his experience, records, and photogenic aptitudes. Promising racer Kate Freeman proved to be an intelligent, helpful editor and critic of the manuscript. Elaine Chatfield was a patient and accurate typist. Josie Ritter provided graphic advice. I'd also like to thank John Fry of *Ski* magazine for his interest and help on the project and Bob Elman of Winchester Press for his friendly and helpful assistance in getting the book published.

FOREWORD

Cross-country skiing has exploded from approximately 100,000 U.S. participants in the early 1970s to between three and five million in the early 1980s. Unfortunately, the number of experts able to disseminate up-to-date information on the sport around our large country has not kept pace with the boom in participants. Communication and media coverage is poor and the majority of the books available are either outdated or too generalized to supply the pertinent and detailed information required by the serious skier.

This book is planned to aid all types of skiers. The ski tourer or mountaineering skier will benefit from the knowledge, physical conditioning, and technical maneuvers used by the top international competitors. In all sports and particularly in cross-country skiing, the newest and most useful theories and techniques are developed among those at the highest levels of competition and gradually filter down to the average and beginning participant. Although this book is geared to the expert and the racer, it will be useful to all skiers.

In my thirty-plus years of skiing, racing, coaching and writing, I've tried to put objectivity into this sport of subjectivity and variables. The athlete doesn't want to be bogged down with extraneous information in his quest to understand his sport, himself, and his program. He needs specific information to obtain the maximum benefits from each hour spent training and racing.

This book reflects the need for specificity and objectivity in cross-country skiing. There is a great deal of information about skiing, physiology and sport that I've chosen not to include because, for one thing, it is available elsewhere and primarily because I want to emphasize the aspects of sport relevant to the skier's efforts to achieve his maximum potential as a cross-country competitor.

The theories, programs, activities and other information presented in this volume are based on my experience in skiing and coaching. It is written as if I were coaching you, the reader. As any coach knows, certain parts of every program must be emphasized and repeated over and over again to the athlete. Therefore, I may seem to be repetitious about subjects such as training logs, stretching, checking your pulse and so forth. This has been done on purpose because these are aspects of training and racing most often ignored or left out of the athlete's regimen.

The goal of this book is to provide you with all the information you need to establish a program, make the best use of your training time and develop the skills, physiological conditioning and mental powers necessary to reach your potential as a cross-country competitor.

If you have the motivation, cross-country racing boils down to one axiom: You'll get out of this sport exactly what you put into it. The dedicated, committed, and hard-working skier is the one who finishes one stride ahead.

Good learning, good laboring, and good luck!

Marty Hall
July, 1980

ONE STRIDE AHEAD

1

CROSS-COUNTRY RACING

Sport's Ultimate Challenge

Cross-country racing involves merely moving from one point to another over the snow with slats attached to your feet and sticks in your hands. What's the challenge in that? After all, it's been said that if you can walk, you can ski.

Don't be fooled by the simplistic statements that float around about cross-country skiing. Skiing well and racing at your potential is complicated, intricate, and above all challenging. If you can walk, you can likely run—but it doesn't mean you can ski.

The challenge of cross-country racing lies in the almost innumerable variables the athlete must overcome to be successful. Not only must the skier master the many complex movements of technique, but he must also be in excellent physical and mental condition to cope with other factors influencing his performance: snow, ski equipment, wax, weather, courses, training, travel, tactics, terrain, pain, health, fear, food, strategy, clothing, et cetera ad infinitum.

The foot runner simply puts on his shoes and runs over a paved, consistent surface. The cross-country skier doesn't have it so easy.

NATURAL AND TANGIBLE VARIABLES

The racer doesn't deal only with the ferocious blizzard that freezes his body and obscures his view of the course. During off-season training he must roller ski in 100-degree temperatures, through rain storms, and into the chill of fall. While under the physical strain of racing and training, the competitor will face every variation of temperature, humidity, wind, and weather. In the winter he'll be racing over terrain that will rise 100 meters over one kilometer, and then he'll have to charge down the other side of the hill using every trick he knows to gain every possible second—and survive. He has to contend with powder snow one race, mashed potatoes the next, and granular snow and solid ice in between. His body must be able to work efficiently at altitudes ranging from sea level to 10,000 feet. But the environment is just one facet of the variables facing the cross-country ski racer.

Although the skier is ultimately dependent only on himself in this individual sport, he

1

The environment creates incredible problems and discomforts for the racer. An icy beard is only a minor distraction.

must first come to grips with tangible variables affecting his performance—his equipment, the course, the wax, his coaching, and the competition.

There have been remarkable advances in ski equipment and in course design and maintenance over the past decade. Today's equipment, from fiberglass skis to wax and even underwear, has combined with better courses and tracks to make our sport more enjoyable and easier. However, these advances have put a great burden on the competitor. The sport scientists and sports medicine people have formulated difficult training programs and technical moves for efficient and powerful skiing. Meanwhile, equipment and well-groomed modern courses encourage higher racing speeds. The competitor must assimilate all the available information, select and care for his sophisticated equipment, train hard with specificity for his sport, and then head out on those speedy courses and do everything possible to be an increasingly efficient and fast skier.

In the old days, the racer trained when he could find time and had only a single pair of skis for racing. He covered the skis with a wax on race day and went out and suffered his way around the narrow, poorly maintained, change-of-direction course. Today, the racer must be a skiing machine, engineer, meteorologist, and chemist. He must select the proper pair of skis and judge the weather and snow conditions to pick the best combinations of wax for his skis so he'll have every possible advantage out on the course.

PHYSICAL AND MENTAL VARIABLES

One of the major appeals and challenges of cross-country racing is the physical demand it makes on the body. The skier must move his body over the snow with technical efficiency and keep at it for hours. He uses every muscle and must be in command of every part of his body. The racer must be a power endurance animal—strong, fast, and able to persist. He must master the demanding and intricate technique, cope with difficult snow conditions, accept the workload of long uphills, and have fast reactions and movements to deal with speeds of up to and over 40 mph. His body must handle the paces of a five-kilometer sprint and a hundred-kilometer marathon.

To satisfy all the demands of ski racing, the competitor must train all year long to adapt

Cross-country racing demands control over the body at high speeds. Bill Koch demonstrates the downhill form that helped him earn an Olympic medal in 1976.

Thomas Wassberg, Olympic gold medalist in the 1980 Games, doesn't take the corner at the 1979 Lake Placid Pre-Olympics with the mastery Bill Koch used. Cross-country racing is always a challenge.

his body specifically to cross-country skiing. He spends much more time training than he does racing. Training tears down the body so it will rebuild stronger and be more oxygen-efficient. To train and ski well, he must know about physiology, diet, health, and rest. He must accept the inevitable illness and injury and know how to find the best medical advice and assistance to overcome such setbacks.

There's a saying among racers: If you ain't hurtin', you ain't goin' fast enough. If we knew how to deal with pain, we'd all be world champions. Pain is individual, and the highly motivated skier knows how to accept the pain resulting from the physical stress of racing. Training teaches him about pain; as he pushes himself harder and harder, he elevates his pain threshold as he elevates his level of conditioning. In time, pain becomes a question of mind over matter.

The best competitors in the world will tell you that cross-country racing develops into more of a mental than a physical test. The top 30 entrants in the Olympics have virtually equal physical and technical abilities. The winner is the skier who pulls every bit of knowledge about skiing together, focuses it on the race, and motivates himself to push to the limits. To achieve this mental state, the skier must overcome all sorts of fear. The dynamic positions of cross-country skiing can create a fear of falling. There is fear of the high speeds and fear of possible injury. The all-encompassing fear of failure can involve everything from falling to disappointing yourself or your peers. All these fears will detract from the skier's ability to focus on the race, which will be reflected in the results.

The skier must overcome any fear in order to give the sport his physical, technical and mental maximum. The best way to dispense with fear is to know everything about cross-country skiing. Read, research, talk to experts, talk to racers, listen to coaches, study films, and learn everything you can. Don't leave anything to chance but know your sport from technique to training, from rules to roller skiing.

Don't look back. Alison Owen charges off after being tagged by Betsy Haines in the 1980 North American Championship relay at Telemark, Wisconsin. She has no fear even though Canada's powerful Firth twins, Sharon and Shirley, are right on her tail.

Learning about skiing is an ongoing process because every aspect of the sport is continually evolving. Keep up on new ski designs, new ways to apply wax, new technical maneuvers, new racing tactics, new training activities. This awareness will make your job easier, put you in control of more of the variables, and speed you to the finish line faster.

Knowledge of the sport will make you a confident and fearless competitor. If you're tuned in to all the aspects of racing and are dedicated in your mental preparations for competition, you'll have no reason to doubt yourself. With knowledge, you reduce the effect of the variables and can be competitive with the less informed but more athletically gifted skier.

Acquiring knowledge of the sport and developing the physical abilities to be an efficient, powerful skier requires motivation, dedication, and commitment. Each individual has his own, unique reasons for committing himself to excellence in cross-country skiing. His motivation will be augmented by external forces such as an enjoyment of the people in the sport and the enthusiasm generated by his coach and teammates.

The individual must decide to commit himself to the challenge of cross-country competition. He must establish his own goals, gain confidence through knowledge, and be physiologically and psychologically prepared and eager to deal successfully with all the variables he faces. He must know himself, know his body, and know his sport.

TAKE UP THE CHALLENGE

The beauty of cross-country racing is that it's an individual sport which appeals to all types of people. Each takes up the challenge for his own personal reasons and interests. The physical fanatic is drawn by conditioning and the opportunity to be outside and active in the winter. The bookworm gets enjoyment from the engineering and chemistry of the equipment and waxing. The physiologist will like the intricacies of technique. The psychologist can learn from his efforts to deal with the variables, the fear, the pain, and the competition.

These intrigued and diverse individuals may then set their own goals as skiers. One 29-year-old may be working to make the Olympic team. Another 29-year-old will challenge himself in short citizen races, while yet another will commit himself to the marathons on the Great American Ski Chase or World Loppet. A fourth 29-year-old will get satisfaction from coaching young skiers in the Bill Koch League. There's something for everyone in cross-country.

There's something for everyone in cross-country skiing, no matter what your age or ability. Here the father and son team of Jack and Tim Armstrong celebrate the completion of the 1978 marathon at Waterville Valley, New Hampshire.

Specificity is the key to success in cross-country racing. The skier can't waste time pursuing extraneous activities and following programs that don't train his body and mind specifically for his sport. Success on the race course is a gradual building process. It takes years of training and racing experience to reach one's potential. Therefore, the beginning or poorly conditioned skier must gradually work his way into training programs. Further, every skier should have a complete physical check-up before engaging in the training and racing program outlined in this book. See a doctor knowledgeable about sport and let him know that you are going to undertake training for the most strenuous and physically demanding sport in the world.

Most often the skier will have little coaching assistance. Because there are few school programs and even fewer ski clubs, the number of qualified coaches available to racers in North America is very limited. Many competitors are self-coached, but the better they get, the more they need a coach who sets up a training and racing program, evaluates the skier's training and technique, times and feeds during a race, provides expertise on racing and waxing, handles logistical problems, and helps motivate the athlete.

The skier who wants to compete now faces a choice. Not long ago, if he raced he would be competing against the best in the country because the limited number of skiers meant there was only one echelon of racing. Now programs are developing for all ages and levels of ability and interest. Ski competition has become a life-long activity because of the diversity of racing programs.

Through competition, the racer discovers his true self. A good race mirrors the challenges in life. The skier must deal with difficulties and variables, overcome them, and work on to the finish line.

Racing is the ultimate test of your skills as a skier. Many tour skiers who enter citizen races insist they don't compete, but everyone ends up competing. You either race against the leaders or someone you've skied with most of the distance. The challenge is in skiing to your potential, regardless of the order of finish. Although there are other skiers listed on the results, the racer is in essence only competing against himself, testing his ability to achieve his potential. Every race finished is a victory over yourself—you are always a winner.

2

OFF-SEASON TRAINING

Education, Motivation, and Specificity

In 1978, Bob Treadwell, then a 23-year-old member of the U.S. World Championship Team, was in Sweden for a series of races. During his stay, he talked with several of Sweden's better junior skiers who were 18 and 19 years old. When Bob asked them how much training they'd done over the past year, they replied they had accumulated 7,000 kilometers. Four and five years their senior, Bob had trained 5,000 km that year. Needless to say, the Swedish juniors were ahead of Bob in the results on race day.

I relate this story to indicate that cross-country skiing is a very young sport in North America. Although the first U.S. National Championships were held for men back in 1907, our sport didn't begin to achieve any real growth until 1974. More cross-country skis were imported to the U.S. in 1974 than there were American skiers during the previous 20 years.

It wasn't until the 1970s that the U.S. began making strides toward catching up with the racing traditions and knowledge of the Europeans and Soviets. We continue in a transition period of growth in numbers of participants and in skier education and expertise. But we head into the 1980s well on our way to catching up. We are developing a foundation of expertise and have an ever-increasing number of athletes motivated and able to handle the volume of training and the racing effort required to be internationally competitive. Most important, U.S. skiers are learning how to train for cross-country ski racing.

The backbone of a training program is commitment. The challenge and enjoyment of sport lies in seeking to achieve one's maximum potential. Personal commitment is the only way to reach that potential. The main thrust of the cross-country skier's commitment must be to a solid and progressive training program.

Race results are in direct proportion to the athlete's level of training.

Adolf Kuss, *1972 U.S. Olympic Nordic Combined Coach*

As Dolf Kuss' axiom indicates, natural ability is not the key to cross-country success. The athlete is born with a certain level of natural ability. Coordination, balance, reaction time, speed of movement, and agility may be refined through training. Beyond refinements, the athlete has little control over his natural ability.

6

The control factor for success in cross-country skiing is physical conditioning. The skier must combine a finely tuned body with his natural ability to reach his potential. Other sports aren't quite as demanding. I play a lot of baseball in the summer. Although I don't train for baseball, I have a certain amount of success playing. This can be traced to natural ability. I can't, however, enter a citizen cross-country race and expect to have the same amount of success from my natural abilities. I'll do well in a ski race only if I am in shape for skiing and have trained specifically for the sport.

Cross-country is a highly technical sport. Without an off-season training program, the skier's race results will be disappointing. Further, he will actually have trouble skiing. Today's equipment and techniques demand a physical conditioning base. Even U.S. Cross-Country Team members can't just go out and tool around on their fiberglass skis; they must be in shape to take advantage of the most efficient techniques, use the most appropriate skis and waxes for the conditions, and handle the difficulties encountered on modern courses. There are no shortcuts to success in cross-country racing. The only route is hard work. You can't depend on your teammates, your coach, or your natural ability. You will get out of cross-country skiing exactly what *you* put into it.

We all begin at ground zero. There was a time when Olympic medalists Bill Koch and Juha Mieto couldn't ski a kilometer or do 20 sit-ups. They attained world-class levels only through many years of hard training. Reaching your potential is a progressive, gradual process. International competitors will tell you that it takes a minimum of five years of hard training to approach high levels of conditioning. This five years comes on top of whatever club or school programs they were involved in before initiating a serious training program.

Fortunately, the dramatic evolution in cross-country skiing over the past decade has included new theories and knowledge about training which have led to more rapid development of skiers. The keys to success are now motivation and education. The athlete must establish his goals and know how to train himself to reach his potential without wasting time and energy on extraneous conditioning methods which don't adapt his body to his sport. It took time for skiers to recognize that they must train all year long to reach their potential. Now this is an accepted fact. As the evolution continues, skiers accept the fact that their training must be geared specifically to the requirements of their sport—training methods must mimic or simulate skiing and its demands.

Modern training programs are no longer hit-and-miss propositions. Specific training activities such as roller skiing and strength training have been developed which allow us to maximize gains from time spent training. Each workout is designed to adapt the body to the demands of skiing. Even if we don't have as much time to train as national team members do, we know we can get maximum benefit out of a single hour of work if we train with specificity. In the old days, skiers would run or bike to train. Now they roller ski, ski hike with poles, and work to condition the *entire body* for skiing movements.

Training must be based on the physical, technical and psychological requirements of cross-country racing. First and foremost, the racer is an oxygen-consuming animal. He must be able to take in oxygen and move it around his body to fuel his muscles. In other words, the racer must be cardiovascularly conditioned. Cross-country is an endurance sport; the skier must be able to persist in physical activity and resist fatigue.

Further, cross-country is a power sport. The velocity with which a skier propels himself down the track is a function of stride length. A long stride depends on power, the ability to move fast or explosively. Today's racers are skiing faster and faster because they are stronger. They are conditioned to the point where they can fully utilize the dynamic position of modern techniques.

In sum, the cross-country skier is an animal of power endurance. Current technique, equipment, and courses demand that the racer possess endurance combined with strength so he can make strong movements and push harder and faster for longer periods of time. His total body must be trained and adapted specifically for his sport.

The first step is to evaluate your current physical status and background (an extensive physical examination by a doctor is recommended). Based on your conditioning level and motivation, you can establish some realistic goals. Decide whether you want to be the next Oddvar Braa or Galina Kulakova or whether you're trying to win your age class in next season's citizen races. Next, develop a solid training program that will put you on the track to reaching your potential. Determine where to plug yourself into the volume for each of the various activities. If you don't have a coach to help in this evaluation, experiment to see what your body can handle. Start a training log immediately—it's the only way to evaluate accurately your program and how your body reacts to it. Through time and evaluation, you will develop a program suited to your needs and goals.

People are always looking for secrets to success in this sport. The truth is that there are none. It's not what you ate the night before the race that will earn you a gold medal, but what you did to prepare in June and July for the past five years. You have to fill the gas tank—build a physiological conditioning base—or you'll run out of gas without achieving your potential or your goals.

Dolf Kuss used to pose the following question: Is training endless, boring repetition, or is it boring, endless repetition? Any successful athlete can find some truth in the question, but the drudgery of conditioning is outweighed by the setting where you train, the atmosphere inherent to the sport, the people involved in the sport, and by cross-country skiing itself. Each day is a new challenge. Training isn't boring or endless if you accept the challenge.

PRINCIPLES OF TRAINING

A good training program tells you what to do and when to do it. Education about sport will put the athlete's motivation to his best advantage. The athlete (and coach) must be educated in the principles of training for cross-country skiing. This is an ongoing education based on the unique facets of the sport and the five basic tenets of training for a power endurance activity: specificity, duration, intensity, load, and frequency.

Specificity. Specificity is performing activities in training which best simulate the demands of cross-country skiing. The advent of roller skis has been perhaps the biggest step forward in specificity training, and the progress continues. In 1979 skiers learned from the sports medicine experts that once-accepted training by running and biking can actually have a detraining effect because the workload and technical application are not adequate preparation for skiing. Ski running with poles, for example, vastly improves the quality of a running workout because the athlete is using his entire body, coordinating his upper and lower body movements and training his body to accept the workloads necessary to compete successfully in the winter. Few of us are on a national team and training full-time for skiing, so specificity is particularly important. We simply can't afford to waste training time biking or running when we can benefit so much more from roller skiing or ski hiking.

Specificity will benefit the skier technically, physiologically, and psychologically. The goal of training is to adapt both the body and the mind to the demands of ski racing. In planning and evaluating your program, it is important that all three aspects of specificity be involved in your training throughout the year.

Technical specificity means that your training should include activities which involve movements related to skiing. Through roller skiing, ski walking with poles, and other specific activities, you can prepare your body for the movements of skiing. Give your body muscle memory and nerve knowledge—a trained awareness of the proper moves ingrained through repetition of those moves. Through training, patterns of movement are stored in the brain and the body repeats them under specific stimulus. Unless the patterns are nearly identical, there is little carry-over of skill, speed, or reaction time between different movements.

For example, a left-handed person can't throw a ball well with his right arm, even if that arm is as strong as his left, because the muscles in the right arm have not been trained in the pattern of the throwing movement. Specific activities allow the skier to improve his technique during dryland training.

Physiological specificity readies your body to accept the stress and effort of skiing. Knowing the physical demands of the sport, you design a training program to include those types of activities that develop a physiological conditioning base which will make successful ski competition possible.

The psychological benefits from a specific training program should not be ignored, although they often are. Training prepares the body for competition and teaches the brain to deal with the stress, discomfort, and pain that are a part of cross-country racing. The Olympic medalist is constantly dealing with total body pain during a winning effort; he is

Off-season training must emphasize the use of proper skiing technique through specificity of training methods. Compare the body position of the athlete in dryland training with the skier in the photo at right.

Muscle memory gained through specific off-season training will develop patterns of movement to perfect the racer's ski technique. This photo was taken six months after the photo on the left, and the body position is virtually identical.

feeling his way along the tracks, determining how hard he can push himself. He knows from pushing himself while training just what he can tolerate. The leading international competitors share an almost equal level of physical conditioning and technical skill. The winner is the athlete who can pull all his capabilities together on race day and deal with the pain of competition, which is greatly a psychological feat. Mental training lets your brain know exactly what will be demanded of your body technically and physiologically so you can best handle the various demands of cross-country competition.

Duration. Duration is the amount of time spent in each workout or in each repetition necessary to achieve the goals of the training session. The required time will vary a great deal depending on the purpose of the activity—endurance, speed, strength. An endurance workout is by its very nature much longer than an interval workout. As the athlete's conditioning improves, the duration of each type of workout will increase. Thus, a September training session will be longer than a May session because the improved physiological base will require increased workloads to make conditioning gains.

Cross-country skiing is an individual sport and this fact carries over into training. One athlete can't expect to accomplish the same goals as another in an equal amount of time. The duration necessary for each athlete's workout is determined by his physical conditioning base and his individual goals for the training session.

Intensity. Intensity is the speed of movement or rate at which each workout or activity is conducted. The level of intensity will vary according to the methods of training because each level of intensity emphasizes benefits to certain physiological areas. For example, when lifting weights to build strength, the pace of the movements is relatively slow, but when lifting to build explosive power, lighter weights are used to allow for quicker movements.

The intensity of endurance and interval workouts is controlled by pulse rate. As in other aspects of training, determining the level of intensity to accomplish the goal of the workout depends on the conditioning level of each athlete. A beginning racer can certainly not be expected to hill run at the same pace as a better-conditioned skier. He must establish his own pace determined by his conditioning base. This pace will vary between workouts and will increase overall as his conditioning level improves.

The athlete should regulate his training by becoming aware of the effects various levels of intensity have on his body. Determine the lengths of the training loops you normally use and then time yourself over those loops during each workout. This way you can keep track of your pace and determine the level of intensity of each workout.

Load. Load is the resistance involved in an activity which determines the amount of effort required to complete the work. A productive workout will often involve a greater load than will be required while skiing. Overloading trains the body to function at optimum levels throughout a race by having the body work against greater resistance during training. For this reason, skiers will lift heavy weights and pull an Exer-Genie with greater resistance than the load involved in poling while skiing. This overload enhances the body's ability to handle the physical load of skiing. On the other hand, some training methods require lighter loads in order to emphasize improvement in speed of movement. An interval workout on the Exer-Genie will involve less resistance than that of a strength workout.

Load or resistance can be varied to fit individual needs in most training activities. In skiing, running, and roller skiing, the amount of vertical in the terrain will determine the load; the length and steepness of uphills used in training may be greater than what you'll face in competition. You may also add load by wearing a weighted pack while training, by limiting the recovery time between repetitions and by increasing the pace or intensity of the workout. In strength training, load is increased by adding more weight, such as doing sit-ups on an inclined plane while holding a weight behind your head. Again, the individual must determine his level of conditioning when planning load into his workouts. The goal is to load his body beyond the level required in skiing without causing undue stress.

Frequency. The tenet of frequency determines how many repetitions should be involved in a workout, how often to do a particular workout each week, and the amount of training time spent on certain activities during different times of the year. The athlete should be aware of the percentage of his training that is spent on each type of activity so that his training is appropriate for the time of the year. You won't, for example, be doing as much interval work in June as you do in October, and strength training will have a different emphasis in the off-season than it has in the winter.

Specificity, duration, intensity, load, and frequency—the five tenets of training—must be involved in the athlete's program throughout the year. A successful training session may not include all five tenets, but the athlete should evaluate each workout to be certain that the five tenets of training are involved in his overall program so that he is meeting the goal of adapting his body and mind to cross-country skiing through a balanced program.

Let's take one workout and see how the tenets apply. In hill running with poles, the three facets of specificity are in play; you can work on technical movements, simulate the physiological effort of skiing, and there is a psychological relationship between what you ask of yourself on the race course and what you're trying to accomplish during the workout. During the workout you may run up the hill five times with a predetermined time for each repetition. The frequency tenet comes with the five repetitions and how often you do this training activity. The workout is interval training and, therefore, is primarily involved with a high level of intensity. Because you are using your whole body and due to the effort of running up the hill at a certain pace, you are pushing your body and training it to accept ever-increasing effort. Load comes from the resistance of running uphill. Duration is the time it takes to complete the workout.

In developing a productive training program, the athlete must determine the purpose and usefulness of each activity. Is the workout planned primarily to train for speed, strength, or endurance? The impact of each of the five tenets of training on the activity will determine its benefit.

The Training Effect Zone

Part of the competitor's job is understanding how his body works and what is required to improve its level of conditioning. During a cross-country race, your body is working to supply oxygen to the muscles. Two systems are at work in this delivery process. The central circulatory system takes in oxygen through the lungs to the heart and delivers it throughout the body. The peripheral system transfers the oxygen from the blood to the muscles. The cross-country skier trains to develop efficiency in both these systems to enhance his body's ability to maintain a maximum level of oxygen uptake and usage for extended periods of time. Although maximum oxygen uptake is limited by the individual's genetic makeup, proper training will improve the body's ability to utilize oxygen.

During the greatest portion of a race, your body is in a submaximal, aerobic state.

When aerobic, your oxygen delivery system, particularly the peripheral system, is supplying enough oxygen to the muscles to meet their demands. With sufficient amounts of oxygen, the muscles can efficiently and completely burn glycogen, the fuel for muscle function.

At other times during a race, your body is under stress. A steep uphill or a sprint to the finish line may create a demand for more oxygen than your central cardiovascular system can supply to your muscles. This is known as the anaerobic state, in which your muscles function in an oxygen debt. Without sufficient oxygen, glycogen is inefficiently utilized, resulting in a buildup of lactic acid. This concentration of lactates causes pain, is perceived as muscle fatigue, and impedes the muscle's ability to work. The goal of your training is to improve your body's efficiency when it is in both aerobic and anaerobic states. By training in each of these states, the body gains this efficiency and is able to accept progressively heavier workloads.

Aerobic training is endurance training in which the body's steady demand for oxygen is being met. Training aerobically improves the body's peripheral circulation efficiency so that the muscle fuels are burned completely, thereby delaying the onset of lactic acid buildup and fatigue. Aerobic training also increases the muscles' ability to store glycogen and the rate at which oxygen is transferred from the bloodstream to the muscles. As your aerobic conditioning progresses, oxygen use by the muscles becomes more efficient so the heart rate and muscle fatigue caused by a workload are decreased.

As you train more intensely, your body moves into an anaerobic state where it learns to function more efficiently without oxygen. Intense effort forces the central cardiovascular system to work harder, training it to accept heavier loads. Anaerobic training enhances the muscles' ability to store fuels so they can make strong movements readily. Intense training increases the rate at which the muscle fuels are used so the muscles can move with speed. It also raises the muscles' tolerance to lactic acid buildup so they can function for longer periods of time without fatigue. Simply put, anaerobic training, such as interval workouts, will increase the body's ability to handle the stress of rapid, strong movements.

After extended periods of effort, the muscles will shift to a secondary, and less efficient, fuel system. The muscles have used up their supply of glycogen and begin to use fat as fuel. The muscles can continue to function with this fuel system, but in time, because it is inefficient, movement will become painful and coordination will become difficult. This state is commonly known as "hitting the wall."

The power and energy expended in anaerobic exercise requires that the body be given time to recover and refuel. When the intensity is decreased, oxygen can pump through the system to remove the lactic acid that has built up in the muscles. Light jogging and stretching will encourage this circulation and removal. Restoring the burned glycogen after intense muscle use requires two days of carbohydrate intake. Commercial glucose and electrolyte replacement fluids will prevent dehydration and exhaustion during and after a workout.

Cross-country competition requires both aerobic and anaerobic efficiency. Therefore, your training program must include the proper balance of endurance and intensity work. Aerobic training allows you to ski for longer periods without succumbing to fatigue: Anaerobic conditioning increases the amount of work you can do so you can undergo more stress at faster paces without collapsing or hitting the wall. A good training program will gradually enhance both your aerobic and anaerobic efficiency, which means your physiological conditioning base improves.

TEZ—Determining Aerobic and Anaerobic States

The intensity of an individual's activity may be delineated into anaerobic and aerobic states according to how his age and conditioning level affect his heartbeat and pulse rate. An aerobic state is known among athletes and physiologists as the training effect zone, or TEZ. The training effect zone varies with each individual and will move upward as his conditioning improves.

In *Physiology of Fitness*, Brian J. Sharkey, a Ph.D. in exercise physiology at the University of Montana, developed guidelines to determine the athlete's TEZ and anaerobic threshold. Chart 1 outlines the average training zones for adults based on their age, level of conditioning, and maximum heart rate. As the dotted lines indicate, a 25-year-old skier on the middle of the hill of conditioning will be in his training effect zone if his pulse rate is between 150 and 160 beats per minute. To determine your training zone, evaluate the level of your conditioning and your age, then check the chart for the heart rate range for your TEZ. You may also use the self-evaluation testing program described later in this chapter to determine if your conditioning level is at the top, middle or bottom of the hill.

Regarding heart rates, women will average about five beats a minute faster than men, because women generally have a smaller heart size. Sharkey indicates that the maximum

CHART 1
Training Effect Zone Guidelines

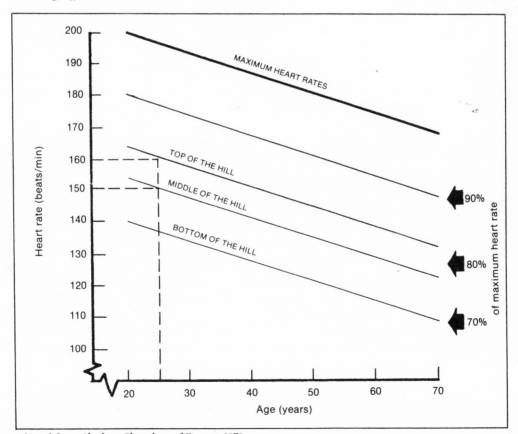

Adapted from: Sharkey, *Physiology of Fitness*, 1979

CHART 2
The Training Effect Zone (Sharkey)

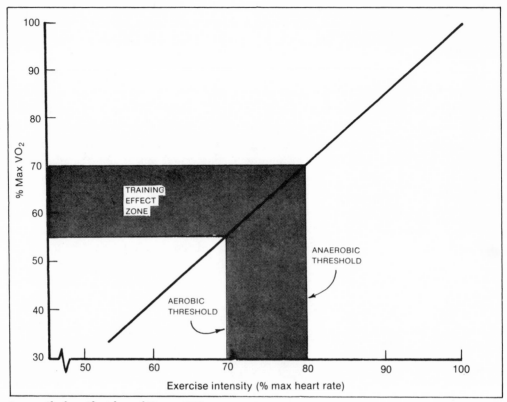

Source: Sharkey, *Physiology of Fitness,* 1979 .

possible heart rate is 200 beats per minute. Many athletes often train anaerobically beyond these assumed maximums, indicating that more research is necessary in defining maximum heart rates.

Sharkey further defines the training effect zone as to the percentage of the athlete's maximum volume of oxygen uptake (mVO_2) as it relates to the intensity of his activity—the percentage of his maximum heart rate he achieves during exercise. Chart 2 was developed by Sharkey to define the effects of various levels of exercise (determined by heart rate) on the cardiovascular system (oxygen usage efficiency, mVO_2). To achieve an aerobic state in training, your heart must be beating between 70% and 80% of its maximum rate. As the athlete's heart rate approaches 80%, his body moves toward an anaerobic state. Therefore, when your heart rate is at or above the upper limits of your training effect zone, you are anaerobic.

When training, you will predetermine the purpose of your activity and know whether you should be aerobic or anaerobic. Your pulse rate will tell you if you are within the desired state. An awareness of your training effect zone is essential to a controlled training program. You will be able to plan a better balance of training activities when you know the effects of training in your aerobic and anaerobic states.

Effective training means that you must be aware of your pulse rate so that you know the

Cross-country skiers are using devices such as the heart monitor to control their training activities and racing pulse rates. Even if you don't have this sophisticated device, stop and check your pulse routinely during training.

state of your body. Some athletes use devices known as heart monitors to check their pulse but it is easy to do this without such a device.

A good training program will gradually raise the level of your conditioning base, which means that your training effect zone will move up—you'll be able to train with a higher pulse rate without reaching your anaerobic threshold. Your training methods must be adjusted as TEZ rises in order to continue improving your conditioning.

Also keep in mind that the break between aerobic and anaerobic states is not this distinct. Training at the upper levels of your TEZ will improve both your aerobic and anaerobic efficiency. The two states cannot be divorced, just as both the central and peripheral cardiovascular systems are continually functioning. Your physiological state during exercise will merely change in emphasis as you train with varying intensity.

Additional Training Guidelines

In addition to the five tenets of training and a knowledge of aerobic and anaerobic fitness, there are several other factors to be considered in planning long-term and day-to-day training programs. Concern for these principles and a bit of common sense will lead to a successful training program in which injury, illness, and disappointment are held to a minimum.

Progression. Skiers, particularly those just entering a serious training program, should be careful not to set training goals that are too high for their level of conditioning. All athletes must recognize that getting into shape is a progressive project. Bill Koch and Tim Caldwell have been training for skiing since they were in their early teens. Other skiers can't expect to reach Koch and Caldwell's levels of conditioning overnight within a year. To be successful internationally, men must train between 8,000 and 10,000 km (4,800 to 6,000 miles) each year. On the other hand, a high school skier or beginning racer might train 2,000 to 3,000 km annually. It will be several years before the inexperienced skier can handle the loads of the international greats.

Getting in shape takes time, patience, and hard work. The new athlete must not play around with the upper levels of his conditioning because he is highly prone to disappointment and discouragement, if not physical breakdowns. Be realistic. Don't run yourself into the ground before you've established years of a training base. Only the experienced and well-conditioned athletes can push themselves to their limits and beyond without fear of long-lasting negative effects. But every skier can make gains through a well planned program. A successful training program allows the athlete to improve his conditioning level progressively from week to week and from year to year.

Hard and Easy. As a rule of thumb, a hard workout should be followed by a relatively easy workout. During physically demanding training, such as intervals or long endurance work, the body is put under a great deal of stress. The muscles are strained and sometimes are mildly injured, requiring time for recovery.

A training program should be designed to allow for recovery. This certainly doesn't mean you have to take a complete rest the day after a hard workout. You can plan your time and alternate types of activity—go ski walking the day after a strenuous session of weight lifting. I often plan my athletes' program so that they have a hard workout in the morning, take the afternoon and the next morning off, then train in the afternoon. This way they train both days and they know they're staying abreast of their training program. Actually they have had a full day off between hard sessions. The trick is to balance high-intensity workouts against low-intensity training to allow for recovery.

Europeans carry this hard/easy concept into a long-range program. If they train eight hours in week one, they train nine hours in week two and ten hours in week three. During the fourth week they return to nine hours and progress by one hour a week for two more weeks and then drop back one hour in the eighth week. This progression continues through the off-season so every fourth week is somewhat of a rest and recovery week. The Finns used this program successfully in the 1970s. Another program would be to alternate hard and easy weeks of training by varying the training hours each week.

Positive and Negative. The nature of each workout may be defined in positive and negative terms. In negative workouts, you feel totally wasted, both mentally and physically, at the end of the session due to the intensity, duration, and/or load involved. Strength training normally falls into the category of a negative workout due to the physiological goals of strength work.

The majority of other types of workouts should be positive; you feel as if you still have a bit left to give at the end of a session. This leaves you ready to face the next day's workout. Many athletes and their coaches are in such a hurry to improve the conditioning base that they end up with too many negative workouts. A constant diet of negative workouts can overtrain the athlete and destroy his enthusiasm for training and his sport. He ends up being a work horse, not a race horse.

Balance. A balanced training program can only be achieved by involving all facets of training to your program all year long. Your conditioning base is improved only if both endurance and intensity work are involved all the time. This is not to say, however, that the emphasis on each activity is equal throughout the year. More time is spent on endurance in the early off-season and then on intensity during the late off-season, but a percentage of each week's training should include all facets of conditioning work.

Warm Up. In order to prepare for a race or a workout and avoid the potential of injury, you must first warm up. When your body is warm, the chemicals and mechanisms associated with muscle function, blood flow, oxygen availability, and reflex timing are activated. Once you've worked up a sweat and your muscles are loose, your body is ready to function and is less subject to injuries, such as torn muscle fibers.

One way to warm up is to run a mile at an easy pace and do stretching exercises. I prefer warming up by gradually working into the activity planned for the workout. If I'm going to ski run, for example, I jog easily with my poles, do some stretching, run a bit harder, and stretch again. Then I know I'm ready for the workout and haven't wasted my time doing nonspecific exercises. I've warmed up the muscles I'll be using during the workout.

Warm Down. Cooling off after a workout is very important to your body. It's always bothered me when athletes take off immediately after a training session, because it's the best time to prevent injury and get ready for the next workout. You should do everything you can to enhance the body's ability to recover from the stress of a workout.

By stretching and jogging easily after your workout, you keep your peripheral circulation moving, allowing your bloodstream to remove lactic acids that have built up in your muscles. This avoids sore and stiff muscles. Stretching after a workout is also the best time to effect complete flexibility because you can gain the most benefits from stretching when the muscles are warm. Spend 10–20 minutes jogging and stretching after each workout.

The warm down is also a good time to recap your workout. Talk with your coach or fellow skiers while you warm down, evaluate the workout, and determine the comments and reactions you will write in your training log. The warm down period is a good time to find out more about yourself, your training and your body.

Dress Properly. Proper clothing is another way to avoid training injuries, sickness, and soreness. Change out of wet clothing immediately after your warm down. Physical problems are often caused by shocking the body—getting cold after a strenuous workout. Always take dry clothing along for a change after a workout and bring along a jacket or warm-up suit if the weather merits it.

The athlete must be prepared for weather changes while training. There is no such thing as bad weather, just bad clothes. A jacket or a rain suit is a must on an extended workout. Getting caught on the top of a windy ridge during a long ski hike is bad news unless you have the proper clothing. During cold weather, it's smart to wear the new polypropylene underwear with its wicking effect that draws sweat away from the body and keeps you warm and dry. The underwear is form-fitting and stretchy, so it's comfortable for training.

Just as in distance races and marathons, I advise skiers to wear a fanny pack during distance workouts. The pack won't hamper training but could help avoid a lot of discomfort. It should contain a rain suit, feed bottles with water, ERG, or Gatorade, a roll of fiberglass tape to repair a broken pole strap, toilet paper, and some money in case the skier gets stranded or needs to buy some food. If roller skiing, the fanny pack should also contain an extra binding and tools to repair any equipment damage. Having a fanny pack on a long roller ski or run can save a lot of aggravation and help ensure a good workout.

Rest. Rest is a fact of life every day of your training. It is necessary in keeping a positive frame of mind and in maintaining a healthy body. Lack of proper rest is the quickest way to get sick. Rest is particularly important for the athlete who is increasing his training load. If he is progressing from one to two workouts a day, a nap between sessions will pay dividends in his body's ability to handle the work and recover. And resting doesn't mean going out and lying in the sun, which saps energy rather than restoring it. Rest means hitting the sack, even if only for 45 minutes.

The athlete in training must have a consistent lifestyle, which includes plenty of rest and full nights of sleep. Skiers in school often find that lack of rest is their downfall. They can't go to bed at 9:00 one night and then stay up studying until 2:00 A.M. the next. The discipline necessary to the sport must be carried into the athlete's lifestyle. His life should be regulated to include adequate rest, or the shocks of an uncontrolled lifestyle will mow down his body.

One way to calculate how much rest your body needs is to check your training logs. See what kind of patterns have developed when you've varied your program. Did you feel better when you trained four days straight and took one day off, or when you alternated morning and afternoon workouts to work in a day off without actually missing a daily workout? Your log should help you determine the best regimen for you.

The important thing is not to become a slave to your training log. Many younger athletes feel they have to record a workout every day and wind up not taking enough time off. Then they wonder why they have no spark for that important race.

PLANNING YOUR PROGRAM

Athletes are goal oriented. They know what they want to accomplish. The successful athlete establishes realistic goals and then systematically pursues them by carefully planning a training and competition program. Developing a good training program is one of your most important tasks as a cross-country competitor. A haphazard program will get you nowhere; an intelligently planned program is an essential aspect of accomplishing your goals. Planning places each and every activity in perspective so the athlete has a concrete and progressive program to achieve the utmost from himself in competition.

The skier should establish his goals for the coming year in April, just after the racing season winds up. He will develop a plan of training and racing based on his objectives and his background. This annual program will then be broken down into monthly, weekly, and daily goals.

Some coaches would argue that you can't plan each day of the athlete's year. I disagree, because I believe it's important for the athlete to have specific objectives for the day, the week, the month, and the entire season. The program is designed for each individual's needs and goals and is the guideline which carries him through the year. By having a plan and following it as closely as possible, the athlete can objectively evaluate his season, learn from mistakes, improve his training, and control his competitive efforts to his best advantage.

The first step in planning a program is evaluating your current physical status. If you're just starting out on an extensive conditioning program, it is imperative that you undergo a complete physical examination by a physician. Let the doctor know that you will be training for the most demanding sport in the world. The exam will give you a concept of where you stand physiologically and what your strengths and weaknesses are.

Evaluate what you've been doing athletically for the past three to five years. The racer will know simply by studying his training logs. The skier just entering a serious program will have to try to recall exactly how much and what type of activity he's had in recent years. This is a time-consuming effort, but you'll be surprised how much you know about your activities. Your goal is to determine the volume of training you had in past seasons because it is the base from which you will develop your training program for the next year.

Once you have a fair idea of where you've been and where you stand physiologically, start figuring what you want to accomplish in the next year. A training volume figure will be based on your self-evaluation and on how much time you have to train. A good program will give you the maximum benefit from each available hour of training time.

To determine the volume of training for the coming year, I prefer to use kilometer, rather than hourly, figures. As a general rule of thumb, a beginning racer will increase his training volume by 10% from one year to the next. For example, if he covered 1,500 km in his 1979–1980 season, he will set a goal of 1,650 km for 1980–1981. The figure of 10% for a beginner's annual volume increase evolved over the years from studies of what type of increases athletes can physically handle. It was determined that the more years an athlete has been in training, the larger the volume increases his body can stand.

Beginning racers too often overextend themselves in their rush to reach the top. The athlete must have a controlled rate of progress to avoid overtraining. Too tough a program will lead to injuries, illness, and continuous breakdowns. Most importantly, the athlete's motivation can be destroyed by overworking his body. A 10% increase in training volume will keep the beginning racer on a program of progressive improvement of his physiological conditioning base without overburdening his physical capacities.

After two or three years of 10% increases, the athlete has established a physiological base and can handle a 15%–20% annual increase in training volume. This rate of increase may continue annually until the athlete reaches what is considered optimum volume. International competitors eventually reach a level where they either hold steady on their training volume or actually decrease it, while increasing the quality and intensity of their training. For men at the international level, this means between 8,000 and 10,000 km each year and 7,000 to 8,000 for women. Not many of us reach this optimum level.

The concern in planning a program is that it be progressive; each year, as your body develops a conditioning base, you add to that base by increasing the volume and quality of your training. The person who trained 2,500 km each year for five years will be hard pressed to equal the race results of the athlete on a progressive program who has increased his training load gradually from 1,500 to 4,000 km over that same period. A 10% or 20% increase may seem like a lot until you break it down to a daily basis, and it might mean an additional 15 minutes of training time a day when spread out over the year.

At some point, of course, the age factor will begin to limit our training volume capabilities. Progress may be defined by being able to handle the same volumes at age 50 that you did when you were 40. As you get older, you will need to monitor your training as carefully as the international stars. You will need to be aware of how to treat your body, because you won't be as flexible nor able to take the pounding you did when you were 25. The more specific your training, the easier it is on your body; roller skiing, for example, is a lot kinder to joints than running. Training and aging is an individual concern.

Once you establish a training volume goal for the year, you can get down to the meat of planning your program. Begin by dividing up your winter and off-season volume based on a fifty-fifty breakdown between on-snow and dry-land activities. This split is a very rough guideline and will certainly vary from skier to skier. But, in general, 50% of your volume will come in the winter months (November through April) and 50% in the off-season (May through October). Thus, if your annual volume goal is 4,000 km, you can plan roughly 2,000 and maybe up to 2,200 km of dryland training.

The next step is to establish a month-by-month program for the off-season. This program is progressive, gradually preparing your body for winter through calculated increases in monthly training volume. Table 1 is a basic guideline for your off-season monthly planning. Take your summer kilometer total and plug it into the percentages indicated for each month to break down your training goals for each month. The percentages should work for all but the skier on very limited training volumes.

After you've determined your monthly volumes, you can plan how much time will be spent on each activity. The experienced athlete who has kept a log in previous years may wish to work in hours to be spent on each activity, rather than kilometers. He will know, from his logs, what his pace was the preceding summer while roller skiing, ski running, ski hiking, rowing, etc. He should plan to increase this pace during the coming year as part of his progressive program. If, for example, he averaged 12 km per hour roller skiing last year, he might shoot for 12.5 km per hour the coming year.

Table 2 provides guidelines for determining the percentage of volume to be spent on each activity during the off-season. The table includes activities I consider vital to a dryland training program. Other activities may be added or substituted. The numbers for roller skiing, ski running, ski hiking, rowing, and intervals are the percentage of time or distance of the monthly volume total to be spent on each activity. The exception is strength training, where the numbers on the table indicate the range of time to be spent each

TABLE 1
Off-Season Monthly Volume Percentages

Month	Percent of Off-Season Volume
May	13%
June	15%
July	16%
August	17%
September	19%
October	20%
	100%

TABLE 2
Off-Season Monthly Activity* Percentages

	Endurance				Intervals	Strength (3 times per week)
	Roller Skiing	Ski Running	Ski Hiking	Rowing		
May	35%	25%	20%	12%	8%	30–45 min.
June	35%	25%	20%	12%	8%	30–45 min.
July	35%	25%	20%	10%	10%	30–45 min.
Aug.	40%	25%	15%	10%	10%	45–60 min.
Sept.	40%	20%	15%	10%	15%	45–60 min.
Oct.	55%	20%	5%	0%	20%†	45–60 min.
Nov.‡	75%	10%	0%	0%	15%§	45–60 min.

*Flexibility work is not included here, but the athlete must have a daily program of stretching exercises.
†Half of October intervals should be on roller skis and the other half on foot.
‡November percentages are included here for the athlete who is *not on snow* this month.
§November dryland intervals should be entirely on roller skis.

workout. You should have three strength workouts within the indicated duration range each week during the off-season.

In developing your monthly plan, remember that all aspects of the training program must be a part of your weekly activities throughout the year. Because the sport is a total body sport, you can't concentrate only on endurance and ignore strength and interval workouts at any point in your training. This doesn't mean that the percentage of time you spend on intervals will be the same in June as in September, but that all phases of your program should be involved to some extent all year long. A common, but mistaken, tendency is for athletes to spend more time and effort at activities they enjoy the most and ignore the areas of their greatest weakness. You have to have a complete program to expect progress and success.

After determining how much of each type of activity is planned for a month, pull out a blank calendar. Block off time periods when you know you have obligations—school, work, social, travel, etc. Fill in the remaining days with a balance of activities to meet your monthly goals. Plan a variety of each type of workout during each week and be certain to include time for rest. This planning lets you know what is to be accomplished during each training day.

To demonstrate how a program is planned, let's take a 22-year-old college woman who's a senior classified racer. Based on a 10% increase over the previous year's volume, she plans to cover 4,000 km during her competitive year from May 1981 to March 1982. For her off-season from May through October, she'll take half that total for her off-season volume. With the 2,000 km figure, she goes to Table 1 to determine her monthly volume. Thus, she comes up with a progressive schedule of 260 km in May, 300 in June, 320 for July, 340 for August, 380 for September, and 400 in October.

At this point, she will take her May volume total of 260 km and plug it into Table 2 to determine what percent of her training will be spent on each endurance and interval activity. For example, her roller skiing for May will be 91 km (35% of 260 km). Based on her average pace in each activity the preceding year, she will establish a pace one kilometer per hour faster for 1981. Then she takes the kilometers she plans to cover roller skiing and divides that figure by her planned pace to determine that she will spend 8.3 hours roller skiing during May. She uses this formula for each activity to come up with figures in Table 3.

TABLE 3
College Racer's Sample Monthly Planning Figures

May Goal: 260 km

Activity	Percent of May Volume	km	Pace	Time
Roller skiing	35%	91 km	11 km/hr	8.3 hr
Ski running	25%	65 km	9 km/hr	7.2 hr
Ski hiking	20%	52 km	6 km/hr	8.6 hr
Rowing	12%	31.2 km	7 km/hr	4.5 hr
Intervals	8%	20.8 km	7 km/hr	3 hr
				31.6 hr

Then our racer, who is just getting into a serious strength training program, determines that she will train three 30-minute sessions of strength work each week. For May of 1981, this means 13 sessions or 6.5 hours of strength work during the month. She also knows she will do flexibility exercises before and after every type of workout, so she doesn't have to make any special plans for that aspect of her training.

Her next step is to set up a calendar for May, dividing the days into morning and afternoon (Chart 3). She puts her strength workouts in place each Monday, Wednesday, and Friday afternoon. Then she adds the school, travel, and social obligations she has during the month. She puts her interval workouts on the calendar next, knowing that she will have three one-hour aerobic sessions. She plans these on alternating Saturday mornings as part of her strategy to schedule her body for race-type efforts on the weekend, the normal time for winter competition. One interval will be on roller skis and the other two will be hill running.

Next she will plan her ski hikes to total 8.6 hours. Because the sessions will be long, she plans them on weekend days not scheduled for intervals when she has time. They will be progressive with the first ski hike 2.1 hours, the second 3.0, and the third 3.5 hours. Now she knows she has 8.3 hours of roller skiing, 7.2 hours of ski running, and 4.5 hours of rowing with a movable seat to complete her May schedule.

She wants to have balance and variety in her program, so she schedules the various endurance workouts so that no one week is particularly hard and that each week has a variety of activities. She also knows that she will be increasing her volume by 40 km in June, so she wants her May schedule to be progressive to build up to the June increase. Thus, she plans the last week in May as the biggest volume week of the month and includes a day of double workouts at the end of the month.

By looking at her May plan in Chart 3, you can see that she has designed a good program which will allow her to meet her monthly goals. It's progressive, balanced, and includes all facets of her training program. Besides, she has a total of 16 days off, including half-days, so she will be rested and recovered from each workout.

Toward the end of May she will follow a similar formula in making her plan for her June training program. Each month will include more volume through the off-season, so she can increase the length of workouts and/or plan more double sessions on certain days while still having plenty of time for rest and recovery.

When evaluating your program and planning your training, keep in mind that, just as in a race, it's not always possible to accomplish the goals you've established. This certainly doesn't mean the end of the world or the failure of the program. An athlete is bound to have "off" days. Similarly, he might go beyond his training goal during an "on" day. Your annual, monthly, and daily plans are simply solid guidelines for your training, not hard-and-fast requirements.

The athlete must be ready to make adjustments in his program to compensate for unexpected changes in his plans. For example, Doug Peterson, a U.S. team member whom I coach, had planned 2,000 km of roller skiing for the summer of 1979. But then he had the opportunity to ski on snow in May and again for an entire month in the early fall, which cut into the time he'd planned for roller skiing and gave him a higher volume in September than we'd planned. To compensate, we reduced his October volume by about 250 km but increased the intensity of his workouts that month.

CHART 3
A College Racer's Sample Monthly Plan

MONTH: MAY   19 81

SUNDAY	MONDAY	TUESDAY	WEDNESDAY	THURSDAY	FRIDAY	SATURDAY
					1 SKI RUN / STRGTH	2 INTERVALS (HILL RUN)
3 CLASS TRIP →	4 STRGTH SKI RUN	5 ROLLER SKI	6	7 ROLLER SKI	8 ROW / STRGTH	9 SKI HIKE 2.1 HRS
10 ROW	11 STRGTH SKI RUN	12 CLASS DAY →	13 STRGTH ROLLER SKI	14 SKI RUN	15 STRGTH ROLLER SKI	16 INTERVALS ROLLER SKI
17 SKI HIKE 3 HRS	18 STRGTH	19 EXAM ROW	20 STRGTH SKI RUN	21 ROLLER SKI	22 STRGTH EXAM	23 WEDDING →
24 SKI HIKE 3 HRS	25 EXAM / STRGTH ROLLER SKI	26 ROW 1.5 HRS	27 GRADUATION STRGTH	28 TRAVEL HOME →	29 STRGTH ROLLERSKI 1.3 HRS	30 INTERVALS (HILL RUN)
31 ROLLER SKI SKI RUN 1.2 HRS						

Be flexible and willing to evaluate and adjust your program on a weekly, if not daily, basis. Perhaps your plan turns out not to be strenuous enough for you, or you've overloaded yourself. Evaluate your program and make the necessary adjustments. After laying out your program for the year, go over the whole plan with a knowledgeable person for some external input in determining a realistic program.

The success of your program depends on your willingness to carry it out. Your plan will be no good if you compromise it with extraneous activities. To accomplish your goals, you must set aside the necessary training time. Following through on the objectives you've set for each day, week, and month will make you a happy, confident athlete and will pay off in big dividends on the race course.

SELF-EVALUATION—TESTING AND LOGGING

Self-evaluation is an essential part of any athlete's training and competition program. Although concrete evaluation is ultimately found on the result lists, self-evaluation must take place throughout the year. The athlete should evaluate himself through physical testing and assess the information recorded in his training logs in order to be objective about his program and his progress. Don't wander through five to seven months of the off-season without stopping routinely to test and evaluate your program.

Testing

There are three types of physical testing currently available to cross-country skiers in the United States.

The athletes on the national team routinely undergo extensive tests directed by sports medicine experts. The tests have been developed over the past decade to determine each athlete's level of conditioning. The tests are conducted with modern sports medicine equipment worth thousands of dollars, such as treadmills to gauge cardiovascular capacity. The series of tests includes a number of different stations which evaluate upper and lower body strength, coordination, percentage of body fat, reflexes, reaction time, speed of movement, etc. These are primary tests and have helped national team members establish individual training programs based on each skier's strengths and weaknesses.

Non-national team members can take advantage of another testing program developed by the U.S. Ski Team for the U.S. Ski Coaches' Association through the sports medicine center at the University of Wisconsin at LaCrosse. The USSCA provides free material and information on how to set up a series of 11 specific secondary tests. The series doesn't require much equipment but takes three days to be run correctly and must be monitored by a few coaches or other individuals. The tests are ideal for club or school programs in evaluating the conditioning level of their athletes. Test results are sent to LaCrosse for evaluation. The group in LaCrosse will determine the results and rank each athlete nationally. This ranking is updated routinely and is exciting for the athlete because it gives him a measure of where he stands. As he undergoes further testing, he can note his personal progress as well as improvements in national ranking.

SET. The third type of testing available to skiers is also a secondary testing program which I call Self-Evaluation Testing, or SET. This program allows the athlete to test himself virtually on his own in order to gauge his conditioning level and, therefore, is the most practical method for many skiers.

TABLE 4

Self-Evaluation Test Score Guidelines

Test	Bottom of the Hill		Middle of the Hill		Top of the Hill	
	Women	Men	Women	Men	Women	Men
Bench press	25–30 lb under body weight	10–15 lb under body weight	Body weight	Body weight	10–20 lb over body weight	20–40 lb over body weight
Sit-ups	20	30	30	40	45	55
Long jump	Less than height	Less than height	12 in. over height	13 in. over height	18 in. over height	22 in. over height
Arm dips	0–3	3–5	4–8	6–15	Over 10	Over 20
15-min. run	1 mi	1½ mi	1½ mi	2 mi	2¼ mi plus	2¾ mi plus

SET is designed as an objective evaluation of the athlete's conditioning and is useful as a guide when adjusting or correcting training deficiencies. The program was used for a number of years by the U.S. Ski Team, and it was successful in determining the skier's training needs. The guidelines indicated on Table 4 are based on the performance of national team members. The results of the Top-of-the Hill gang of U.S. team skiers are used as parameters by which skiers can measure their progress.

The five tests in SET could be more specific for skiers, but I believe they relate enough to the physical requirements of the cross-country racer to be a good indication of his conditioning level. You may wish to develop your own SET program with different activities. The main concern is that the activities test all physical aspects important to skiers and that they are standardized. Any change in equipment or activity will invalidate the program because one testing session won't relate to the next. Also, as you reach a high level of conditioning, gains in the results will be minimal. By keeping the tests standardized, you can note even small gains.

Plan to undergo SET four times during the off-season, beginning in early May when your training program is just underway. This initial test, together with past years' training volumes, will determine your training base for the coming year. Other tests should be scheduled in late June, mid-August, and just prior to your return to on-snow training. The timing of the final test is important; be certain there is time to rectify any deficiencies in your program before the snow flies.

1. *Bench press.* This is an upper-body strength test of the triceps and latisimus dorsi muscles, which are the prime movers in the poling motion. The bench press stations on Universal Gyms are preferred for this test because they are safe and will be standard from test to test. The athlete lifts the maximum amount of weight he can, being certain to complete a full range of motion. He is allowed three attempts and can rest as long as he wants between attempts. The heaviest lift is recorded. As Table 4 indicates, the well-conditioned skier can lift many pounds more than his body weight.

2. *Sit-ups.* This exercise tests muscle strength, speed, and endurance of the abdominal area. The stomach muscles are important to the skier because they connect the upper and lower body movements, influence breathing, and aid in poling. The athlete lies flat on his

back on a flat surface with his knees bent, his feet held stationary, and his hands locked behind his head. Making a complete sit-up motion—his elbows touch his knees and his head returns to the floor—the skier has 60 seconds to do as many sit-ups as he can.

3. *Arm dips.* Dips are a test of arm and shoulder girdle endurance, which are important in the poling motion. The test may be done on parallel bars, dipbars or a dip station on the Universal Gym. The athlete may build his own dip station with parallel 2 by 4s set at about chest height and a bit over shoulder distance apart. The athlete lifts himself off the ground, lowers himself until his arms are bent at a 90° angle, then raises himself until his arms are straight—at no time should his feet touch the ground. (Be certain to do a full range of motion on each dip.) There is no time limit on this test but is continuous with the athlete attempting as many dips as possible.

4. *Standing long jump.* This is a test of explosive leg power. Because skiing is a power endurance event, leg strength, particularly in the quadriceps, must be developed. In this test, use the jump facilities at a track to avoid injuries on landing. The athlete stands at an established starting line with his feet spread about shoulder width. To prepare, he can make any amount of swinging and squatting movements he wants, as long as his feet remain stationary and he jumps evenly from both feet. The athlete takes three jumps, and his longest jump is recorded.

5. *15-minute run.* The run gauges the athlete's overall cardiovascular endurance. The test should be conducted on a 440-yard track. The goal is to run as far as possible during the 15-minute time limit.

The SET program will take about 45 minutes to complete. Remember that you are testing yourself, not your fellow skiers. The goal is to improve your scores each time you're tested, not compete against someone else. Race results in the winter will compare you to others. SET is a test of your training progress. You're not training to do well in the tests, but training to be in shape for skiing.

The SET program serves both the athlete and the coach. A lack of progress in the test results can indicate that the athlete is not training hard enough, merely going through the motions. Another function of SET is to determine specific weaknesses in the athlete. For

TABLE 5
Testing Record

Test	Date			
Bench press				
Sit-ups				
Dips				
Standing long jump				
15-minute run				

example, if you can't do any more dips in July SET than you did in June, it's obvious that you need to increase the amount of training in that area. The test often convinces the athlete that he's been training hardest in areas where he excells at the expense of his weaker areas. The series of self-evaluation tests during the off-season should provide you with the information you need to alter your training to be certain you are totally ready for winter. Be sure to record your SET results in a testing log. Table 5 is a sample log. You may want to use the back side of your log to record any comments about each series of tests.

The testing log should be encouraging as you note concrete gains made in the different SET activities over the off-season. As you reach the upper level of conditioning, however, the gains demonstrated by SET will be smaller. I often tell beginning racers that it's easy to gain laps, but the inches will come hard. When you approach the Top of the Hill, or the conditioning level of the national team, the increase in the distance you cover in the 15-minute run will not be as great as the increases you made early in your training program.

Training Logs

Success in sport requires self-discipline. No matter what the level of competition—international, national, divisional, school, or citizen—the athlete must be disciplined in his training and in recording his program. Logs record your activities, from which you can objectively evaluate your program—who you are, where you've been, and possibly where you're going.

Every racer should have sets of five basic logs to record his activities—weekly, monthly, annual, four-year summaries, and competition logs. Chart 4 and Tables 6 to 9 are similar to those developed by the U.S. Ski Team. The U.S. Ski Coaches' Association sells a one-year supply of USST logs with instructions at a very reasonable rate. The logs in this book are a bit more specific than the ski team logs because I include all the activities essential to a cross-country training program. The athlete may devise his own system of logs geared to the particulars of his training program.

Weekly Log. The weekly training summary (Chart 4) is fairly self-explanatory. The skier makes a daily record of his activities, including his rested pulse rate, body weight during the week, hours of sleep, and training workouts. Training data should be recorded in kilometers. The skier should record the vertical climb covered and the amount of time spent climbing to determine his training pace. The reverse side of the weekly summary is used for comments on how training went each day and may include factors such as weather conditions that affected training. Be accurate when recording in your logs. This is difficult after a bad day of training, but information, even about bad days, will be extremely helpful to you in the long run.

A few comments about the value of keeping track of your pulse rate are necessary. Pulse is an indicator of the body's well-being. As you get into the routine of taking your daily resting pulse, you will establish your own normal rate. When you're into a heavy training program, when you aren't getting enough rest, when you're bothered by psychological problems or are sick, your resting pulse rate will jump perhaps five beats above normal. It's possible that this rise is only a temporary situation and you can continue training. However, if the upward trend continues, you know that something is wrong and you might need to get more rest, cut back on training, or take a complete break from training.

CHART 4
Weekly Training Summary

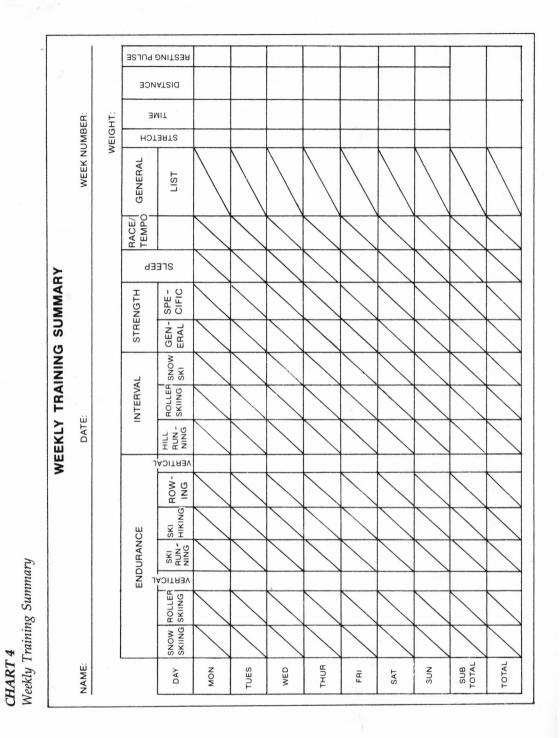

WEEKLY TRAINING SUMMARY

NAME: DATE: WEEK NUMBER:

WEIGHT:

Monitoring your pulse is one more way of being objective about your training. If you wake up one morning feeling tired but your pulse rate is normal, you know your body is rested and ready to train. The pulse rate is the best way to plan a rest day, rather than arbitrarily deciding to take Sunday off. Let your body, via your pulse, tell you when you need a break. Don't become a slave to your training log and feel you have to record workouts every day. If your body says you're tired, take a break.

Get into the routine of taking your pulse as a regular part of your life. Take your pulse at the same time every day; the best time is in the morning just as you wake up. Have a clock or watch with a second hand by your bed so you can take your pulse first thing. Using the arteries in your neck, chest, or wrist, count how many times your heart beats in six seconds and multipy that by ten to determine your pulse rate. Elite racers, as a gauge, have resting pulses of 35–40 beats per minute for men and 40–45 for women.

However, some people get nervous about taking their pulse. As soon as they put their hand on their wrist, their pulse rate goes up as much as 20 beats above their resting pulse. Because these people can't rely on their pulse, they must be very sensitive to and aware of other body signs.

The weekly training log includes columns for figuring your daily totals for all activity on the left in both time spent and distance covered. At the bottom of the log, weekly totals for each specific activity are calculated in the subtotal column. Below that is a line marked Total, where you determine the cumulative totals for all your training during the year through the current week. These figures will keep you apprised of the progress you've made and whether you're on course to accomplishing the goals you set for your training in your annual and monthly planning.

The daily comments made on the back of the weekly log are very important when you sit down to evaluate your program. The comments should include facts about your training—times for intervals, training pulse rates, recovery times, weather, etc.—as well as your feelings about each workout. These comments will tell you and your coach how you are reacting to your training. Next spring when you go over your logs to plan the next year, they won't mean much to you unless you have a buzzword or key to evaluate each workout: was it a good workout, was the location bad, were you exhausted, or did you feel you could have done one more repetition. This feedback and the thought process involved in commenting on each workout are important parts of educating yourself about training and racing. If you're aware of how your body reacted to a particularly strenuous workout, you'll know how hard you can push yourself during a race. You'll be able to say during a race, "I felt this way last summer doing intervals and it means I'm about to go under, so I'd better ease up a bit."

Monthly Logs. Table 6 is a sample of how to set up a monthly training summary. This log provides an overview of the training you've accomplished in the month so you'll know which goals you have and haven't accomplished and can make any adjustments in planning your program for the coming months.

Competition Logs. The competition log is the record that evaluates the purpose of all your training—racing. It's the main indicator of whether your training program is working and will help plan a better program for coming years.

Table 7 is a sample competition log which has room for only a few competitions. I would hope that any serious racer would need more than one of these logs—North American racers should compete in 25–40 races a year. The log has a column to record your time out

TABLE 6
Monthly Training Summary

Name: _____ Calendar Month: _____ Year: _____

Weight Fluctuations: _____ Percent Fat: Covering Week Numbers:

	Distance	Hours	Vertical	Comments
Distance Training				
Ski running				
Roller skiing				
Ski hiking				
Rowing				
Snow skiing				
SUBTOTAL				
Interval Training				
_____				
_____				
SUBTOTAL				
Strength Training				
_____				
_____				
_____				
SUBTOTAL				
Racing				
_____				
_____				
_____				
SUBTOTAL				
TOTAL				

TABLE 7

Competition Log

Name: _____ Season: _____

Date	Name of Race	Location	Distance	Time/Place	Time Out of First	Winner	Comments

of first place. You may wish to expand this to indicate how you did in relation to the winner of your class or to a competitor who is ranked a bit better than you, particularly if the overall winner won by a wide margin. You might be ten minutes out of first place but only three minutes out of second place.

Recording comments on your race is an important aspect of the competition log. How you felt about your effort, how your body reacted, etc., will be helpful in determining which type of prerace training is effective and what you can do to prepare for important races. The comments will also indicate other aspects of strategy and racing tactics which were successful for you.

Yearly Log. A smart racer will fill in his yearly training summary at the end of each month in order to evaluate his ongoing program. Don't wait until the end of the training year to work on this log or you'll miss another opportunity to be certain that your training and racing program is heading in the direction of your goals.

Table 8 is an annual summary log. Information from your monthly logs will be transferred to your annual summary. You will then determine the percentage of your total volume spent on each activity. You also will include the rate at which you performed each activity each month in terms of kilometers per hour.

Another factor to be determined on your annual summary is your vertical workload. The U.S. team developed the following formula to indicate how hard your workouts were through a measure of intensity and load:

$$\frac{\text{Rate} \times \text{Vertical feet}}{3,280 \text{ feet/km}} = \text{Vertical workload factor}$$

This figure won't mean much until you compare it with the VWL factors from other training periods. After a time, you should be able to see an increase in this factor, indicating that your workouts are progressive. The figure is more indicative than other totals because it accounts for the amount of vertical covered in training.

TABLE 8
Yearly Training Summary

Name: _____ Year: _____

Month	Endurance training—Distance (km), Time (hr), Rates (km/hr), Vertical Work Load (VWL)																	
	Ski Running				Roller Skiing			Ski Hiking				Rowing			Snow Skiing		
	km	hr	Rate	VWL	km	hr	Rate	km	hr	Rate	VWL	km	hr	Rate	km	hr	Rate
April																	
May																	
June																	
July																	
Aug.																	
Sept.																	
Oct.																	
Nov.																	
Dec.																	
Jan.																	
Feb.																	
March																	
April																	
TOTALS FOR YEAR (Dry and Training Only)																	
TOTALS FOR YEAR (All Training)																	

Racing			Intervals (km/hr)		Strength	Totals (km/hr) (exclude strength hrs.)		Total Kilometer Percentages						Total Hour Percentages			
								Ski Running	Roller Skiing	Ski Hiking	Rowing	Skiing	Racing	% Endurance	% Strength	% Interval	% Race
km	hr	Rate	km	hr	hr	km	hr	% km	% km	% km	% km	% km	% km	% hr	% hr	% hr	% hr
							Total km for year							Total hr for year			

TABLE 9

Four-Year Training Summary

Name: _____

	19___					19___					19___					19___				
	km	hr	Rate	%	Avg. VWL	km	hr	Rate	%	Avg. VWL	km	hr	Rate	%	Avg. VWL	km	hr	Rate	%	Avg. VWL
Endurance training																				
Rowing																				
Roller skiing																				
Ski hiking																				
Ski running																				
Skiing																				
Racing																				
Intervals																				
Strength																				
TOTALS																				

Four-Year Logs. The most important aspect of the four-year training summary comes from the concrete evaluation it allows you to make of your program. This log is a strong indicator of who you are and where you're going as a competitor. It will help determine the success of your training program and what changes must be made to make your program more progressive.

The four-year log (Table 9) isolates annual totals of each type of activity. These totals and your success in competition will be an objective indication of the strengths and weaknesses of your programs.

Evaluation. The serious skier will spend a great deal of time studying his logs. This evaluation is essential in planning training for the days and weeks ahead and is a particularly important gauge during the racing season. The log will warn you when fatigue is setting in, when you are overtraining and when you are getting sick. Logs also work positively to let you know when you are reaching a peak and how to control it as well as what has worked best for you in recovering from a race or from illness. It will show you what regimen is most successful those important few days before a race. The log will also tell you if you've been training too much in one area and too little in another. This type of evaluation will allow you to adjust your program when necessary.

Evaluation and adjustment are based on where you stand as recorded in your training and racing logs. The following are a few things you look for in your logs when evaluating your program.

- Resting pulse rate fluxuations.
- Diet patterns—is your diet apathetic or enthusiastic?
- Sleep pattern fluxuations.
- Psychological affects—did a personal problem affect your attitude toward training?
- Weight loss or gain.
- Mental and physical reactions to a particularly heavy period of training or racing.

From these factors recorded in your log, try to establish some patterns. If you had a period where you felt your training or racing was going particularly well, try to determine what led up to the period and what you did to maintain it. Equally important, try to establish a pattern for what led up to a period of poor training and racing or to an illness. Was your resting pulse rate rising? Did you feel tired after each training session, indicating overtraining? Did you change your diet? Did problems with a personal relationship interfere with your training? Then determine what you did to recover from this down period. How fast did your pulse rate readjust? What type of training load were you under? What was your reaction to this training?

Getting a grip on patterns which lead to both high and low training and racing periods will help determine how to plan your season and your week-to-week training. You may never come up with concrete patterns, but studying your log will indicate trends and the type of training that will best keep you on track toward your training and racing goals.

In sum, the athlete must sit down and plan his training season. He must continually evaluate his training through testing and monitoring of his training logs. And he must train hard with intelligence in order to progress toward fulfilling his potential.

METHODS OF TRAINING

Training methods are as varied as there are numbers of coaches. No matter what the idiosyncracies of a program, the athlete can undoubtedly find a book or a coach to support the training methods he has chosen. There are many ways to achieve success in cross-country skiing. Individual preference rules the choice, but it must be tempered by the physiological, psychological, and technical demands of the sport and needs of each athlete. The athlete should establish his training methods after evaluating the options, educating himself in the basics of training and determining his goals.

For the 1980s, at least, the basic rule in athletic training is specificity. The best way to prepare for a sport is to train in that sport. Of course, this rule presents difficulties to those of us involved in a seasonal sport like skiing. Most of us can't ski all year long, so we must devise other methods of training which will best condition our bodies for the specific requirements of skiing.

METHOD ONE—ENDURANCE TRAINING

Endurance training has, naturally, always been the major part of the cross-country skier's conditioning program. As I said, endurance is the ability to persist in physical activity and resist fatigue. What better describes the athlete's ability to complete a 50-km race? Having expended his last ounce of energy, his training background and the continuous evaluation of how hard he can push himself get him across the finish line.

Endurance training conditions your body to push harder and harder during competition while resisting fatigue. Physiologically, endurance training gradually elevates your anaerobic threshold so you can ski more intensely for longer periods in an aerobic state where your oxygen intake meets your body's demands for it. The goal of endurance training is to push your aerobic level higher and higher.

There are no two ways about it—endurance training is time-consuming but essential. Because the athlete is staying within his training effect zone, he must work for long periods of time to gain physiological benefits from an endurance workout. Further, improving his endurance level is a continuous process taking years to develop fully. To be competitive nationally, the beginning racer must spend between three and five years developing his conditioning base. International winners train intensely for five to seven years before being competitive. Look at Alison Owen, for example. She started racing at age thirteen in 1966. It wasn't until the 1979 and 1980 seasons that she gained ranking among the top ten or twelve women in the world.

There are two guidelines commonly used to define an endurance workout. One states that a junior skier must train continuously for 45 minutes while a senior skier will train for 60 or more minutes. This guideline is generally accepted, although it must be adjusted to the conditioning level of each athlete. The beginning racer might have difficulty working continuously for 15 minutes and the well-conditioned skier may have a four- or five-hour workout.

A second useful guideline in determining the upper limits of the length of an endurance session is that the workout should be 1½–2 times longer than your longest races. This guideline best applies to top-level athletes. Men who ski 50-km events in 2½ hours should workout for 3½–5 hours. Women who ski their longest race, 20-km, in about one hour might train for 90 minutes to 2 hours.

Each athlete must evaluate his conditioning level and plan workouts to improve that level without overtraining. The idea is not to come out of every session totally exhausted, but to push yourself to the fine line between feeling good and going under. Your body signs will control your program and each workout. If you plan a long workout, push yourself but be realistic. If your body doesn't have it, cool it. On other days, you may train longer than you planned because you find you have it in you.

The beginning racer will initially have difficulty meeting his goals in a continuous endurance workout until he reaches a certain level of conditioning. He may need to adjust the terrain or pace of the workout to accomplish his goals. Just remember that endurance workouts must be continuous—no stopping to chat with friends or take a break. The harder you work the sooner you'll be able to handle the load of endurance training and realize improvement in your conditioning base. As your training progresses, your training effect zone will move up. This means that your body will be able to handle heavier workloads at a higher heart rate. A good indication that TEZ has moved up will be from improvements made in your SET or other testing results. As you move toward the top of the hill of conditioning, you must recalculate your training effect zone and anaerobic threshold pulse rates according to the guidelines in Chart 1.

Your pulse rate is the control factor in endurance training. Once you've established your training effect zone, you monitor your pulse rate during training to be certain you don't reach your anaerobic threshold. Again, this is individual, depending on the level of conditioning, and may vary from 130–180 beats per minute. Many people are surprised with how slow their pace must be to stay within TEZ. A clue to being in TEZ, other than the concrete factor of your pulse, is if you are breathing easily enough to carry on a conversation while training.

It's important for the athlete to develop a feel for pace so that he knows that a certain pace will keep his heart beat at a certain level. In time, you will educate yourself to the relationship between your pace and your pulse rate by monitoring your heart beat. Remember that training will raise your training effect zone, so you must adjust your pace accordingly to achieve the goals of an endurance workout. This adjustment will come fairly rapidly to the beginning racer, while the top eschelon athlete will notice only small gains because he is reaching his upper limits.

Terrain is a big factor in most dryland endurance training activities because it determines the load and type of workout. During the off-season months, the terrain should gradually become more difficult as your body adjusts to the workloads. In the spring and early summer, terrain should be fairly gentle with gradual uphills and downhills. The amount of vertical should gradually increase so you are training in steeply undulating terrain by the fall. Chart 8 in Chapter 3 is a useful guideline in planning the terrain for your off-season workouts.

Training builds both physiological and psychological endurance. The mind often gives up before the body, so you often need to psych yourself up to go the distance in an endurance workout. However, it's important to keep track of mental signs of fatigue while training, as well as physical ones. The brain will often warn the athlete that he is overtraining before his pulse rate rises and before he gets sick. Be honest with yourself in evaluating all the signs.

There are many activities which qualify as endurance training. I limit these activities and classify them into two groups, based on their benefit to cross-country skiers. First-Class Activities are those which are specific to the sport and involve total body usage. Second-Class Activities are not as specific to skiing and usually involve use of only the upper body or only the lower body.

Most of the Second-Class Activities were accepted as good training, even for world-class racers, just a few years ago. Biking and foot running were traditionally a major part of the skier's training program. Then sports medicine experts determined that Second-Class Activities are simply not specific enough for cross-country skiing. They do have a conditioning effect on the body, but they can actually decondition cross-country skiers. Many people who ski in the winter are runners in the summer and spend most of their training time running. There is nothing wrong with this, depending on your goals as a skier. Second-Class Activities provide variety for the athlete and, although they are not the best training for skiers, they are certainly better than doing nothing.

Skiers have to train specifically for their sport using their entire bodies. This was demonstrated back in 1975 when the U.S. team's sports medicine staff ran a series of tests on the team members. The racers were tested in the late spring when their dryland training began, in the fall during their transition to on-snow training, in early January, and again at the end of the racing season. The tests showed that the athletes were in the best physical shape in January because they had spent the preceding two months on-snow training their entire bodies. They weren't strongest in the summer because there wasn't as much emphasis on full-body workouts. The tests proved that total body usage led to higher levels of conditioning.

First-Class Activities

The best dryland endurance training activities for the cross-country skier are roller skiing, ski hiking with poles, ski running with poles, ski walking with poles, and rowing with a movable seat. The First-Class Activities all involve total body usage and require the athlete to coordinate his upper and lower body movements, both technically and physiologically.

The First-Class Activities provide specific training for cross-country skiing. All are related to the skiing motion, most allow the athlete to work on ski technique, and all have a workload comparable to skiing. Only rowing does not involve the use of ski poles but does substitute oars. All five activities relate to skiing in terms of the tenets of training— specificity, duration, intensity, load, and frequency of movement.

The four activities requiring poles are particularly important to the skier because they allow him to work on technique during the off-season. Many people think you can't improve technique over the summer, but I know from working with athletes that you can with First-Class Activities. Muscle memory and nerve knowledge—adapting the body to skiing—is developed in the summer, and the athlete should spend time improving his technique while roller skiing and ski hiking, walking, and running.

Roller Skiing. Roller skiing is the most important activity in the skier's off-season training program. Roller skiing is the closest you can come to actually skiing, making it particularly important to North Americans with our limited access to off-season snow. In the past, North Americans haven't taken full advantage of the benefits to be gained from roller skiing, but the interest and enthusiasm for this activity are growing.

Roller skis take some adjusting to before you feel comfortable on them. You're not skiing in tracks, so it's up to you to control the direction of the roller skis. Because they are elevated on three wheels, balance is even more of a factor that it is in snow skiing. You must simply relax, take it easy at first, and gradually adjust to the feel of roller skis. The quicker you become comfortable on the skis, the more you'll gain from your training time. When roller skiing, the smoother the pavement, the better the workout. Concrete is almost impossible, however, because the tips of your poles can't dig in. The warmer the pavement, the easier it is to pole. Carbide pole tips are essential to a successful workout.

Roller skis are ideal for all types of training activities—endurance, intervals, technique work, tempo training, and racing. The terrain will often dictate the type of training and technique, so you need to locate terrain to suit the type of workout you have planned. Distance isn't a limiting factor—skiers are covering up to 50 km a day on roller skis. For a normal endurance workout, the guideline of 45 minutes for juniors and an hour or more for seniors applies.

Given the five tenets of training, you can use your imagination to apply them to a variety of workouts. Three typical workouts would involve (1) double poling over flat terrain, (2) skiing over undulating terrain to accomplish a natural interval effect and use a variety of techniques, and (3) skiing on a gradual to steep uphill using diagonal striding and hill technique. Because the skier should devote 35%–75% of his off-season training time to roller skiing, it's important to devise a number of workouts in differing locations to avoid boredom.

Endurance training on roller skis offers an excellent opportunity to work on technique. A good roller skier can do whatever the terrain demands—double pole, single stick, snowplow, and downhill. At a minimum, the athlete can master the double pole on roller skis. The diagonal stride is a bit more difficult without coaching supervision but certainly is possible. The more confident the athlete is on his roller skis, the better he'll be able to mimic ski technique. We've clocked national team members going 40 mph on downhills. Many are able to snowplow. You have to get into the plow while your skis are under control; if you're going too fast, it's too late to go into a plow and you simply have to ride out the hill or telemark off the pavement, using undergrowth to slow you down.

When working on technique, it's best to have a coach observing and correcting. This means self-coached racers and those involved in school programs are often at a disadvantage. It's easy to get into bad habits roller skiing that will carry over to your on-show technique.

Bad technique habits often result if the skis are too slow or too heavy, if your poles lack sharp carbide tips, or if you ski on rough pavement. Common bad habits include a poor weight transfer to the gliding ski, bad balance, dropping the kicking ski behind too fast, incomplete single poling movements, and squatting or not dropping your arm through the knee when double poling. Be conscious of technical errors and work to correct them.

Take the time to work on technique while roller skiing. Too often coaches ignore technique in dryland training. Video tapes or Polarvision is particularly helpful to the athlete. Set up a situation where the terrain demands a variety of double poling, diagonal and downhill. A loop works well so the coach can move around and observe the athlete doing the various techniques several times during a workout. It's also useful to show films of snow skiing during the summer so the athlete has a fresh mental image of what he should look like while roller skiing. I've also found that shopping mall windows are great mirrors at night—you can ski along and watch your technique reflected in the store windows. (Be certain to note the technique carry over illustrated in the accompanying roller ski photos with their on-snow counterparts in Chapter 5.)

Roller skiing diagonal stride, free glide position. Both poles are off the pavement and the arms are fully extended so the two hands are in a line nearly parallel with the ground. The lower right leg is perpendicular to the ground and the upper right leg is raised. Compare these roller skiing photos with their respective counterparts in Chapter 5.

Roller skiing diagonal stride, poling while standing. Be certain that the poling arm is levered or angled in a strong working position. The trunk is moving downward to aid the arm in the poling action. The left leg and right arm are in a relaxed recovery phase.

Roller skiing diagonal stride, poling while kicking. As the legs come together, the right roller ski has ended its glide and the leg is preparing to initiate a kick. The angle behind the right knee is decreasing as the body squats or compresses, aiding the poling and preparing to kick.

Roller skiing diagonal stride, kick completion. As the skier completes the kick off his right leg, he extends his arms and shifts his weight completely to the left ski.

Roller skiing double pole no kick, compression. Initially, the body is fairly upright but moves forward as the skier prepares to plant his poles. The legs remain fairly straight as the body angulates at the hips. The arms are levered and remain at this angle from pole implantation until they reach down near the knees. The driving force behind the poling is the compression of the upper body. Timing is important, so try it slowly the first time out.

Roller skiing double pole no kick, follow-through. The skier has angulated at the hips a bit too far; his upper body should only compress to about 105°. The skier has his weight a bit back to gain maximum glide, and his arms have straightened out.

Roller skiing double pole no kick, arm extension. The arms have followed through to their complete extension and the upper body is starting to raise up. The knee angle has remained the same throughout the poling motion.

Roller skiing double pole with kick, pole delivery. As the skier extends his arm forward, he initiates a kick off either foot. This drives his body forward to the position for poling. Be aggressive and ignore any fear of falling forward or you'll develop bad poling habits.

Roller skiing double pole with kick, compression. Because the skier was aggressive in his pole delivery, his body is generating energy on the poles as it compresses. The right leg is driving forward. Don't be lazy in this movement.

Roller skiing double pole with kick, gliding. Keep the head up to prevent compressing the body too far.

Roller skiing double pole with kick, follow-through. The arms are following through from the poling motion and the upper body is rising out of its compression. Notice that the front wheel on the right ski is off the ground; the skier has his weight back to enhance his forward velocity. He'll kick off his left leg on his next poling motion.

Roller skiing uphill, pole implantation. When roller skiing uphill, the skier uses the technique known as hill running only on very steep hills. In this photo the skier is on a moderate hill, so he uses a diagonal stride but shortens the arm and leg movements.

Roller skiing uphill, poling while kicking. As the body compresses, the poling right arm drives down to the knee and the left moves forward to be ready for the next poling motion.

Roller skiing uphill, pole delivery. The skier is actually in a free glide phase, but only briefly due to the resistance of the hill. The right arm is extended but not as far as it would be in a true diagonal stride, nor is the left ski off the ground.

Roller ski skating. Skating on roller skis requires a bit of confidence and a lot of practice. The key is to commit your weight fully on one ski as you step forward with the other. The skier has transferred his weight completely to his right ski after pushing off the left. As he brings the left ski forward he will prepare to initiate a poling motion. Stay forward.

Pole Simulation Movements and Workouts. Training without poles can lead to detraining for the skier, which is why ski hiking and ski running workouts have become an increasingly important part of cross-country training since 1979. Putting poles in my hands seems to improve my spirits and interest in training because I know I'm accomplishing more physically and technically, and that my efforts will pay bigger dividends come winter. Besides, those uphills seem easier when I use my arms to help me.

There are three basic pole simulation movements for training on uphills—ski walking, ski running, and ski striding—which are used during endurance workouts known as ski hiking and ski running. The terminology in common use seems to overlap, but remember that there's a difference between the three movements and what is actually done during a workout.

Ski walking is a long-gaited, heel-striking walking movement coordinated with the use of poles. The pace should be 2.1 to 2.3 strides per second. Check your pace by being certain to make about 33 strides each 15 seconds. This stride rate will be decreased over steeper terrain—remember that your pulse rate is the primary control. By leaning your upper body forward, you will obtain better use of the poles. Conversely, an erect body position will result in less pole use.

Ski running is simply a natural running movement coordinated with pole use. Run naturally and don't force ski-type movements because the primary concern is physiological (heart/lung) output. Again, pole use increases with forward lean of the upper body. Ski running is most commonly used on gradual uphills to increase the workload. In late summer and fall, ski running becomes a bigger part of training as workloads increase in response to improved conditioning levels.

Ski striding is a cross between the ski walking and ski running movements. Heel striking is emphasized, but the pace is faster and the stride more elongated than in ski walking. Because this is the most demanding of the three pole simulation movements, ski striding is used for endurance training in the late summer and fall when you really want to increase your workloads. It is an anaerobic effort when done for a period of time much beyond 30 seconds. Ski striding is most often used in hill-running interval workouts.

Endurance workouts involving these three pole simulation movements include ski hiking and ski running. A ski hiking workout is conducted in mountainous terrain involving long uphill sections. A workout will run from one to four hours with stretches of uphills taking 5–20 minutes to cover when the ski walking movement is used. Pace is controlled so the athlete stays within his training effect zone. Poles are used continuously.

An endurance ski run workout is conducted in undulating terrain typical of a cross-country ski trail. You run on the flats and downhills while carrying poles in your hands since the pace is too fast for effective poling. The ski walking movement is most often used on uphills. Depending on the steepness of the uphills and the desired workload, the ski running and ski striding movements may be used on uphill sections. Terrain load should increase during the late summer and fall.

The poles used in these activities should be aluminum and about five centimeters shorter than the poles used in snow skiing to compensate for the fact that tips don't sink into the ground. The baskets should be cut down in size to avoid the potential of injury should the basket catch on a branch while you're training.

Ski walking. Don't go out the door without your poles for off-season training. Over the flats and on downhills, run naturally and simply carry your poles off the ground. As you move into a hill, let the poles start working for you. Shorten and quicken your steps to adjust speed down to a walking tempo.

Ski walking. The pole is planted and the skier begins rotating over the left leg and ankle, just as in hill running on snow. The left leg is preparing to "kick."

Ski striding. Ski striding is very beneficial for conditioning level and technique. The emphasis is on making a long stride following the gradient of the terrain without any significant vertical movement. The movement most closely relates to the diagonal stride of any of the pole simulation movements. This photo illustrates poling while kicking. The right arm is pushing and the left leg is beginning the kick movement. Keep your head up.

Ski running. On an uphill, the skier runs naturally and is able to use his poles. This workout on a gradual hill increases the physiological load over ski walking. The movement is not contrived, but each foot lands naturally on the ball rather than with a heel strike. By increasing the forward lean of the upper body, you'll increase the push off the poles.

Ski striding. This position is as close as you'll get to free glide off skis. Without a glide, the right arm can't be fully extended. Notice the heel strike of the right foot.

Rowing with a Movable Seat. Rowing is becoming more and more popular as a training device for skiers in the U.S. The world-class rowing organization in the U.S. completed a biomechanical study comparing rowing and cross-country skiing and determined a great similarity between the physiological demands and muscle usages in the two sports. Elite U.S. rowers have been encouraged to train for their sport by skiing in the winter. If the crossover is good for the rowers, it must be good for skiers as well.

This activity requires a movable seat or slide, which is normally placed in a type of boat known as a shell, although the seat may be adapted to other types of small boats. The feet are held stationary by a harness apparatus while the seat moves on rollers. Rowing in this rig coordinates the use of the upper and lower body. The leg action is similar to the demands on the leg while skiing, and the push and pull of the arms simulates poling.

I enjoy rowing because it's easy on the joints and gives the body a break from the pounding of running. In fact, it can be good activity when you're injured or just sore. Besides, it's a pleasant change of atmosphere to head out on a lake or river, and you can cool off by hopping overboard.

Rowing can be used for interval workouts as well as for endurance. The load, which comes from resistance against the water, may be increased by towing something, bringing a passenger along, or rowing against the current.

Shell rowing. In a boat of this type, it's vital to establish a sense of balance while rowing. Begin by working only with the arms to get a feel for the mechanics of the movements and then work on the timing of the coordinated arm and leg movements. In this photo, Doug Peterson is in a position known as the catch—the pull of the arms and push of the legs is about to begin. Notice the length of the runners behind Doug, which indicates how far the seat will move.

Shell rowing. Doug has completed one stroke and fully extended his legs. He will now feather the oars (flatten the blades parallel to the water) for the recovery.

Second-Class Activities

The change in direction of cross-country training away from Second-Class Activities has been validated by sports medicine testing. Some coaches and athletes have fought the change. It takes time for new concepts to reach all parts of the U.S. and more time for them to be fully accepted. But the fact is that specific, full-body activities have been deemed the best training methods for skiers by the sports medicine experts.

Second-Class Activities concentrate on either upper or lower body work, with limited coordination between the two and limited specificity to skiing. They are not the best type of workouts for a skier but do offer variety to a training program and, again, are better than doing nothing. The three Second-Class Activities which were a big part of training for skiing in the past are running, biking, and hiking. Other Second-Class Activities are swimming, kayaking, canoeing, rowing with a nonmovable seat, and orienteering.

I don't include many other activities which some coaches consider part of a skier's training program. Chopping wood and digging ditches are not specific enough for the skier. They may contribute to general conditioning and may be a good mental outlet, but the athlete can't rely on this type of activity to prepare him for cross-country skiing.

Biking. I've disapproved of bike riding since the early 1970s when I watched skiers get injured on bikes and other skiers train for bike racing rather than for ski racing. I'm so convinced it's nearly a useless activity for skiers that I put only enough biking in my athletes' programs to give them sore rear ends so they end up wanting to stay away from it.

Let me further explain my prejudice. The lack of upper body use in biking is detrimental to skiers. The leg muscles developed by biking are not the same as those needed for skiing. Leg flexibility is hampered because biking shortens the hamstring and calf muscles. Because the body weight is supported by a seat and you often train in packs, the effort expended is 20%–30% below maximum. Therefore, time becomes a factor if you're training at high levels. To equal the physiological load of 60–90 minutes of roller skiing, you need to bike for three or four hours. The roller skier will be getting some needed rest while the biker is still out pedaling.

The best thing I can say is that biking provides some variety when a skier goes stale doing First-Class Activities and can be used during rehabilitation from certain injuries.

Running and Hiking. Both running and hiking can be useful as cardiovascular workouts; but without poles, coordination and arm use are limited. These activities may be upgraded by incorporating leg movements similar to skiing—long strides and ski walking up hills on the heels. A full, poling-type arm swing may be coordinated with leg movement. These additions will make running and hiking a bit more specific for skiing.

I'm certain, despite the discouraging facts, that running will remain a part of skiers' training programs. However, the athlete who wants to reach his full potential as a skier will give running a backseat to ski walking, ski running, and ski hiking with poles.

Swimming. Swimming might become an important part of a skier's training program if he is injured or if he is traveling and doesn't have the time or equipment to roller ski or ski run. Swimming is a good mental break and adds variety to a program.

Orienteering. A lot of skiers orienteer during the off-season. It's fun and educational in terms of learning to use a compass and a map and in developing teamwork and camaraderie. It's a good cardiovascular activity for the skier, particularly if the course is set over ski terrain. I know I've put myself under while orienteering.

Kayaking and Canoeing. These activities are good for upper body work, but because the legs are virtually static their value to skiers is limited. Kayaking is more intense than canoeing, but you'll still have to use some imagination to make it useful for ski training. If the skier has a leg injury, however, kayaking and canoeing could become an important part of his program during recovery. While canoeing and kayaking, check your pulse. It will take a good amount of time and effort at these activities to reach the training effect zone. But for all of us non-Olympians, a good canoe trip or a kayak through the rapids is a fun mental break and makes us feel like we've accomplished a little something.

METHOD TWO—INTERVAL TRAINING

Interval training is a significant part of the education and conditioning of the competitor. Because a cross-country race may be viewed as a series of connected intervals, interval training is educational for both the brain and the body. The athlete must know his physical and mental limits in order to raise those limits. Through interval training you will gain an increased body awareness. You'll learn the effects that various speeds, stress, and pain have on your body, so when these same sensations occur in competition you will know how to deal with them.

Many athletes overlook the relationship between what they experience in training and what they experience in competition. They view training only as physiological conditioning and ignore the valuable lessons to be carried over from training to racing. Because intervals approximate the physical demands of racing, the wise athlete knows the value of interval training and will use it to prepare both physically and mentally for competition. He will remember the body signs encountered in a July workout when the same signs occur in a January race. Those signs will tell him when he is pushing his body too hard and when it is time to press harder. Further, intervals improve your cardiovascular system so your muscles are better supplied with oxygen. Aerobic intervals improve the body's peripheral circulatory efficiency,and anaerobic intervals improve its central system. This is accomplished while the body learns to function with the speeds and loads of racing.

Interval training involves periods of strenuous activity alternated with periods of recovery which involve light activity or rest. The workouts are controlled by a stopwatch and the skier's pulse rate. The body is trained to accept progressively heavier workloads and recover from them quickly.

Endurance training is the foundation for the cross-country skier, and interval training is the stairway to the top of his physical capability. Because of their importance, intervals must be a part of the skier's training program throughout the year. The emphasis on intervals will, of course, vary at different times of the year, gaining increasing importance as the racing season approaches and gets underway. During the off-season, the amount of time spent on intervals should increase from 8% of the skier's training program in May to 20% in October (Table 2).

Interval training is one of the most misunderstood, misused, and ignored methods of training. Some American coaches and athletes dislike the regimentation of intervals, so they fail to include them in their programs. Other coaches rely on intervals daily because they believe using the stopwatch will motivate athletes, particularly skiers in a school program. However, training can become so intense that it not only harms the skier's body but kills his enthusiasm for training and for his sport.

In planning productive interval workouts, you must apply the tenets of training, know the guidelines for controlling intervals, and determine the goals of each training session. With these factors in hand, many different types of activities may be used for interval training. As with endurance training activities, I qualify the types of activities for intervals into two classes. First-Class Activities include roller skiing, grass skiing, and hill running—a combination of ski walking, ski striding, ski sprinting, ski running, the hesitation walk, and the Indian dance. All these activities are specific to the demands of cross-country skiing. Second-Class Activities for intervals would include rowing, running, biking, kayaking, canoeing, and swimming. Again, these activities provide variety to a training program but are definitely not as beneficial to the skier as First-Class Activities. If biking or running is a major part of your training program, you should be aware that this activity can be used in intervals.

Aerobic Intervals

With the aim of improving peripheral circulation efficiency, aerobic intervals involve fairly long work periods within the athlete's training effect zone alternated with periods of recovery. Any First- or Second-Class Activity may be used for aerobic intervals.

In planning an aerobic interval workout, locate terrain which is gentle and plan on a pace which will keep your pulse rate in TEZ. Set up a loop which will take 3–10 minutes to cover. After warming up, cover the loop as fast as possible without going anaerobic. If the terrain is variable, you may need to slow to a walk on uphills to keep your pulse rate below your anaerobic threshold. After completing each trip over the loop, rest. You may want to stretch and jog or ski around easily. Check your pulse rate every 30–60 seconds during this recovery period. When your heart rate is down to 120 beats per minute, you're ready to cover the loop again. Athletes in good physical condition will require a recovery period of two minutes or less. Be certain to record the time it takes you to cover each loop and to recover between each loop.

Anaerobic intervals

Many sports medicine experts and physiologists believe that the next breakthrough in cross-country competition will come from those athletes able to spend an increasing amount of time doing anaerobic training. Such training raises the skier's anaerobic threshold, increasing his ability to ski faster for longer periods of time at or near anaerobic levels. However, anaerobic training must be kept in balance with all the other training methods useful to the skier.

Anaerobic intervals are short and very intense work periods in which the athlete is operating at 80% of his maximum pulse rate and above, meaning that he is at or above his anaerobic threshold. The goal is to improve his central cardiovascular efficiency while working under an oxygen debt. The workout may involve First- or Second-Class Activities conducted over a loop between 30 seconds and three minutes long. The terrain does not need to be gentle. You cover the loop at race pace or above so your pulse rate reaches 80% or more of its maximum rate. Heart monitors are particularly useful in anaerobic intervals. Between efforts, rest or exercise lightly until your pulse rate is down to 100 beats per minute. Again, be certain to record your pulse rates and the time it takes to cover the loop and to recover.

Controlling Interval Workouts

A very important consideration in interval training is accurately determining when the workout should end. There are basically two rules of thumb to use when deciding how many repetitions signal the end of a workout.

The first approach is to compare the length of time it takes an athlete to cover the interval. For example, if the skier covers the first four repetitions in two minutes each and his time on the fifth repetition increases by only a couple of seconds, the workout should be continued. But when the time on a repetition increases by 15 seconds or more, it's time to stop the workout.

The second guideline to controlling intervals is by recovery time. I prefer this method because it's a true indication of the athlete's physical state. If the workout involves two-minute intervals and it takes the athlete 60 seconds for his pulse to return to 100 (for an anaerobic workout) or 120 (for aerobic) between repetitions, the workout continues as long as the 60-second recovery time remains fairly constant. When his recovery time increases significantly, perhaps up to 80–90 seconds, the workout should be ended.

The guidelines for controlling intervals—repetition time and recovery time—are flexible. The increase in repetition time may vary quite a bit, depending on the length of the interval and each athlete's level of conditioning. Also, the athlete might vary his pace, deliberately or not. An intense pace will lead to a quick increase in repetition time. The recovery rate may actually improve for a time before increasing.

Controlling the workout requires good communication between the coach and the athlete. The coach must carefully monitor how each athlete is responding to the workload. He should watch for telltale signs that an athlete might be over his head physiologically. An obvious sign, in addition to pulse rate and heavy breathing, is a loss of coordination. I can look into the eyes of athletes I know well and tell by a glazed look if they are going under.

Athletes can be destroyed by poorly controlled intervals. It is particularly important to monitor interval workouts of well conditioned athletes because they could psychologically continue intervals all day long. Over-training can be very destructive. Be aware of the goals of the workout, the type of training over the preceding few days, and upcoming training plans. Some days the athlete will need to push hard and other times take it a bit easier. Generally, he should feel like he might be able to complete one or two more repetitions when the workout is over. The workout should be positive and individual. It must be set up for each skier's needs so he can call it quits when his body signs say he should, not continue because others in the group are. It's important to conduct positive intervals geared to the individual so he doesn't come to hate interval training because he's been buried too many times by an inconsiderate program.

Interval Workouts

Coaches and athletes should use their imaginations to create a variety of interval workouts which are interesting as well as physiologically beneficial. Early in the off-season when the athlete might be doing just one interval workout a week, rotate the type of workout from week to week. As the summer progresses into fall and the athlete is doing two or three interval workouts each week, try to avoid duplicating the same workouts too often. Rotate the workouts and change locations to avoid boredom and keep up enthusiasm.

Table 2 (p. 20) includes a guideline to the percentage of time you should devote to intervals during the off-season. A good interval workout, depending on the level of the athlete, usually takes an hour, including warm up and warm down. The workouts can be adjusted to suit the level of conditioning by combining both anaerobic and aerobic work and by setting an appropriate pace, load (via terrain), and number of repetitions. Establish good locations for the various types of interval work planned. I often use the same hill for

Grass skiing. By comparing Doug Peterson's grass skiing to the on-snow hill running technique photos in Chapter 5, you can see the obvious similarity of the movements. Grass skiing is not widely accepted as an off season workout yet, but it would be a good addition to everyone's fall interval program.

grass skiing and hill running because I've found a good one which offers a variety of ways to negotiate the climb from bottom to top. The hill can be used for intervals anywhere from 15 seconds to four minutes in length and has a variety of terrain available.

Grass Skiing. A fairly recent addition to dryland training activities is grass skiing. I've used it successfully the past couple summers and found it to be a fantastic workout technically, physiologically, and psychologically. Hopefully, at some point there will be plastic trails developed for off-season ski training since grass skiing requires a bit of work to set up. In the meantime, grass skiing is a great addition to off-season training because there is no way to overrate the importance of training on skis for coordination of upper and lower body, timing, full-body use and just the mental boost of being on skis in July.

To set up a grass skiing workout, find a suitable hay meadow or logging road with a moderate uphill suitable for intervals. To make things easier on yourself, gather a group of skiers to lay down pine needles, hay, or sawdust in tracks. Try to find an area which will require a minimum of maintenance over the summer.

Use some old fiberglass rock skis or even an old pair of wood skis, aluminum poles a bit shorter than your on-snow poles and normal cross-country boots and bindings. The skis will be waxed according to the type of workout. When I want to concentrate on lower body effort, I heat in a durable binder wax. With no wax, the upper body will come into play more as the skis are now more slippery.

Grass skiing is a great time to work on technique because you don't have a 100% kick as you do in all other dry-land activities. Therefore, grass skiing is very similar to snow skiing because you must use your arms and be conscious of getting on your ski correctly; you can't be sloppy like you can while roller skiing. Using a video or sequence photos is a good aid in technique work.

Grass skiing is strenuous anaerobic interval training. We often warm up and warm down by doing ski walking. Sliding back down the hill should suffice as the recovery period.

Hill Running. Hill running is a great conglomeration of all types of activities with various training benefits. The workout includes dryland activities used by skiers throughout the Nordic world, plus a couple of moves we dreamed up in the U.S. All the activities are specific, and the training can be a mix of anaerobic and aerobic with a good dose of technique work as an added benefit. Because of this combination of advantages, hill running, along with roller skiing, is the backbone of many skiers' off-season program.

Take your aluminum ski poles and find a fairly long hill about the steepness of a typical uphill on a cross-country course. A grassy meadow or a seldom-used dirt road will work. Six activities are involved in hill running: ski walking, hill striding, Indian dancing, ski sprinting, ski running, and the hesitation walk. In planning a workout, you can pick just one of these activities. I usually include all six so I can work on anaerobic and aerobic conditioning, explosive strength, technique, pace adjustment, etc.

Ski walking is primarily aerobic with a stride rate of 2.1 to 2.2 strides per second, as in uphill snow skiing. This is definitely a technique exercise. With each stride, be in a dynamic position and concentrate on rolling over the ankle so your shin-ankle angle changes and the angle of your knee remain pretty static. This technique will simulate the kick in hill skiing. The step is primarily one where the heel strikes the ground first. Use your poles. Each repetition of ski walking may last between one and four minutes.

Hill striding with poles, or ski striding, is a fairly traditional training activity but is currently held in tenuous esteem because biomechanical studies determined that Americans were too upright while skiing. I think hill striding is still beneficial, provided you assume a dynamic position and stay close to the ground. The motion is a springing one and you land on the heel of your foot. The poling arm should make a thrusting, downward motion toward the knee, not the hips. Striding correctly often puts you in an anaerobic state because of the natural pace, but a gentle uphill will make it possible for the exercise to be aerobic. Each repetition will last 30–90 seconds.

The Indian dance is the only one of these activities in which you don't use poles. The dance is basically a skipping motion with a vertical emphasis, which requires explosive lower leg action. Be certain to coordinate movement of your opposing arm and leg as in skiing. This requires a bit of coordination and is harder than it looks. The Indian dance should be done in 30- to 60-second repetitions. It is beneficial in developing the explosive power of your gastroc (calf) and quadricep (thigh) muscles, which are important in the explosion of the cross-country kick.

The ski sprint is an all-out effort for 15–45 seconds. The emphasis isn't on technique, other than coordinating the arm and leg movements, but is anaerobic work for speed and quickness of movement.

Ski running, on the other hand, involves some control of your pace. You will be able to use your poles more than in sprinting, although the motion is shortened up a bit. The emphasis is again on cardiovascular conditioning rather than technique. Each repetition will be from one to three minutes.

The hesitation walk is a strength movement at a very slow pace. It involves going through the ski striding motion with a hesitation or pause each time you step on the lead foot. The emphasis is on making correctly timed strong movements. It may look pretty dumb, but after you do it for a minute, you'll learn the effort it requires. The forced slowness is good for both strength and timing. Because of the slow pace, it's a great opportunity to concentrate on technique—you can watch each pole plant, where you place your foot on each stride, where your arms are moving, etc. Each repetition of the hesitation walk should last 1–4 minutes.

Hill running workouts can be designed in a number of ways and can be used for both formal (timed) intervals and informal training. Set up a program which alternates anaerobic speed work with aerobic exercises emphasizing technique. As your conditioning improves, you can add more time to each activity and more repetitions to each set of activities. Between repetitions, remember to recover to 100 heartbeats per minute for anaerobic work and 120 for aerobic effort.

Ski striding. The right arm is moving up and into a levered position so it's ready to work upon pole implantation. Note the length of the stride.

Indian dance. A Hall invention to develop strength and explosiveness in the kicking motion. Be certain to coordinate the arm and leg movements correctly; like the diagonal stride, the opposite arm and leg move together. Learn the movement by simply skipping, then increase your arm use and vertical thrust.

Indian dance. Keep the arms relaxed and work to achieve as much height off the "kick" as possible. Point the toe of the kicking foot down when you're in the air. This exercise uses all the leg muscles involved in the kicking movement of skiing.

Ski sprint. Used mainly in hill runni workouts, the ski sprint is anaerobic trai ing with little concern for technique. T skier works to build maximum speed for 15–40 second sprint.

Hesitation walk. This is a useful movement for both technique work and strength. The athlete is in the position where he momentarily hesitates before making his next poling and kicking motions. As he hesitates, he checks his pole placement, angulation, and alignment and gets set for a well-timed and very strong poling and kicking motion. After doing the hesitation walk uphill for 1–4 minutes, you'll feel why it builds strength.

Fartlek and Natural Intervals

All too many coaches and athletes accept fartlek and natural intervals as interval training. In fact, they are part of endurance training and do not qualify as intervals. They are hit-and-miss activities because they are informal and subjective.

Fartlek is a Swedish term which loosely translates as speed play. The athlete runs or skis or roller skis, increasing his pace and/or terrain when he feels like it. When he tires, he slows the pace until he recovers. This is obviously a very informal, subjective workout. Any conditioning benefits will come only if the athlete knows his body and is willing to push himself for 45 minutes to an hour. In natural intervals, the athlete lets variations in terrain create the workload. While moving at the same pace, the terrain changes will affect his pulse rate. On the flat, his pulse might be 120, on an uphill it will be 170 or so, and then the downhills are used for recovery. The difficulty of the workload depends on the terrain, although pace could be adjusted to affect a greater training load.

Natural intervals are a process occurring constantly in training, unless the terrain is totally flat. Therefore, natural intervals are simply a part of endurance training and do not constitute a true interval workout. Accepting natural intervals as anything beyond endurance training is a copout. Anyone who relies only on fartlek and natural intervals for interval training doesn't have a good grasp of training principles.

Tips on Interval Training

■ As should be obvious, it's almost necessary to have someone else time intervals. It's possible to time yourself, but it's more beneficial if you don't have to worry about this aspect of your training session. When I run interval workouts for athletes, I record their time on slips of paper and hand the slips to them at the end of the workout so they can record their times in their training logs.

■ It's not always necessary to time intervals and keep track of pulse rates, although these steps add control and objectivity to the workout. Another method is to establish a certain pace for covering a specific distance. This trains the athlete to have a feel for pace and its affects on his body after several repetitions at the same speed.

■ The athlete should put particular effort into recording information about his interval workouts in his training log. Include facts such as the type of workout, the number of repetitions completed, the pulse rates reached, recovery times after each repetition, and the time it took to cover each repetition. Record feelings about how your body reacted to the workout—whether you felt you were going under, when your muscles started burning—so you can relate to these reactions when they occur in a race. This will add perspective to your daily and long-term training plans and goals. The interval log will let you evaluate your progress and plan your training in terms of volumes, percentages, and types of workouts needed. Comparing your records of interval workouts is an objective gauge of improvement.

■ Remember, the recovery rate for aerobic intervals is a pulse rate of 120 and 100 for anaerobic. These figures apply to all athletes. The pulse rate doesn't need to be exact but should be within five beats.

■ Get plenty of rest after interval training. Your body has been under stress and it will take time and rest for it to recover.

■ Don't forget to warm up before and warm down after interval workouts. Dress properly.

■ During the fall, participate in roller ski races and other fast, timed workouts which classify as tempo training.

■ If you're training intervals with other athletes, don't worry about comparing or competing with them. They might need a 170 heart beat to be anaerobic, while you reach your threshold at 160. There are times when it's helpful to be pushed by another athlete, but you must evaluate your training based on your own level of conditioning, training effect zone, and pace. The only valid comparison between skiers comes during competition in the winter.

■ The more athletes involved in an interval workout, the more coaches and/or timers required. When one coach tries to handle 15 or 20 skiers, the workout becomes an effort in mediocrity. The coach can't deal with each athlete individually, so he must gear the workout to the average level of conditioning, which is a disservice to all. There are several ways to involve a group in interval training, particularly anaerobic intervals. The coach must be concerned with each skier's needs and conditioning level. The lesser athlete may do the same workout, but it's important that he do fewer repetitions. Or the stronger athlete might be handicapped by going farther or starting a specified number of seconds behind the lesser athlete. The two can still train together, as long as the needs and limits of each are considered.

Many athletes and coaches don't like intervals. Granted, they are hard work. But the athlete shouldn't be afraid of them because they are an excellent evaluation of his conditioning progress. It always amazes me when athletes don't want to find out exactly how they're doing—just like skiers who love to train but hate to race. Because intervals are objective, they are an accurate indication of what is good and bad about a training program. Intervals let the skier know where his training is weak along his route to the winter of racing so he can alter his program, if need be, before the season arrives. Intervals are a true education of mind and body. Don't ignore them.

METHOD THREE—STRENGTH TRAINING

Because cross-country skiing is a power endurance sport and because of the technical demands of modern skis, strength training has become an increasingly important part of the serious skier's program. A portion of the skier's training time must be set aside for strength training because other activities, such as roller skiing and rowing, can't adequately improve his overall strength.

The explosive power necessary for a strong, long stride on skis is best developed through a specific strength training program. Such a program will also improve speed of movement, decrease the possibility of injury, and enhance muscle endurance, the ability of the muscle to contract repeatedly with power. Strength training will give you both a physical and a psychological advantage over the skier who has ignored this aspect of conditioning. Further, the self-discipline required for pursuing a strength program will carry over into all of your activities.

Some athletes, particularly Europeans and women, are still concerned about becoming muscle-bound from weight lifting and other strength work. This simply won't happen in a program for skiing. If you use specific exercises with a full range of motion, you won't get muscle-bound—you'll get strong! And you'll come out of a good program more flexible

These photos of Doug Peterson grass skiing illustrate and identify the muscles and muscle groups which are the prime movers in cross-country skiing. Although just about every muscle is involved in skiing and training, the ones identified here are the ones deserving concentrated development in a strength training program.

than ever before. Women should be the last skiers to shy away from strength training. Due to their physiology and training backgrounds, women can gain tremendous benefits from strength work, particularly in their upper bodies.

Strength training used to be synonomous with weight lifting. Actually, there are a number of activities outside the weight room which can build a skier's strength. The individual must decide how he can best and most comfortably accomplish improvements in his skiing strength by evaluating the various available activities. There are two basic strength training methods: formal and informal.

The basis of a formal program is lifting in the weight room with either Nautilus or Universal Gym machines or lifting with free weights (barbells). The skier suppliments weight lifting with the Exer-Genie and the roller board, both used to specifically strengthen skiing muscles.

The informal strength program is based on using the athlete's body weight as the main source of resistance rather than weights. The training might involve a circuit loop in which you run through the woods, stopping at stations to perform various exercises. Good exercises for skiers include arm dips, leaning wall leg squats, sit-ups and back extensors. The Exer-Genie and roller board are also a part of an informal program.

Many athletes use a combination of both formal and informal strength programs, varying the emphasis on each during the off-season. Other skiers with limited time and/or equipment devise a series of strength activities they can perform in their own living room. The options are varied and selection is up to the individual. I would advise the athlete to read books on strength training and weight lifting before establishing his own program. The more knowledgeable the athlete, the more successful he will be.

During the off-season, the athlete should do a strength workout three times a week. There's an old axiom about developing strength: if you work out once a week you make no gains, twice a week you maintain, and three times a week you gain. When planning each weekly training program, the strength workouts should be included first. Work the other activities around the strength work, alternating days. Don't do strength work two days in a row. Strength workouts are, by their nature, negative because the loads, intensity, and muscle stress involved leave you physically exhausted. Also be certain to work gradually into a strength program. Even well conditioned athletes must let their bodies gradually adjust to the training as they begin their off-season strength work each spring.

Before and after the strength workout, the athlete must warm up and warm down to avoid injury. A good strength workout will include 15 minutes of warm up and 15 minutes of warm down. Run to get the circulation going and do some stretching exercises to loosen up the muscles and hasten recovery from muscle stress before and after the workout.

If the late summer or fall arrives and the athlete hasn't made the progress he'd planned in his strength program, he can go into a crash program. Instead of strength work Monday, Wednesday, and Friday with the weekends off, do strength workouts on every other day through the weekends. I've had my athletes successfully so through such a program just before the season started to improve their strength levels.

The serious athlete will want to develop a separate log just to record his strength training. The accomplishments in each workout will be recorded. The strength log will be especially helpful if the athlete is starting a new program or if he has an extensive workout involving a number of different activities. It's important to record everything about a strength program, so the athlete is aware of progress, plateaus, and problems with certain activities.

The Weight Room

The first step in the weight room is to become familiar with the equipment, just as in any training program. Start slowly by going through the total circuit of exercises easily with light weights. Get used to the movements involved in each lift and be certain to go through the full range of motion. The worst thing the athlete can do is charge ahead—he'll likely strain muscles and wind up being so sore he won't be able to work out for a week. He should go easy the first couple of sessions and educate himself on how the equipment works and what demands the workout will make on his body.

The Universal Gym and Nautilus machines are the most ideal equipment for weight training. They are self-contained, don't require spotters, and are easy to adjust. They save time and mental energy and can be adjusted to be more specific for cross-country training compared to free weights. Just be certain to familiarize yourself with how each machine and each station works—how to adjust the seats, how to strap yourself in, how to adjust the weights—so you properly isolate the muscle groups to be worked and avoid injury.

The Nautilus is said to do the best job of isolating muscle groups, allowing you to make the greatest gains in the least amount of time. Further, the Nautilus works on an elipse mechanism so the workout is isokenetic—resistance is progressive as you move through the motion. Isokenetics compensate for the fact that the limb can lift weight in proportion to the accuteness of the angle. As the angle increases, more weight can be lifted. Thus, the athlete may lift 80 lb in the first stage of a military press on the Nautilus, but the resistance will increase to 150 lb as the motion is completed.

Free weights and some Universal Gym machines provide only isotonic work in which the level of resistance is constant throughout the entire range of motion. Isometric strength work, such as sitting against the wall in the phantom chair, involves the muscle contracting against resistance without going through the full range of motion. Isokenetic work is most useful for the skier because he lifts the optimum weight through a full range of motion and gains full strength in all phases of the movement. Newer Universal Gyms include a levering system which allows for isokenetic strength training.

The principle in developing strength is to reach a state of total muscle fatigue. We often joke about this and call it total muscle failure. You work until your muscles are exhausted. You'll know when this happens because your muscles tremble and there's no way you can do that last lift or pull yourself up the roller board once more. Strength increases when the muscle is worked to its maximum.

Progression on the Nautilus starts by establishing a weight on each station which you can handle. At each station you complete a set of 8–11 lifts. The weight should be adjusted so that by the final repetition the muscles involved are totally exhausted. Each time you can complete the number of repetitions recommended for a station, you increase the weight by one plate during your next workout. This progression continues.

When using free weights or a Universal Gym, I recommend the following program, which was developed for the U.S. Ski Team. At each station, or for each muscle group exercise, do three sets of ten repetitions with progressive resistance. For example, if the first set has a resistance of 100 lb, the second set should be increased to 110. For the third set, lift 120 lb as many times as possible. When you can lift the 120 lb ten times on the third set, begin your next workout with 110 lb in the first set, 120 on the second and 130 on the third. This progression is repeated at each station as you can handle 10 repetitions of the third set. Table 10 is an abbreviated sample of a weight training log for use with free weights or the Universal Gym. Note the progression of resistance through the sets and over the time period.

When working with free weights, you must have a spotter on hand to avoid injury. You don't want to end up pinned to the bench with 150 lb on your chest when you can't quite make that last repetition. The last lift will build your strength, and a spotter can help you make that final inch to complete the motion. Having a spotter is simply the smart and safe thing to do when working with barbells.

Rest periods during weight lifting or any type of strength workout should be no longer than the time it takes you to complete one set. Thus, the rest period may be as short as 15 seconds, depending on how much weight you are moving and how fast you're lifting it. During the rest period, do some stretching, particularly those muscles you just worked. The short rest periods mean you move right along through your weight lifting. You'll be exhausted at the end of the workout.

Everyone, particularly beginners and even the athlete who has been lifting weights for a long time, eventually reaches a plateau in lifting. The athlete achieves a certain level of resistance and finds it difficult to increase the load. The body becomes a bit resistive to progress and the plateau could last a week or ten days, but he has to fight his way off the plateau and into heavier weights or his training progress will come to a standstill. The problem most often occurs with the athlete's weakest lift, proving again that the athlete tries least at activities he doesn't like. I know that I don't like the military press—it drives me crazy—but I also know that I must drive myself hardest at it.

One method of getting off the weight-lifting plateau is to back off in other areas of training so you have more energy for your strength program; don't back off on your weights. Then you should enter the weight room totally psyched to pull out of the plateau. Another way to move on is to lift with a friend who is near your level, which may give you the competitive incentive to tough it out and move on. Try yelling and screaming like the discus throwers to get the adrenalin flowing.

TABLE 10
Sample Weight Training Log

Lift		Military Press			Leg Press			Bench Press			Sit-Ups		
Date	Sets	1	2	3	1	2	3	1	2	3	1	2	3
6/22	Reps	10	10	10	10	10	10	10	10	9	25	25	25
	Wt	125	135	145	225	235	245	135	145	155	0	0	0
6/24	Reps	10	8	7	10	9	8	10	10	10	25	20	15
	Wt	135	145	155	235	245	255	135	145	155	5	5	5
6/26	Reps	10	9	8									
	Wt	135	145	155									

There are several ways to put variety into a weight lifting program. Rotate from station to station or from exercise to exercise within the program. Do each set once and move through the entire routine three times instead of completing three sets at each station. Or complete the sets at a station, go outside and run a bit, then return for the next station. You may also add variety by mixing the three types of weight lifting—power, endurance, and pure strength lifting. Strength lifting is basically the progressive program where you do a maximum of ten lifts per station and increase the weight progressively. Endurance lifting is when you continue the repetitions beyond eight or ten; progression is measured by the number of lifts you can do rather than by added resistance. Power lifting is when you work with lighter resistance and lift as fast as you can.

Some skiers do a combination of the three types of lifting during each workout. Others begin the off-season by doing endurance lifting, move into pure strength lifting in mid-summer, and switch to power lifting three or four weeks before going on snow. Still other skiers stick with one type of lifting throughout the off-season. The choice is yours.

But the athlete should not limit his strength training just to weight lifting. Other more specific activities should suppliment his program. The Exer-Genie and roller board are excellent activities to develop strengths necessary for cross-country skiing. Finish off your strength workout by using the roller board (for double poling) and Exer-genie (for diagonal stride poling) to develop muscle memory specific to skiing. Muscle memory, simply put, is getting the muscles conditioned to working in the same planes as they will while skiing. You want your muscles to remember how to perform best during a race when they are tired, and by using the roller board and Exer-Genie after weight lifting they will develop a memory of how to perform.

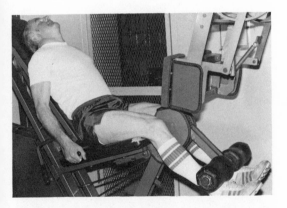

NAUTILUS KNEE EXTENSION

Load: *Select the number of plates that will cause total muscle fatigue after 8–11 repetitions.*

Position: *Sit in seat and adjust backboard for good support. Place legs so ankle joints are behind lifting pads.*

Movement: *Raise legs directly upward until knee joint is fully extended and legs are straight. Return to starting position and repeat.*

Main Muscle Benefits: *Quadriceps* (front thigh muscles; primary in kicking motion)

UNIVERSAL KNEE EXTENSION

Load: *Men start with 25% of body weight; women with 20%. Weight increased by 5 lb each set.*

Workout: *3 sets of 15 repetitions each leg.*

Position: *Sit upright on lifting bench with lower legs at right angles to upper legs.*

Movement: *Lift lower leg until knee joint is fully extended and leg parallel to floor. Lower leg slowly. Repeat, alternating legs.*

Main Muscle Benefits: *Quadriceps* (front thigh muscles; primary in kicking motion)

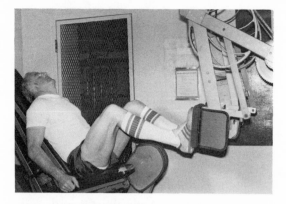

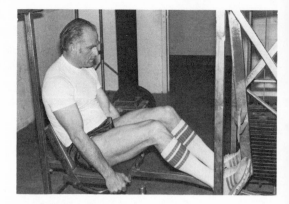

NAUTILUS LEG PRESS

Load: *Select the number of plates that will cause total muscle fatigue after 8–11 repetitions.*

Position: *Sit in seat and adjust backrest for firm support. Place feet evenly on pad to ensure equal pressure in movement.*

Movement: *Keep head and back in contact with backrest. Push feet directly out until legs are straight and knees are locked. Return to starting position and repeat.*

Main Muscle Benefits: *Quadriceps* (front thigh muscles; primary in kicking motion), *gastrocnemius* (calf muscles)

UNIVERSAL LEG PRESS

Load: *Start with weights equal to body weight; increase by 10 lb each set.*

Workout: *3 sets of 10 repetitions.*

Position: *Sit securely in seat, knees bent, holding on with hands for support.*

Movement: *Pushing evenly with both feet, extend knees until legs are completely straight. Return slowly to starting position and repeat.*

Main Muscle Benefits: *Quadriceps* (front thigh muscles), *gluteus maximus* (buttocks muscles), *gastrocnemius* (calf muscles)

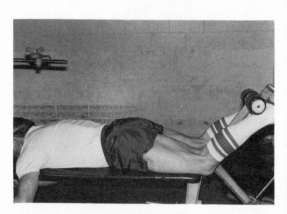

UNIVERSAL ANKLE EXTENSION

Load: *Men start with 60% of body weight; women with 50%. Weight increased by 10 lb each set.*

Workout: *3 sets of 10 repetitions.*

Position: *Stand with balls of feet resting on board 1–3 in. high; heels on floor. Hold lift in rest position.*

Movement: *Lift by raising heels off the floor until the weight is bearing on the balls of the feet. Slowly lower heels to floor and repeat.*

Main Muscle Benefits: *Gastrocnemius* (calf muscles; used in completing kicking motion)

UNIVERSAL KNEE CURL

Load: *Men start with 20% of body weight; women with 10%. Weight increased by 5–10 lb each set.*

Workout: *3 sets of 15 repetitions.*

Position: *Raise the lower legs as far as possible toward buttocks. Lower slowly to starting position and repeat.*

Main Muscle Benefits: *Biceps femoris* (back thigh muscle; used to straighten leg at end of kicking motion), *semitendinosus* (back thigh muscle), *gracilis* (back thigh muscle)

NAUTILUS HAMSTRING PULL

Load: *Select the number of plates that will cause total muscle fatigue after 8–11 repetitions.*

Position: *Lie back down on bench, firmly cinch support belt, and activate by pushing both pads under hamstrings down to a position parallel to floor.*

Movement: *With one leg held in start position, raise the other toward the chest in a bent position. Straighten raised leg and push it back to start position.*

Main Muscle Benefits: *Biceps femoris* (hamstring, back thigh muscle; used to straighten leg at end of kicking motion), *gluteus maximus* (buttocks muscles)

UNIVERSAL LATS BAR

Load: *Men start with 20% of body weight; women with 10%. Weight increased by 5–10 lb each set.*

Workout: *3 sets of 10 repetitions.*

Position: *Instead of pulling on bar, wrap a towel over top of bar to simulate double poling motion. Grab towel and stand in ready position.*

Movement: *Keeping back rigid, pull hands toward hips. Slowly return to starting position and repeat.*

Main Muscle Benefits: *Triceps and latissimus dorsi* (back of upper arm muscle and side of back muscle; primary in poling motion)

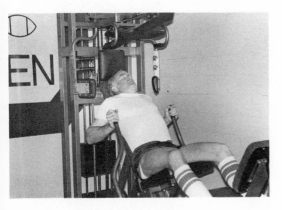

NAUTILUS ELBOW EXTENSION

Load: *Select the number of plates that will cause total muscle fatigue after 8–11 repetitions.*

Position: *Firmly strap into seat with support belt. Activate machine by pushing against foot pad, raising handles. Release foot pad after placing hands in position on handles.*

Movement: *Push the handles away from chest until arms are fully extended in locked position. Slowly return to starting position and repeat.*

Main Muscle Benefits: *Triceps* (back of upper arm muscle; primary in poling motion), *latissimus dorsi* (side of back muscles)

NAUTILUS MILITARY PRESS

Load: *Select the number of plates that will cause total muscle fatigue after 8–11 repetitions.*

Position: *Sitting upright, grasp handles just above shoulders.*

Movement: *Pushing straight up, extend arms until they are straight and in a locked position. Return slowly to starting position and repeat.*

Main Muscle Benefits: *Triceps* (back of upper arm muscle; primary in poling motion), *deltoids and trapezius* (muscles in shoulder and upper back)

FREE WEIGHT BENCH PRESS

Load: *Men start with 50% of body weight; women with 40%. Weight increased by 10 lb each set.*

Workout: *3 sets of 10 repetitions.*

Position: *Lie back down on bench so knees are bent and feet are on floor. Hold barbell on chest.*

Movement: *Press the barbell directly upward until arms are fully extended. Slowly lower to chest and repeat.*

Main Muscle Benefits: *Triceps* (back of upper arm muscle; primary poling muscle), *pectoralis major and serratus anterior* (chest muscles)

NAUTILUS TRICEPS PULLOVER

Load: *Select the number of plates that will cause total muscle fatigue after 8–11 repetitions.*

Position: *Sit upright, firmly pressed against seat back, with hands holding wooden bar and elbows pressed to pads.*

Movement: *Being certain to keep elbows on pads, push up and forward until arms are parallel with floor. Return slowly to starting position and repeat.*

Main Muscle Benefits: *Triceps* (back of upper arm muscle; primary in poling motion), *latissimus dorsi* (side of back muscles)

NAUTILUS COMBINATION PULLOVER

Load: *Select the number of plates that will cause total muscle fatigue after 8–11 repetitions.*

Position: *Sitting upright with support belt tightly fastened, activate machine with foot bar and place elbows on pads of lifting bar. Remove feet from foot bar.*

Movement: *Let the lifting bar move back as far as possible, stretching triceps. Pushing against elbows, move the bar toward the thighs. Slowly return the bar to the starting position and repeat.*

Main Muscle Benefits: *Triceps* (back of upper arm muscle; primary in poling motion)

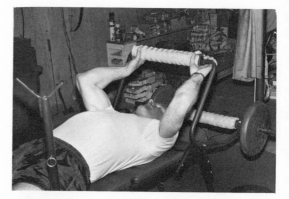

BENT ARM PULLOVER

Load: *Men start with 15% of body weight; women with 10%. Weight increased by 5 lb each set.*

Workout: *3 sets of 10 repetitions.*

Position: *Lying back down on weight training bench with feet on the floor, grab bar overhead.*

Movement: *After lowering the weight as far as is comfortable over and behind head, pull bar toward chest with arms bent until it reaches chest. Slowly return bar to start position and repeat.*

Main Muscle Benefits: *Triceps* (back of upper arm muscle; primary in poling motion), *pectoralis major and serratus anterior* (chest muscles)

Exer-Genie. Compare the similarity of arm movement in these photos with that of the diagonal stride. Set the Exer-Genie high enough so that you pull down, not back. Stand far enough away so that full arm extension on the follow-through is possible. Note the pole straps on the ropes that provide for poling simulation.

Exer-Genie

The Exer-Genie is a patented device which can be used almost anywhere for strength, endurance, and interval training. It costs about $35 and is small enough that it can—and should—be taken with the skier on his travels throughout the year. This flexible device can be set up in numerous ways to add specificity to the skier's training. Resistance from the device is adjustable to fit each individual. Through a simple adaptation of adding pole straps to the ends of the rope, the Exer-Genie allows the skier to simulate the diagonal poling motion during strength, interval and endurance workouts.

For an Exer-Genie strength workout, adjust the resistance level high enough so you can complete only 8–12 pulls with each arm before muscle fatigue sets in. Then do three sets of pulls, resting between sets for an amount of time equal to the time of completing one set. For an endurance workout, reduce the resistance so you can pull continuously for 10–30 minutes, depending on your conditioning level and sex. Exer-Genie intervals can be set up by adjusting the resistance level quite high and pulling hard for 30 seconds to two minutes. This will really get your heart pumping. Be certain to place the Exer-Genie high enough to allow for an accurate simulation of poling.

A new type of activity we're trying with the Exer-Genie is to use rope about 100 meters long with a harness attached to add resistance while grass skiing, ski walking, and snow skiing. Football players do this type of thing all the time to build strength and power. For skiers, this added resistance would slow speed but require stronger movements than needed skiing. A weighted sled might be more useful for winter strength training on snow.

Actually, the Exer-Genie can be used for any number of exercises. It comes with three sets of handles and a plate to stand on, which allows for back work. A manual on the various exercises comes with each Exer-Genie. One of its beauties is that it may be set up outdoors on a tree or indoors in front of the television set or in range of a stereo. Watching TV or listening to music while working out can make those 15–30 minutes more positive.

Roller Board

The roller board is an inclined plane with a sled and ropes used to simulate double poling. It's relatively inexpensive ($30 to $40 in materials), easy to make (an hour or two for anyone with some carpentry skills), and excellent for upper body strength, particularly double pole musculature.

The roller board may be used in sitting, kneeling, or lying positions. In a strength workout, do three sets of pulls, increasing the number of repetitions in each set. Resistance may be added by increasing the angle of the board. The first set, for example, may include 10 repetitions. For the second set, the number of repetitions should either be increased to 20 or the angle of the board should be increased. The third set is either 30 repetitions or 10 at an even more elevated angle. As strength is developed, add resistance by doing the pulls with a pack on your back which carries an increasing amount of weight each set.

For an endurance workout, place the roller board at a relatively low angle but high enough so your hands don't hit the ground. Then repeat the poling motion until you reach total muscle fatigue. Do two or three sets. Top skiers can complete three sets of about six minutes each.

When using the roller board, concentrate on completing the follow-through motion, raising your hands behind your back on each pull. When first trying the roller board, start with it at a low angle to familiarize yourself with the correct movement. Pull down, not back, to use the triceps. It's very important that the hands drop below the board, not right back to the shoulders.

Roller board, lying. Get comfortable on the sled, face down, and fully extend your arms overhead.

Roller board, lying. Keeping the arms slightly levered at the elbows, pull downward. The arms move straight down from the shoulders below the inclined plane of the roller board.

Roller board, lying. Finish the poling motion with a good follow-through. Your hands should be higher than your hips. Lower the sled slowly by reversing the arm motion.

Roller board, kneeling. Be certain to have the feet draped over the back of the sled and the back rounded. With arms levered, pull downward toward the knees, not back to the hips. Complete the follow through. If you can't, lower the roller board. This position is more specific than lying face down.

Roller board, sitting. Pull down and through as far as possible. Don't bend the elbows too much.

Weight Room Alternatives

Many athletes simply don't like the atmosphere of the weight room, but this doesn't mean they should ignore a strength training program. There are several alternatives to pumping iron in the gym.

One alternative is to set up a training room in your cellar, garage, or spare room. The Exer-Genie and roller board will be the two basic stations of a workout. Barbells are another good training investment, although not necessary. A variety of exercises will complete the program. Another alternative would be to set up a circuit training loop outside. You run to various stations, stopping for strength exercises. Because of the specificity of muscle memory developed by the Exer-Genie and roller board, I would advise the skier to concentrate on these two activities if he lacks the time or inclination for a more complete strength program.

As a bare minimum, skiers should plan three half-hour sessions each week for strength exercises in the living room. Even this bare-boned strength program will undoubtedly aid the skier come winter. Don't leave a blank spot under the strength column in your training log. Exercises which will build strength for skiing, in addition to the roller board and Exer-Genie, include back extensors, chair dips, arm dips, sit-ups, and leaning wall squats. Be creative in developing a strength training program that is meaningful to you.

Arm dips. Begin with the elbows straight and the body elevated. In the lowered position, the feet don't touch the ground, and the angle at the elbows should be 90° with the upper arm parallel to the ground. Return to the starting position and repeat. A workout includes three sets of 10 repetitions. When you can handle this load, increase resistance by wearing a pack weighted in five-pound increments.

Leaning leg squat. This is a great leg strength exercise because it works on the quadriceps, hamstrings, and gastroc muscles. With your head three inches from a wall or tree, place one foot about three feet from the tree and squat until the knee is at a 90° angle. Keep the opposite foot off the ground.

Leaning leg squat. Keeping your head three inches from the tree, straighten the weighted leg. Repeat continuously for a set of 25, then switch to the other leg. When you can do three sets on each leg, wear a weighted pack in increments of 10 pounds.

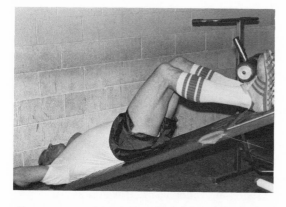

Sit-ups, or stomach curls. The main beneficiary of the sit-up is the rectus abdominus and other muscles used to aid breathing and poling and that work to hinge the upper and lower body. Curls can be performed on a flat surface or add resistance by using an inclined plane such as the roller board or the device on the Universal Gym pictured here. Firmly secure the feet, bend the knees, clasp the hands behind the head, and sit-up to about one third of the distance to your knees.

Back extensors. This exercise is vital to the skier because it strengthens the erector spinae, which is the major muscle in the lower back responsible for supporting you in the dynamic positions of skiing. Lie on the stomach with legs held down and the upper body hanging at a 90° angle below the legs, with hands clasped behind your head.

Back extensors. Continue to raise the body until it is horizontal to the ground. Lower slowly and repeat. A workout includes three sets of 15 repetitions. Hold weights of five-pound increments when you can perform the three sets.

Plyometrics

A relatively new concept in strength training, plyometrics, has been used successfully by track and field athletes in the Soviet Union and East Germany and has been added to the training program of U.S. jumpers. The goal of plyometrics is to bridge the gap between the strength and the power required in producing explosive movements. Explosive strength and power are essential in increasing the skier's stride length.

Loosely defined, plyometrics follows the rubber-band theory—the faster and further a rubber band is stretched, the more forcefully it will snap back. Similarly, by prestretching a muscle before it is contracted, the muscle will be able to handle a heavier workload faster. In other words, a muscle's concentric contraction (shortening) is much stronger if it immediately follows the same muscle's eccentric contraction (prestretching). Plyometric training develops the muscle's capacity to accept a load and carry it quickly. This capacity is very useful in increasing the skier's stride length while maintaining his stride rate.

Plyometric drills should be done outside on grass or dirt, not on pavement. The athlete should wear orthotic plastic cups on his heels. Both of these suggestions are geared to prevent injuries because of the tremendous forces generated in plyometric exercises. Typical plyometric drills include the frog hop in which you jump from a crouched (prestretched) position as far as you can continuously for a specified distance. The goal is to decrease the number of jumps it takes you to cover the distance by increasing the length of each jump. The exercise serves to develop leg strength and power. A second sample plyometric exercise is jumping from a crouched position on a single leg up a long series of steep steps. Alternate legs on each repetition. In time you will be able to jump up two or three steps in one hop. This also develops explosive leg strength.

METHOD FOUR—FLEXIBILITY AND STRETCHING

Flexibility is often an ignored part of cross-country training. Perhaps this is because it's not as satisfying as other training methods which lead to concrete, obvious progress. It's vital that a skier be flexible, but it's difficult to note tangible gains from a stretching program.

Stretching improves flexibility so that you can perform the movements of your sport through a full range of motion without muscle tension. Stretching keeps you relaxed while training and racing. It also develops your kinesthetic sense, an awareness of where each part of your body is and what it's doing. Lastly, stretching encourages muscle recovery from stress and strain by removing the lactic acid build up in fatigued muscles.

I believe the addition of flexibility exercises to the U.S. team program in the late 1970s contributed significantly to the team's physiological development. Take Stan Dunklee. In the old days, he would get on skis and often wind up plowing his own course through the woods because he had such a poor kinesthetic sense. He wasn't relaxed on his skis and fell all too frequently during competition. Then he got into stretching. I've never seen anybody else work as hard to improve his flexibility and kinesthetic sense. His work paid off; he rarely falls while skiing now because he's relaxed, knows where his body is and what it's doing, and has a better sense of balance and agility.

There are a number of ways to develop flexibility. Some skiers use yoga, others ballet, and others use the basic stretching exercises familiar to any athlete. Athletes with a special need for improving their flexibility will develop their own program of stretching exercises they do daily. Others find stretching before, during, and after workouts sufficient.

Stretching is no longer a group effort where everyone lines up for calisthenics during a workout. For skiers, stretching is an individual program. Before a workout, run easily and stretch until you feel your muscles are warm and loose and prepared for a full range of motion under stress. Particular attention is paid to the muscle groups to be worked hardest during the training session. Your stretching movements are passive: slow and controlled, applying smooth tension to the muscles, no bouncing or harsh movements. After the workout when your muscles are warm and receptive, stretching is especially important. It will improve your flexibility and help your muscles recover and get ready for tomorrow's training session.

This series illustrates just a few of the hundreds of stretching exercises. The relaxed hang from the hips is a good place to start. Hang for 15–30 seconds to stretch the back side of the body.

Stretching. Reach for the sky from a single kneeling position to stretch the front of the body. Switch legs after 20–40 seconds.

Stretching. Hang sideways from the waist for 20–30 seconds each direction to stretch the large muscles on the side of the trunk.

Stretching. Don't strain or bounce in grabbing your toes for 20–40 seconds. This will help the back, hamstrings, and achilles tendons.

Stretching. Leaning against a wall for 15–30 seconds to stretch the arms, shoulders, abdomen, and back of the legs.

Stretching. The emphasis here is to let the knees collapse toward the ground to stretch the groin muscles. Pressure from the elbows will help. Also work on bringing the feet toward the groin. Do this for 20–40 seconds.

Stretching. Roll back and forth easily on your shoulders 5–7 times.

Stretching. Start with your feet on the ground over and behind your head. Swing the legs slowly over your body and down to the ground one vertebrae at a time. Raise the legs overhead slowly and hold in the starting position for 10–15 seconds. Do this twice.

Stretching. Stretch the legs and trunk by becoming a human pretzel. Hold for 20–25 seconds and reverse position.

Stretching. This is another good one for your backside. Duck your head to increase the stretch on the back and push on your heels to work on the legs for 20–30 seconds.

Stretching. Rock back and forth on the front leg for 20–30 seconds and then switch legs. This helps the quadriceps, hamstrings, and buttocks.

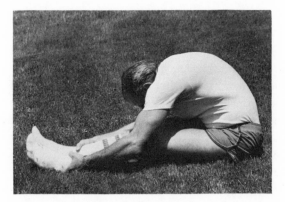

Stretching. Work on the backside one more time by pulling steadily but easily on your legs for 20–30 seconds. Now work yourself through all the exercises one more time.

METHOD FIVE—MENTAL TRAINING

In addition to the self-discipline and psychological strengths for skiing gained through workouts, many skiers complete their programs with specific mental training. Mental training is one more aspect of a good training program. Anything the athlete can do to help clear his mind while resting will leave him more energy to focus on his sport. Mental energy is easily siphoned off into extraneous areas unless the athlete has a firm grasp on his goals and can focus on them with discipline and concentration.

There are many methods for mental training. Yoga, for example, has been used by U.S. team members primarily for flexibility, but it may be expanded to psychological levels which give the athlete better control over his mind in focusing on his sport and in relaxing.

Transcendental meditation, when used by skiers for 20–30 minutes twice a day, clears the mind and rests the brain, leaving it with more energy to focus on skiing. TM actually rests the brain better than sleeping since the brain remains active during sleep. It is particularly good for intense athletes who have a hard time relaxing. TM improves the quality of the athlete's rest and relaxation so he can use his time more productively.

Imagery has probably been the most useful method of mental training. It was introduced to the team in the mid-1970s by Dr. Richard Suinn, a psychologist at Colorado State University. A formal imagery program involves being put in a very relaxed state. Through the power of suggestion, you work to solve problems by mentally picturing yourself mastering them.

Although it's helpful to have supervision in reaching a relaxed state, you can work to develop it on your own. Being totally relaxed is the primary step in a successful imagery program. Lie down in a quiet place and begin by concentrating on your extremities. Tense up the muscles in your toes and feet, then relax them. Repeat this and move up the legs, tensing and relaxing and concentrating on each portion of the body. Then move to your arms and then to the core of your body. Finally, tense the muscles in your head—grimmace, knit your brows, squint—and then relax. Repeat this and then concentrate on being relaxed. Once your entire body is relaxed, imagine yourself overcoming problems. Practice in your mind how you will handle certain situations on the race course, such as an icy section or a particularly difficult downhill, or how you will look when you make improved technical moves. Then when you get out on the course, you'll know exactly what you have to do so you will immediately know now to react without wasting time and energy thinking and being tense.

I encourage my athletes to use imagery in both the winter and summer, especially when they are trying to make technique changes. Just before they go to sleep at night, I have them create a mental image of the proper moves, based on what they've been shown by demonstrations, films, and video tapes. By using imagery during the off-season, they are not only able to improve their technique and tactics but are developing a form of mental training that will be useful to them during the racing season. I also encourage athletes to use imagery in making strategic preparations for racing. Just like tournament golfers take notes on the different holes of a golf course before competition, racers can ski around the race course and take notes on difficult sections—where they should change tracks, how to deal with other competitors in dual and mass starts, etc. With these notes, they can plan strategy and use imagery to prepare for competition. When the race is underway, they'll be able to anticipate what's coming up so they don't make errors costing 5–10 seconds each. Everything they know about the race and the course will be to their advantage, and mental training is one more way to be fully prepared for competition.

METHOD SIX—OFF-SEASON ON-SNOW TRAINING

The ideal conditioning program for a competitive skier would be to train on snow all year. This, of course, is nearly impossible, but more and more national teams are taking advantage of the benefits of off-season training on glaciers and snowfields around the world.

Off-season skiing is no longer limited to national team members. In 1976 when the U.S. team first went to the glaciers in Europe during the off-season, the glaciers drew only Alpine skiers. In time, other national cross-country teams were there each summer, and now all levels of Nordic skiers are using the glaciers. At the Dachstein Glacier in Austria during the summer of 1979, I saw junior racers, club skiers, and tour skiers. This trend is bound to grow and involve more and more North American skiers.

Off-season skiing provides both a psychological and physiological lift for the athlete. It creates a spiritual uplift for the athlelte (all cross-country skiers love to ski) as well as a welcome break from dryland training. Skiing can actually increase the longevity of an athlete's racing career because the break also helps him avoid potential injuries from long periods of dryland training—joint fatigue, torn Achilles tendons, ankle injuries—caused by running in the woods, hiking in the mountains, and roller skiing.

The prime value of off-season skiing lies in conditioning and technique work in a low-pressured environment. It keeps the muscles trained for skiing and is a fantastic time to evaluate and correct technique. The training emphasis should be on distance work with little intensity training.

Because skiing involves the use of the entire body, every time the athlete trains on snow, his ability to take in oxygen (aerobic ability) improves. Then when he returns to dryland training, his oxygen uptake level is better so he can handle greater work loads.

INJURIES AND ILLNESS

Injuries, illness, and other physical problems are unfortunately part of the athlete's life. They are almost impossible to avoid at some time or other during a sports career, despite the best preventative medicines, i.e., a good training program, attention to body signs, proper dress and equipment, a balanced diet, and plenty of rest. Athletes learn to live with soreness and pain; but when injury, illness or other complications strike, you must be certain to take action for a prompt and complete recovery.

Doctors

When you have a physical problem, isolate that problem and see a specialist who is sports oriented. Don't simply see the family doctor or general practitioner, but see a specialist in the area of your particular problem.

Because it's important for the serious athlete to continue training, if possible, while injured or ill, it's best to deal with a physician who can speed you on your way to recovery. Most doctors deal with physically average sick people and advise rest as the route to recovery. Rest may be the correct advice, but there also may be ways to train while recovering. This is why I suggest you establish relationships with specialists who are familiar with sports and, perhaps, sports medicine. Such a doctor will better understand your physical condition, your need to train, and the causes of your physical problem.

Anytime you deal with a doctor, be certain he is aware of the level of your training and the seriousness of your efforts. Don't be afraid of doctors; you're paying for their services and it's important they know who you are and what you're doing so they can prescribe the appropriate treatment for your problem. When you find a good, sports-oriented physician, establish a good relationship and stick with him. Don't switch around, but also don't hesitate to get a second opinion. In addition, athletic trainers and physical therapists can be of great help in planning a rehabilitation program which will keep you happy and allow you to maintain a level of training if the injury or illness isn't too severe.

Pay attention to your body signs. If bad signs persist, seek medical help. Too many athletes run around with minor problems and fail to see a physician who could remedy the situation.

Orthotics

An important consideration for the skier is his feet. Because of the time you spend on your feet training and racing, you are prone to injuries of the foot, ankle, and leg. Many of these types of injuries end up causing back problems as well. Athletes with an injury in these areas should consider seeing a podiatrist, or foot doctor, skilled in the use of orthotics.

God doesn't make every body perfect. Further, the athlete has no control over past injuries. The pounding of training and the increase in physical activity may exacerbate any physical deficiencies and past injuries. Because of a past injury or simply because of the way an athlete was born, he may have one leg shorter than the other, may be more knockkneed in one leg, or have one leg that is stronger than the other. Orthotics are devices which can correct these deficiencies. The doctor molds special pads or lifts for the foot to compensate for such imbalances.

The average person doesn't notice physical imbalances, but thoses imbalances are likely to cause a lot of problems with an increase in physical activity. A lot of people have been driven out of sport due to problems which could have been corrected by orthotics.

Cryonetics

Cryonetics is a therapy for muscle trauma, using cold to limit the swelling, decrease the bleeding in injured muscles, and decrease fluid build up in injured joints. The theory of cryonetics may be applied to normal training. After a strenuous workout, a swim in a cool pool or pond followed by stretching will halt muscle damage and help sore muscles recover. Cold penetrates the body, shutting down the circulatory system and decreasing the potential of fluids pooling in the muscle. Stretching will then warm the body, improving circulation at deeper levels so lactic acids and other unwanted fluids are quickly removed from the muscle.

Cold works the same way on injuries. If you sprain an ankle, for example, immediately put an ice pack on the injured area. Wrap the ice in a towel or something so it is not in direct contact with the skin. Cryonetics speeds recovery and, thereby, can potentially increase the longevity of an athlete's career. However, an athlete should research cryonetics and discuss it with a doctor before applying it. Any serious injury should be examined by a physician. Signs that it's time to see a doctor include prolonged pain, joint injury, infection, and injuries that don't heal despite correct rehabilitation procedures.

Anemia and Menstruation

Anemia and menstrual problems are common among women athletes. If an athlete feels she is anemic, she should consult a doctor. The physician can determine the type of iron supplements suited for the cause of the anemia and whether an iron supplement will help. If there is any one pill that I would recommend to a female athlete to take, it would be a daily vitamin with an iron supplement.

The effect of the menstrual cycle on the female athlete is very individual. Some women are capable of winning gold medals during any phase of the cycle, while others are physically incapacitated during their periods. I know of athletes who are normally unbeatable in competition but who can really take a beating just before their period. Menstruation is a difficult problem for a lot of athletes, and there simply hasn't been enough research in the area to solve many of the difficulties some women athletes face.

When I coached the women on the national team, we spent a great deal of time consulting with gynecologists, trying to control or temporarily stop some athletes' problem menstrual cycles. Other women experienced amenorrhea for up to six years while they were on the team, which is fairly common among women in strenuous training programs. Any athlete with problems or abnormalities in her menstrual cycle should consult a good gynecologist. Find a doctor who understands sport and can relate to the level of training the athlete is following.

It is extremely difficult psychologically as well as physically for many women to deal with menstrual problems. Some women simply cannot perform well if a race coincides with the beginning of their period. They just have to ski the best they can. It's important for a coach to be sensitive to menstrual problems and to open a good level of communication with the athlete.

Colds

Colds are the curse of the skier. A baseball player might be able to play with a cold, but not skiers or distance runners who depend on their lungs so heavily. The skier simply has to take time off from training to rest and recover or the cold will only linger.

Colds are an indication that the body is tired and overworked. They may be caused by exhaustion and lack of rest, by a bad diet, or from forgetting to change to dry clothes after a workout. Temperature contrasts and fatigue are the most common causes of colds.

The best cure for a cold is rest. The athlete must take off two to five days from training, rest, and eat well. If he's had success with cold medicines, the skier should take them as well. The day the scientists come up with a cure for the common cold will be a great day for cross-country skiers and all endurance-sport athletes.

Until then, rest a cold. It's hard to convince athletes to take time off from training or skiing, but they must be convinced to rest and not panic. A well-conditioned athlete won't lose his conditioning in a few days. Of course he won't gain, but the better care he takes of himself the sooner he'll be able to get back to his training. Don't push a cold; wait it out.

Bronchitis, Pneumonia, and Mononucleosis

These three ailments are extremely dangerous to the skier. There is nothing that can be done except to see a doctor right away and take an extended break from activity.

Don't be looking for any short-term recoveries. I know athletes who have lost an entire racing season because they failed to accept the fact they simply had to stop all activity when they caught bronchitis, mono or pneumonia. The athlete must rest and stay in close contact with his doctor. Don't ignore the symptoms of approaching mono or pneumonia. Mono is particularly obvious. The athlete is run down, can't get enough sleep, has no interest in eating, loses weight, has swollen glands, and has a higher pulse rate. Go to a doctor immediately for blood tests and proper care.

Asthma and Allergies

It seems as though everyone is allergic to something. If your allergies or asthma are bad enough to affect your training and racing efforts, see a doctor. Of particular interest to skiers is what is known as exercise-induced asthma. The asthmatic suffers from wheezing and shortness of breath during periods of strenuous activity. The symptoms can be as bad as pneumonia in reducing the athlete's ability to perform; however, it can be controlled through medications prescribed by a physician.

MONTH-BY-MONTH OFF-SEASON TRAINING GUIDELINES

The following are guidelines for the types of activities the cross-country skier should pursue during each month of the off-season, April through October. The guidelines are based on the principles of training and the physical demands of the sport. The program is progressive. The athlete slowly fills his physical conditioning base by increasing his training hours, volumes, and terrain gradually over the May-to-October period (Table 1). By November, normally the heaviest training month of the year, the skier is ready to take on the loads that will ensure a successful and improved winter racing season.

The program is balanced. All aspects of training are involved throughout the off-season. Each method of training is part of the athlete's weekly regimen, with the percentage of time spent on each varying according to the month. The breakdown on activities is provided in Table 2 as a general guideline, which may be varied according to the individual athlete's training desires.

Don't feel strapped in by the guidelines. Cross-country skiing is an evolutionary and individual sport. The skier must be flexible in adjusting his program to the lastest training methods and to his own physical and mental needs. Remember, training isn't endless, boring repetition unless you let it be. Training is a challenge and should provide enjoyment and satisfaction along with good results in the winter.

April

April can be a pretty innocuous month in the skier's year. The racing season is ending; the off-season training hasn't begun. But don't waste this month—there are four activities that can beneficially occupy your time: skiing, resting, planning, and preparing. Stay on skis as long as possible in April. Chase down races, go touring, and have fun bushwhacking. Extend the on-snow season as long as possible, work on technique, and enjoy your sport. April is a great time to relax and have fun on skis without the pressures of the serious competition of mid-winter.

April is also the time to pull your training logs together and plan your program for the coming season. Do this while the past season is still fresh in your mind and while your enthusiasm for racing is still high. Don't plan your coming season too long after the racing is over or you might forget that the point is to prepare for competition.

When the snow is gone, take a rest. For many skiers, an April rest is more psychological than physical. Due to the nature of the people involved in this sport, most will stay physically active while their brain recovers from the strain of the racing season. April is a transition month, and the brain needs a break from last season before getting into next season.

I treat April a bit differently than many coaches because I feel it's a good time to put your muscles through the transition from on-snow activity to dryland training. Many coaches use May for this, but I like to get ready for the off-season in April so full-blown training can begin in early May. The transition is slow. Toward the end of April, get your roller skis and other dryland equipment out and tuned up and begin a light training program so you don't end up spending the first two weeks of May stiff and sore from the shock of your dryland training. Don't try to start were you left off last October or November but ease yourself into dryland training with a relaxed program of light roller skiing, ski running, and ski walking and a few easy strength workouts. A stretching program will help get you through this transition period with less stress and strain. You may still feel some soreness in your muscles, so pay attention to your body signs and don't overdo.

You needn't establish any specific training goals for the month, which in itself is a mental rest. Your only mental strain for the month will be planning your program for the coming year. Enjoy yourself and get your body ready for your dryland program.

May/June/July

May, June, and July boil down to similar training months because endurance is the focus in this time period. Up to 80% of your training time is spent on endurance, while the rest of your time is split almost evenly between intervals, strength training, and flexibility work. Intervals should be aerobic with only an occasional push over the anaerobic threshold. Set up a good program of stretching exercises for before and after each workout. Your strength program should last 30–45 minutes each workout with three sessions a week.

The endurance program during these months should be as varied as possible because it is 80% of your training effort. Rotate workouts between the First-Class Activities. If you can get on snow during a training camp, all the better. Second-Class Activities may be used for added variety, but make an effort to train with poles in your hands as much as possible.

During the first week of May, undergo a testing program, such as the Self-Evaluation Testing. You'll be surprised at how high your conditioning level is. After the long, tiring racing season, many skiers are convinced they have no conditioning base left. It's hard to convince them until they see from their test results that their physical conditioning base is never destroyed. With each new season you take a step up from where you were the year before. You can train longer and harder—add more quantity and quality—than ever before.

Ideally, testing should be conducted on the first day of your dryland program. But if you haven't made the muscle transition from on snow to dry land, it's best to train a bit first. The May test is the base for your summer program. Compare the results with those from the previous May's testing to see where you stand. Evaluate the current scores to determine which areas need the most work. Make whatever adjustments necessary to your program. Toward the end of June, test again to be certain your training is taking you in the right direction. Adjust your program if the tests indicate any new or continuing weaknesses.

July activity almost mirrors that of May and June, although the balance between aerobic and anaerobic intervals will begin to equal. The emphasis remains strongly on endurance training. Workouts should become even more exclusively limited to First-Class Activities for the serious ski racer.

August/September/October

The August-September-October period marks the move into your fall training program. There is a gradual shift from the heavy emphasis on endurance training toward more intensity work through intervals, particularly anaerobic intervals, as you put more speed work into your program. The emphasis on specificity increases so 40%–55% of your endurance training is done on roller skis. Intervals increase to 20% of your training by October.

The effects of the increase in volume and the gradual increase in interval training should be apparent when you undergo SET in the second or third week of August. Compare your results with those of May and June and also with results from the previous August. The tests may indicate you need to increase your strength training. Your strength sessions should last 45–60 minutes from August through October.

September is a good time to enter roller ski races as part of your tempo work. The lucky skiers on the national team will likely be on snow during at least part of September. By October, roller skiing is up to 75% of your training, including at least half of your interval work. Enter as many roller ski races as possible—perhaps one a week—to improve your pace and tempo.

As the days get shorter, your work volumes are increasing, so you must be more conscientious about organizing your training time to accomplish your goals. Also, the weather works against you; it's not pleasant to roller ski in the rain when the pavement is so cold the tips of your poles don't dig in well. But you have to persist and be dedicated or all your good summer training will be for naught.

Toward the end of October (or later if you don't expect to be on snow for a time), undergo your final testing of the off-season. This is a particularly important evaluation as it's the last time to assess your program and make necessary adjustments before the snow flies. Take time to evaluate your results and plan your next few weeks of training so that any weaknesses will be worked out and you'll be in the best shape of your life for the winter season.

Training for cross-country skiers is no longer the hit-and-miss proposition it was during the early 1970s and before. Skiers are racing faster for longer periods because of the knowledge about training that has been acquired through experience, testing various methods, and input from sports medicine and physiology research. The athlete knows how to design a progressive training program, what activities will best prepare him physically, mentally, and technically for his sport, and how to monitor and evaluate his training. The results of modern training methods have been obvious on the race course. Competitors are skiing with better technique, more skill, and ever-increasing speeds.

Importantly, the modern training methods which have allowed international competitors to improve are filtering down to all levels of racing. Even without a meticulously designed program, the weekend racer now has training methods available that will give him the best return on the race course for each hour he spends training in the off-season. Skiers are becoming increasingly sophisticated about their sport; they are not only skiing better and faster, but they are gaining even more pleasure from cross-country skiing.

A basic piece of concluding advice: You never learn by undertraining. As the athlete accumulates a conditioning base and gains an understanding of himself and of training, it's best to overtrain. Push yourself through the pain barrier and learn your limits. Ideally, the serious athlete will train at the fine line between doing too much and not doing enough. But you can't determine that fine line or, more importantly, know your limits unless you overtrain. Overtraining, with concern for the principles of training and the controls dictated by your pulse rate, will give you the maximum physiological and psychological benefits. As I like to say, the uphills will feel like downhills.

3

WINTER TRAINING

Racing is not Refueling

The ideal winter program for the cross-country competitor involves a coordinated schedule of racing and training which leads to a true racing peak, or series of peaks, during the height of the racing season. The fact is, you can't race yourself into shape, nor is it likely that racing will keep you in shape. So, a competitor must have a winter training program to carry him through the competitive season.

It's the gas tank principle: You only get out of yourself what you've put in. The tank, or physiological conditioning base, you filled in the off-season will be empty before March if you don't continue to refuel. Racing is not refueling. The competitor who trains between races is the skier who will achieve consistent results through the season and is most likely to build and maintain a peak. The skier who doesn't train in the winter will never realize his competitive potential.

Despite all of this, winter training is one of the most ignored aspects of cross-country skiing. At coaching clinics and in talking to skiers, the subject of keeping in shape during the season is often sidestepped or generalized because many racers and coaches have a limited understanding of winter conditioning.

Winter training must be put in perspective to the season's prime activity, racing. The competitor, whether he has a coach or is self-coached, must carefully plan a training program in coordination with his racing and travel schedule. The season must be balanced. Some skiers race their winter away and have no fuel for those final competitions in March and April. Others get so involved in training they forget to race.

An appropriate balance of racing, training, and rest comes from time spent planning your season in April and continuous evaluation of your program throughout the year. Solid planning is the best thing you can do to control your racing season and to reach a competitive peak or series of peaks for the important events on your racing calendar. Evaluation is based on the records you keep in your training and racing logs. The stopwatch used in both racing and training serves as a gauge of your progress.

The racer's winter schedule must include adequate time slots for training, which is worked in around his races. To keep in racing form, continue a program of endurance work, intervals, tempo training, flexibility work, and strength or muscle maintenance.

A beneficial winter training program is a function of knowing enough about training and about yourself to know what to do to keep fit from November through April. This chapter will provide guidelines and direction with which you can plan, evaluate, and control a winter conditioning program geared toward a successful racing season.

ON-GOING CONCERNS

During the winter, the racer is trying to peak, not panic. An awareness of several aspects of training for racing will keep you on track toward your goals so you don't find yourself facing unsolvable problems mid-season. Planning your winter months and keeping training and racing logs will give focus to the season and to each day's activities from November through the spring. Attention to the five tenets of training will keep your conditioning progressive and successful. Confidence in your program will prevent panic when there's no snow or you've had a disappointing race. Strength and flexibility training will help keep your body ready for racing. Organization and attention to training will pay off with peaking.

Peaking

The prime goal of the cross-country skier is to compete up to his potential. A successful effort on the race course requires the athlete be in top physical, technical, and psychological form—to be at a racing peak.

Peaking is probably the most elusive goal in all of sport. I'd love to be able to provide skiers with a secret formula for a day-by-day plan to reach a peak, but no such formula has been discovered. In fact, it's difficult to even define or describe peaking. It's like trying to define love. Most athletes will tell you that when they're at a peak, they feel as though the top of the world is just around the corner; they simply feel great and are ready to take on anything.

The most concrete advice I can provide to an athlete who is seeking this state is to plan your program carefully and execute it with intelligence and self-awareness. The bottom line on peaking is knowing yourself and your body well enough to develop a training and racing schedule which will bring out the very best you have to offer during your important competitions.

You're at a peak when all the indicators tell you that you're in perfect readiness for those important races. Your resting pulse rate is low and steady. Your eating and sleeping habits are stable and healthy. You've had a number of outstanding workouts in which your recovery times are much improved, your efforts don't strain you physically, and you psychologically deal easily with the training load. You're mentally on a high and your race results are even better than expected.

Achieving this state of readiness is the payoff for all the effort you've put out in training and for all the time spent planning your program, filing information in training logs, and evaluating your progress. You've learned how to train up to the fine line which divides progress from overtraining; how to recognize a peak and how to maintain it. Then you cruise through those important races at the top of your abilities, getting the maximum return from the energy you produce. This is the ultimate goal in cross-country competition. Your season will look something like Chart 5, depending on the scheduling of your important races.

The international greats can reach a peak and hold it for long periods of time. Or they

CHART 5
Yearly Overview of Peaking

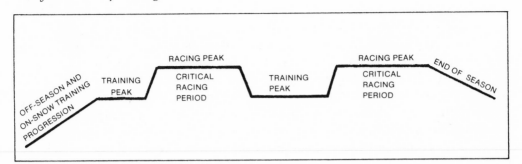

can plan their season to reach multiple peaks for the various important competitions of the season. They do this through physical conditioning, determined mental effort, careful planning, and daily evaluation. They are in control of their situation. Cross-country skiers, such as America's Bill Koch and Norway's Oddvar Braa, have attained amazing peaks. During the 1976 season, Koch began peaking in December during the Olympic tryouts, carried it through two third places in Europe in mid-January and then was second, sixth and thirteenth, respectively, in the 30 km, 15 km, and 50 km and had one of the fastest relay legs at the Olympics. Koch continued to ski well in Sweden after the Olympics until he got sick in late February. His peak had lasted about seven weeks.

Braa raced at a peak from December through April 12 during the 1979 season. He entered 41 races during this period, won 27 times, finished no lower than sixth place, and dropped out of only one race—a truly incredible performance. Unfortunately, neither Koch nor Braa was able to repeat in the 1980 Olympic season. Achieving such peaks is no simple task.

It's difficult to reach a racing peak and all too easy to lose it. Many times athletes reach a zenith and race through it before they realize what's happened. They are either insensitive to their body signs and reactions to training and racing efforts or define peaking in terms of winning.

Expecting victory is often a bit unrealistic for most of us. There is only one first place in a race and, more to the point, skiing at a peak is synonomous with skiing to your potential. A skier who believes he hasn't peaked because he didn't win an Olympic gold medal is being unrealistic if his 15th-place finish came when he was skiing at the maximum of his potential.

In many cases, the athlete is his own worst enemy in recognizing a peak and maintaining the delicate balance between success and disaster. When all the indicators point to a peak—when you're feeling great physically and mentally and skiing technically well—the trick is to control it. Don't try to go around that next corner. If you press on, you may lose that good feeling. Recognize the signs and stay cool; don't go for the top of the world or be unrealistic about your abilities. The athlete who pushes too hard is likely to topple off his peak.

Good racers can go stale psychologically. A break off skis or a change in environment might revive the good feeling. Top form can also be destroyed by a hectic travel situation or a change of plans which costs a rest day. With proper planning and time off from racing for training and rest, the careful racer can avoid the topple. Daily evaluation is the key here. Have a plan but be ready to adjust it.

Developing racers usually go stale physiologically because they've raced and trained beyond their current conditioning level. This doesn't need to happen. Be honest in evaluating who you are and where you are physically. Don't be adversely influenced by what other skiers are saying and doing. This is particularly important if you're in a group or team situation. Don't let a prescribed training program for the group overload you, and don't let training sessions turn into racing sessions where you try to keep up with the best skiers in the group. If you go stale physiologically because you ran out of conditioning background, take a break from racing and either train or rest. Watch for body signs, because you might get sick (a clear symptom of pushing too hard) before you've determined that you're simply tired.

Failing to reach a peak is usually the result of poor planning, preparation, and evaluation during the season. A solid program with a good balance of racing and training and time taken for assessment of the indicators is the best route to a peak. And you can't reach that zenith without racing.

Although this philosophy is not totally accepted in the U.S., I believe a racing peak can only be achieved through racing. There is a definite difference between a racing peak and a training peak. Outstanding periods of training immediately precede a racing peak, but none of these activities matches the adrenalin rush, the psych, the level of competition, the energy, or the excitement of putting on a bib and racing.

Be smart, realistic, and objective about reaching your racing potential. When you've hit a peak or missed it, go back to your training and racing logs to find out why you ignored or failed to develop the indicators of top form. The black and white records of what you've been doing and how you've been feeling will be the best indication of why you hit or missed.

Peaking Program. Physiology experts have determined that it takes an athlete four to six weeks to achieve a peak. What follows is an ideal program which may be used during the six weeks prior to the racing season or to an important series of competitions. The program involves a gradual increase in stress workouts—intervals and tempo training or races used as tempo workouts—over a six-week period. The activities in the program may be compressed into a four-week time period, but six weeks is best. It will often be difficult for racers to carry out the scheduled activities when they don't have complete control over their programs. Adjustments may be made, of course, to fit the athlete's travel, racing, and other obligations, but the level of peaking achieved may be compromised.

In the weekly outlines below, keep in mind that on days of intensity workouts you may also want to ski easy distance for a second training session. Days of endurance training could involve a single workout (15–30 km) or double workouts (covering a total of 20–40 km during the day).

- *Week 1* is spent on endurance. Your first interval workout is added with an aerobic interval session on Saturday or Sunday (likely race day).
- *Week 2* continues to emphasize endurance training but two aerobic intervals are planned—one on the weekend and the other Wednesday or Thursday.
- *Week 3* continues endurance training around two interval workouts and one session of tempo training. The tempo workout should be on the weekend, with one anaerobic interval workout planned for Thursday and an aerobic interval workout on Tues-

day. Easy endurance training should be held between days of interval and tempo training.

- *Week 4* is basically a repeat of the activities in Week 3. The weekend tempo workout could be a short race.

- *Week 5* is the most active week of the program. Two anaerobic interval workouts should be held Tuesday and Thursday with tempo training or a short race on the weekend. Easy distance skiing should be planned between intensity training sessions.

- *Week 6* is an easy week because the important races will begin over the weekend. Plan one anaerobic interval workout on either Wednesday or Thursday, depending on whether the first competition is on Saturday or Sunday. The interval training should be fairly strenuous (anaerobic), but it should leave you in a positive psychological and physiological state. The rest of the week through the day before the first race should involve easy endurance training.

Planning and Logging

Head into the racing season with a plan. Without a carefully considered program of racing and training, the athlete will have an almost impossible time peaking for important competitions and will likely end up with a helter-skelter schedule that makes all his training and preparation futile.

As discussed previously, the skier plans his year in April after the close of the preceding season. This yearly plan is an ideal program based on the racer's goals, objectives, and experience. The plan includes his racing schedule, which normally can be worked out as early as April. You should know the major events you'll want to enter and can fill in additional competitions as the racing schedules become available from your ski association. With at least a general racing schedule, you can plan your training program around the competitions, keeping your individual status, finances, and work or school obligations in mind.

Your goal for winter training and racing volumes (roughly half of the total volume of kilometers to be covered in the year) should be broken down according to the percentages in Table 11. The table presents a guideline for the amount of training and racing kilometers to be covered each month. You'll note that the percentages decrease from November to March because you have less time for training as your racing and travel schedules increase.

TABLE 11
Winter Monthly Volume Percentages

Month	Percent of Total Winter Volume
November	27%
December	23%
January	18%
February	18%
March	14%
April	

*Some racing, transition from snow to dry land.

TABLE 12
Winter Monthly Activity Percentages

	Endurance	Intervals and Tempo Training	Racing
November*	85%	15%	0%
December	70%	20%	10%
January	60%	10%	30%
February	50%	10%	40%
March	50%	0%	50%

NOTE: Muscle maintenance and flexibility programs continue throughout.
*On snow. If off snow in November, refer to off-season activity percentages chart.

As an example, take an international racer who plans to cover 3,000 km during the winter. Using the percentage formula in Table 11, he will cover 990 km in November which will be entirely training. In December, his volume of racing and training will be 690 km as the handful of races he enters will begin to cut into his training time. In both January and February he will cover 480 km of training and racing with the major emphasis on racing because these are the most important competition months of the year. March will involve 360 km, 60% of which will be in competition.

Once you've determined your ideal master plan for the winter, draw up monthly plans as each month approaches. During the last week in November, for example, lay out a racing program for December and then plan how to train around those races. The percentages of time to be spent on each activity are presented in Table 12 as a guideline in designing your monthly plan. In addition to endurance training, intervals, and tempo training and racing, you must include a flexibility program in your daily regimen and plan up to three sessions of muscle maintenance work each week. Fewer sessions may be held, depending on your weekly racing schedule.

When planning the month of December, you may not know the racing schedule or, as often happens, snow conditions make races tentative. Plan a race on Saturday or Sunday of each week anyway. If a race is canceled, your training schedule proceeds—simply substitute tempo training or an interval workout on the day of the canceled race. If there's no snow, jump on your roller skis to accomplish the objectives of the on-snow workout you'd planned.

As you look further into January, February, and March, select the competitions for which you want to peak. Plan a training and racing program to peak for those events. This may mean that you'll use some races simply for training or to work on technique and others which will be treated with less than a full effort. Determine your critical racing periods and those time periods that will be used basically for training and race tune-up and devise a plan similar to the overview found in Chart 5 (p. 81). Develop a program using the six-week guideline by which you can work up to a training peak as the important time periods approach and then race into a competition peak for your main events.

Tables 13 and 14 are the November through March plans I helped Doug Peterson and Kate Freeman develop for the winter of 1980. The charts are included to provide examples of how two athletes of different experience and conditioning levels planned their seasons.

TABLE 13
Sample Winter Plan: Doug Peterson, 1980 Season

Month	Snow Skiing	Roller Skiing*	Ski Running*	Strength	Totals
Nov. Planned	900/60	100/5.5	24.5/2	4	1039.5/73.5
Actual	835/50.3	30/1.5	65/3.75	1.5	930/55.5
		Race and Interval			
Dec. Planned	460/30	100/6.5	(7r, 6i)†	3	560/36.5
Actual	600/37.5	95/4.7	(5r, 1i)	0	695/42.3
Jan. Planned	460/30	200/10	(10r, 5i)	3	660/40
Actual	425/28.3	136/6.7	(7r, 1i)	0	660/35
Feb. Planned	460/30	200/10	(10r, 5i)	3	660/40
Actual	295/21.3	120/6.3	(3r, 1i)	0	415/27.5
Mar. Planned	350/20	250/13	(12r, 1i)	3	610/33
Actual	285/19	160/7.7	(10r, 0i)	0	445/26.7
Apr. Planned	100/5	100/5	(5r, 1i)	0	200/10
Actual	100/7	100/5	(3r, 0i)	0	200/12

NOTE: Most of the figures involve km/hr spent. Thus, Doug was to snow ski 900 km in November and spend 60 hours. He actually covered 835 km and spent 50.3 hours. Strength work is all in hours (Doug neglected his muscle maintenance program entirely from December through March).
*Off snow.
†r = Race; i = Intervals or tempo training.

TABLE 14
Sample Winter Plan: Kate Freeman, 1980 Season

Month	Snow Skiing*	Roller Skiing	Ski Running	Tempo/Race	Strength	General	Totals
Nov. Planned	0	335/27	215/25		6.5	2	550/60.5
Actual	0	234/16.4	178/20.9	32.8/2.2	6.7	1.3	444.8/47.5
Dec. Planned	384/32	0	0	40/2.5	3	1	425/38.5
Actual	155.5/12.4	78.1/5.7	99/10	37.5/2.3	1.9	1.3	369.5/33.5
Jan. Planned	360/30	0	0	60/4	2.5	0	420/36.5
Actual	144/13.6	67.8/4.6	79.6/8	55/3.7	2.3	13/0.5	359.4/32.7
Feb. Planned	360/30	0	0	90/5	2.5	0	450/37.5
Actual	293/19.5	25.8/2.1	8.9/0.8	80/4.8	1.1	16/0.5	423.7/28.8
Mar. Planned	300/25	0	0	90/5	2	0	390/32
Actual	204/17.5	0	13.2/1.3	74/5.7	0.5	0	291.2/25.1

NOTE: The majority of the figures involve kilometers/hours spent. Thus, Kate was to roller ski 335 km in November over 27 hrs. She actually roller skied 235 km and spent 16.4 hrs. Strength and most figures in the General column relate only to hours spent.
*Because there was little or no snow in New Hampshire where Kate lives, she substituted hours and km at other activities for many of those planned for snow skiing. Given the conditions, Kate came reasonably close to accomplishing her training and racing goals for the winter.

You'll note that although the volume goals for each are different, the training progressions are quite similar. The top line in each month is the goal and the lower line is what they actually accomplished, measured in km/hr. Single figures relate only to hours. Also note that their training plans varied because Peterson, as a national team member, could anticipate being on snow for the entire five-month period while Freeman was limited to a great deal of dry-land training.

As I mentioned, plans—particularly the yearly plan—are ideal programs. Goals and objectives will be accomplished if everything falls into place, if your body reacts as you hope it will, and if the races and snow come as anticipated. Normally, however, adjustments must be made to the annual plan. If you understand the tenets of training and have confidence in your overall program, adjustments are easily made and you keep on track toward your goals.

If your training load is too light or too heavy, you must adjust your program. If the race schedule changes, your schedule must follow. Injury, illness, travel exhaustion, and weather will force other changes. For example, if you have a 600-km training goal for the month but are sick and can't train for four days, you have to decrease your goal to compensate for the time you lost. Such adjustments will not panic the athlete who understands training and can evaluate his program.

A smart racer keeps logs all year long. Many athletes do a beautiful job recording their off-season training, but let their logs slide during the hectic winter months. This is a critical mistake because the winter logs are the racer's most important records. Hindsight, as they say, is 100%. Logs give you the perfect hindsight to avoid mistakes. They are a recorded imprint of your progress and bodily reactions and are necessary to evaluate a program, make midseason changes, and develop a valid program for the next season. Further, logs evaluate your status on a week-to-week basis. If you feel you're reaching a peak, your logs will tell you what you've done to get there, how to maintain the peak and how to attain other peaks in the future.

Winter Training Tenets

As discussed in Chapter 2, there are five basic tenets of training to be considered when developing a program to prepare the athlete for cross-country competition: specificity, duration, intensity, load, and frequency. These tenets must be involved during the winter months as much as they are during the off-season to insure a well-balanced and successful season. The winter training program should be designed to give emphasis to each of the five tenets in the athlete's conditioning regimen. The athlete should be aware of the purpose and function of each training session, keeping the daily, weekly, monthly, and seasonal goals in mind. In a productive training program, the athlete and coach know what to do and when to do it.

In-Season, Off-Snow Training

Skiing is by no means the only way to prepare for ski racing. The past few seasons of coaching skiers not on the national team have been very interesting and educational for me. The U.S. team always manages to find good early season on-snow training situations. Most of us don't have that luxury, but it's been proven that being on snow early isn't as necessary as had been thought.

*The East's snowless winter of 1980 brought out al-
ternative training methods. Here I'm practicing
double pole technique while ice skating.*

In 1980 Eastern skiers were stepping off their roller skis to race on snow but were forced to return to dry land training. Many skied well in relation to those who had been on snow because they trained their entire bodies for skiing. Roller skiing, hiking with poles, ski walking, roller board, and Exer-Genie workouts kept many Eastern skiers in shape for trips to on-snow competition. They had fun coming up with different means of challenging themselves. For example, when the lakes froze, they went ice skating with ski poles and found they could simulate skiing motions while on skates, including double poling and the diagonal stride. They were even racing on skates as an added diversion, providing them with good tempo training.

The important thing to remember is to change your training program as the racing season approaches and gets underway, whether you're on snow or not. When it's time to race, the athlete must be ready, even if he hasn't had any on-snow training. In November, switch to high-volume specificity training, primarily on roller skis. As December and the racing season approach, concentrate on high intensity, good volume, and tempo work. The same principles for preparing for the race season apply whether the athlete is on snow skis or roller skis. Roller skis are important during the entire off-season but are vital in November and during the season if there is no snow.

Don't be overanxious to get on snow. Be certain conditions will allow for a good workout. Spending an hour or two roller skiing is much more beneficial than an hour spent floundering around on three inches of untracked snow. If you have no snow or get hit by a mid-winter thaw, don't panic. Get back on your roller skis and stick with the same program you had planned for your on-snow training.

To get a better idea of the adjustments made for training in a snowless winter, I've included two sample training logs for the week of January 21–27, 1980. One log is for Kate Freeman, a divisional racer who was off snow most of the week, and the other is Doug Peterson's log. Both skiers were preparing for the U.S. National Championships the following week.

Peterson, as a member of the national team, was able to be on snow at the race site during the entire week and was in control of his situation. You may note the types of workouts he did, including intervals and some twice-daily training sessions. His sleep pattern indicates that he was in a good situation. The week worked out well for Doug because he had his best-ever results in national championship competition, highlighted by his first medal for a third in the 30 km.

Kate, on the other hand, was home in New Hampshire most of the week. She's a nurse at the local hospital and worked double shifts on one day to arrange for time off to attend the nationals. This, combined with her travel to Quebec for the nationals, left her sleep patterns irregular. Her training involved a wide range of activities: biking, roller skiing, ski running, weight lifting, and intervals on snow skis. Despite the nontypical January training

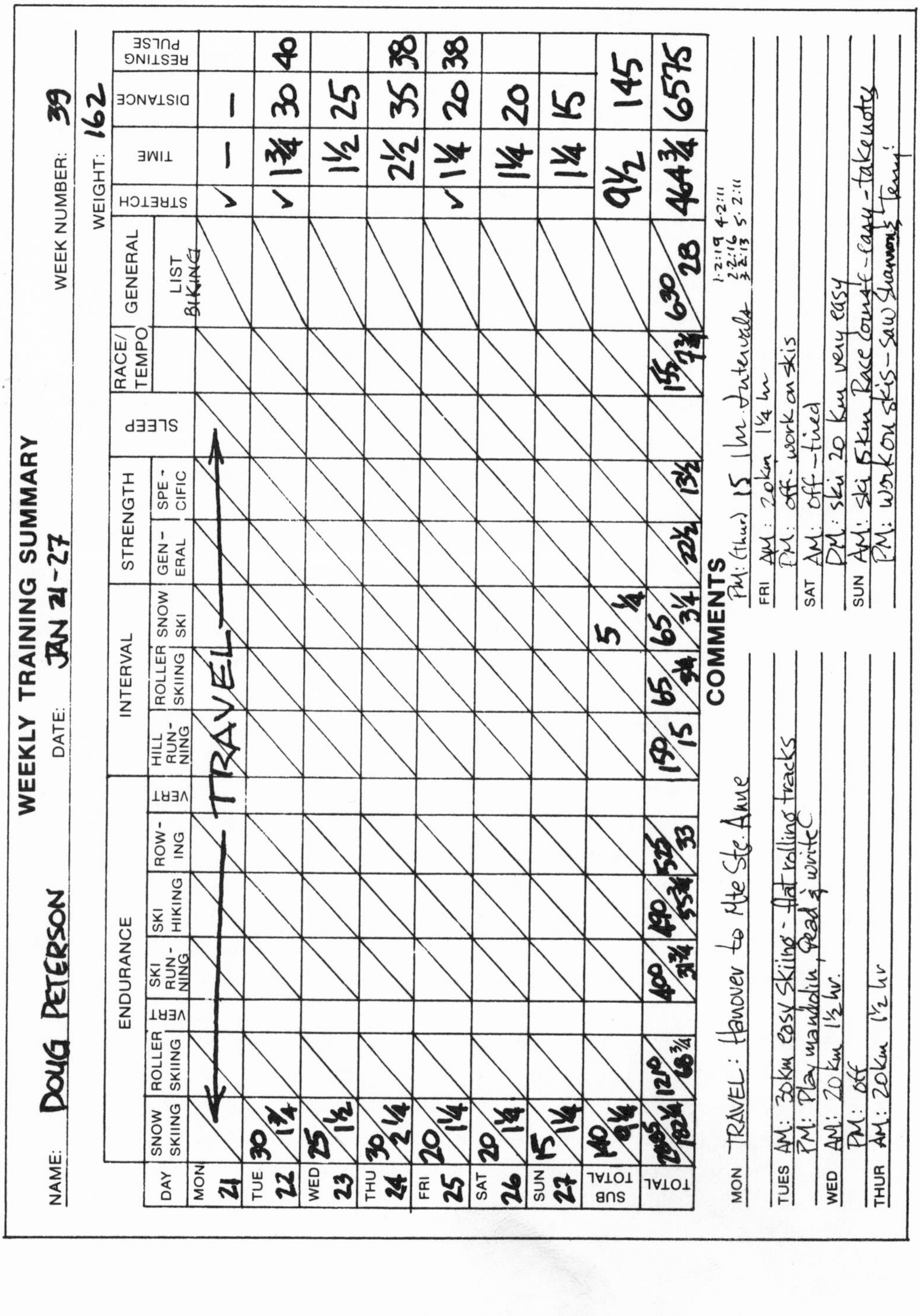

WEEKLY TRAINING SUMMARY

NAME: DOUG PETERSON DATE: JAN 21-27 WEEK NUMBER: 39

WEIGHT: 162

DAY	ENDURANCE: SNOW SKIING	ENDURANCE: ROLLER SKIING	ENDURANCE: VERT	ENDURANCE: SKI RUNNING	ENDURANCE: SKI HIKING	ENDURANCE: ROWING	ENDURANCE: VERT	INTERVAL: HILL RUNNING	INTERVAL: ROLLER SKIING	INTERVAL: SNOW SKI	STRENGTH: GENERAL	STRENGTH: SPECIFIC	SLEEP	RACE/TEMPO	GENERAL: LIST BIKING	STRETCH	TIME	DISTANCE	RESTING PULSE
MON 21	← TRAVEL →															✓	—	—	
TUE 22	30 / 1¾															✓	1¾	30	40
WED 23	25 / 1½																1½	25	
THU 24	30 / 2¼																2½	35	38
FRI 25	20 / 1¼															✓	1¼	20	38
SAT 26	20 / 1¼																1¼	20	
SUN 27	15 / 1¼																1¼	15	
SUB TOTAL	140 / 9¼									5 / ¼							9½	145	
TOTAL	2005 / 182¼	1210 / 68¾		400 / 31¾	490 / 55¾	525 / 33		150 / 15	65 / 5¾	65 / 3¼	22½	13½		155 / 7¾	630 / 28		464¾	6575	

COMMENTS

MON TRAVEL: Hanover to Mte Ste. Anne

TUES AM: 30km easy skiing - flat rolling tracks
PM: Play mandolin, read & write

WED AM: 20km 1½ hr.
PM: off

THUR AM: 20km 1½ hr
PM: (thur) 15 1 hr. Intervals 1·2:19 2·2:16 3·2:13 4·2:11 5·2:11

FRI AM: 20km 1¼ hr
PM: off · work on skis

SAT AM: off — tired
PM: ski 20 km very easy

SUN AM: ski 15km Race course — easy — take notes
PM: work on skis — saw Shannon & Terry!

CHART 6
Weekly Training Summary

week, Kate performed well at the nationals with results at the same level of national point rating that she earned the rest of the season.

By comparing the two logs, you can see the range of possibilities available to the racer and his coach to adjust to uncooperative weather and situations. Both Kate and Doug accomplished similar training objectives through widely divergent programs.

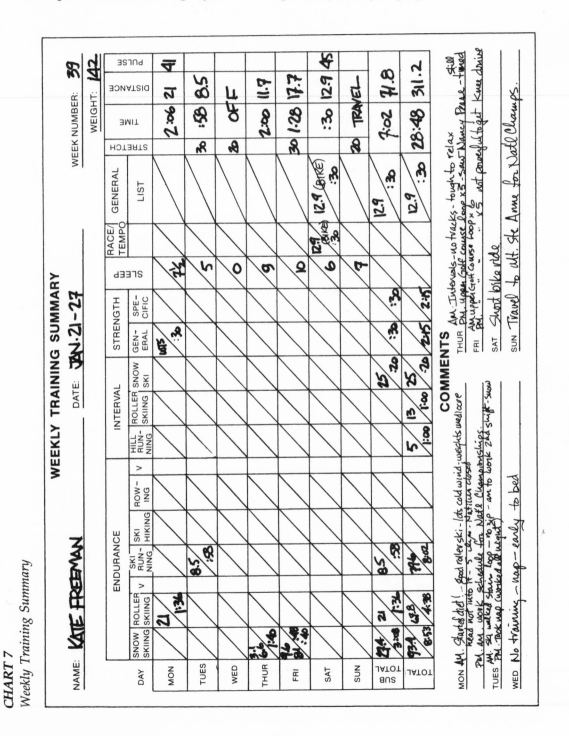

CHART 7
Weekly Training Summary

Muscle Maintenance

I'd hate to count the times I've heard racers moaning about aching backs. Sore backs are almost always a symptom of a lack of a winter muscle maintenance or strength program.

When a racer fails to keep all his muscle groups in shape during the season, he ends up with problems such as a sore back when skiing in varying snow conditions. An aching back often results when making a transition from racing on fast snow to slow snow. The back gets strained because the skier is coming from a situation where he is doing a lot of double poling and gliding to snow which demands more single poling and more use of his lower back muscles in pushing his skis.

The two main muscle groups which require season-long maintenance are the anterior and posterior hinge areas—the stomach and back. These muscles are vital because they connect the upper and lower body and because of the dynamic position of cross-country striding and their involvement in the function of double and single poling. If either of these muscle groups is weak, the cross-country skier is in trouble.

Muscle maintenance is also important in improving the muscle imbalance which develops in cross-country skiers. Due to the nature of the movements in the sport, the quadriceps in the legs become very strong because they are the primary movers, while the hamstrings are underdeveloped. In the upper body, where the arms hinge off the back muscles and due to the dynamic position, certain back muscles become highly developed while the stomach muscles are underdeveloped. Thus, a sudden shift to a great deal of double poling conditions can, for example, cause stomach cramps.

There will always be somewhat of an imbalance between the often-used and seldom-used muscle groups in the cross-country skier's body. However, there is much that can be done through a muscle maintenance program to improve this imbalance.

Winter Muscle Maintenance Activities

Arm dips *(3 sets of 10 repetitions)*
> When you can complete three full sets, wear a pack weighted with 5 lb for women and 10 for men. If dip bars are unavailable, substitute chair dips with a weighted pack.

Stomach curls *(3 sets of 25 repetitions)*
> To add resistance, do sit-ups on an inclined plane or hold a 5-lb weight on your chest or behind your head.

Leaning leg squats *(3 sets of 25 repetitions for each leg)*
> When you can handle the workload, add a weighted pack to increase resistance.

Back extensors *(3 sets of 25 repetitions)*
> When you can complete three full sets, add resistance by holding a 5-lb weight behind your head.

Exer-Genie *(strength, endurance, intervals)*
> Strength—3 sets of 10 arm pull repetitions with high resistance.
> Endurance—Adjust the resistance so you can pull continuously for 5–30 minutes.
> Intervals—Set the resistance at a medium-to-high level and pull very rapidly for 2–5 minutes with 3–5 repetitions alternated with recovery periods.

Include a schedule for winter muscle maintenance in your monthly plan. If there are no races during the week, do muscle maintenance two or three times. If you are racing once in the week, exercise once or twice. If there are two or three races, you may want to pass up muscle maintenance entirely or do it just once. A good time to do muscle maintenance exercises is in the evening along with your flexibility work. Do some stretching, then your muscle maintenance program, then some more flexibility work. Muscle maintenance will make a difference in your race results.

Flexibility and Stretching

Along with a muscle maintenance program, cross-country skiers should incorporate a daily flexibility exercise routine into their winter training schedule. Although the main emphasis on flexibility work is in the summer and fall, stretching exercises should continue throughout the year as a part of your daily activities. Not only does it hasten recovery of fatigued muscles, but it gives the athlete a better kinesthetic sense, enhancing his balance and agility on skis. The flexibility of a full range of motion will allow the skier to adapt more easily to position and technique changes.

WINTER TRAINING METHODS

The season of snow has arrived, the tracks are set, and your off-season training program has you excited to put on your skis and get at it. The racer welcomes winter with a training program which will make the best use of his noncompetitive hours in preparing him for a successful racing season. The basics of his winter plan include adjusting his body to skiing, endurance training, interval training, tempo workouts, and achieving the best results possible on the race course.

First Strides on Snow

When a cross-country skier first steps on snow each winter, the main concern is endurance training. However, you must first let your body adjust to the physical activity through a careful selection of skiing terrain. Just as you adjusted your body gradually to heavier workloads and undulating terrain during your off-season, you must slowly break into the effort of skiing when you get on snow. Chart 8 indicates the relative types of terrain the skier should use during early on-snow endurance training.

CHART 8
Terrain Considerations for Early Season Endurance Work

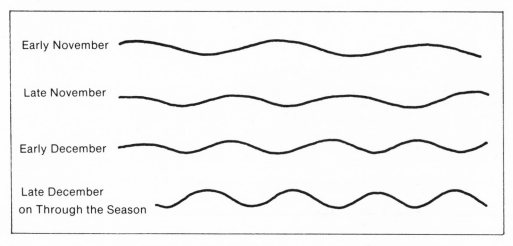

Early November

Late November

Early December

Late December
on Through the Season

While your body is adjusting to training on snow, gentle terrain is advised to avoid strain and overloading. After a time on snow, you build a skiing base and are ready to add greater variety of terrain to your endurance workouts. As the body adjusts, gradually incorporate more undulating terrain and ski at faster paces to increase the load and intensity of your training.

Endurance Training

Endurance is the cornerstone of the skier's training base. Without endurance training, his house will crumble—he'll be unable to persist and resist fatigue during competition. Endurance training will push the athlete's aerobic level progressively higher so he can continue physical activity for long periods of time without succumbing to fatigue.

Effective endurance-building programs vary between individuals. In general, a 45-minute workout qualifies as an endurance session for juniors, while seniors would ski continuously for an hour or more. The workout is controlled by pulse rate, and the skier must remain aerobic and within his training effect zone. A clue to an anaerobic pulse rate is heavy breathing. You should be breathing at a level allowing you to carry on a conversation if you're in TEZ.

An endurance workout may be determined by either the length of the training period or by pace. As in track, the athlete can establish a certain pace—the number of minutes it will take him to ski a kilometer. After you become familiar with your training effect zone and with the terrain where you train, you can determine your kilometer-per-minute pace as it relates to your TEZ. In other words, you will develop a feeling for how fast you should ski over certain terrain to stay within TEZ. Instead of just going out and skiing 15 km, you can determine that your endurance workout will involve skiing five-minute kilometers until your pulse rate indicates fatigue and the end of the workout.

As your training progresses, your training effect zone will raise. This means you will have to increase the intensity of your workouts to gain physiological benefits. Intensity may be increased through use of more difficult terrain or by skiing at a faster pace.

Too often skiers train for endurance with too much intensity (too rapid a pace) and too much load (determined by the amount of verticle in the terrain). Such training is counterproductive because it can lead to mental and physical fatigue and, ultimately, to overtraining. Therefore, it's important to pay close attention to your pulse rate. Your pulse will tell you when the terrain is too steep, when to pick up or slow your pace and whether to keep skiing or end the workout.

Monitor your winter training by checking your pulse (take it for six seconds and add a zero). You can use your chest, arm, or wrist to find your pulse.

Because endurance training is conducted at a controlled pace, it's a good time to concentrate on technique. Work to ski properly, but remember that endurance training is continuous. Don't stop to chat with a teammate or spend much time talking with your coach.

Interval Training

The muscles do not change when you do interval work, but the mind changes very drastically to accept pain. If you train to absorb the pain, you are never going to be good. But if you train to break the pain, you advance to a new level.

Henry Rono, *who set four distance world records in track in 1978*

Serious cross-country racing involves the athlete's ability to deal with pain—the discomfort caused by the cardiovascular stress of skiing hard for extended periods. Dealing with this discomfort is one of the important lessons to be gained from interval training, as Henry Rono's comment affirms. Not only do intervals improve the body's ability to handle workloads and recover from them quickly, but interval training is one aspect of a conditioning program which, along with tempo training, best simulates racing.

While competing, whether in the Olympics or in a citizen race, the skier is constantly balancing his pace with his pain threshold. How much discomfort can he tolerate without going under? How many times can he go into an anaerobic state and finish the race at an optimum pace? The goal is to cross the finish line in a state of complete exhaustion. The athlete knows he got the most out of himself physically, mentally and technically during the race.

During interval training, you experience the sensations faced in racing: burning muscles, pain, exhaustion, etc. Intervals will educate you on how to deal with these sensations during competition. The lessons learned from running intervals in the off-season will carry over to your winter training and racing. Your body and brain continue to learn how to deal with pain, adjust your pace and accept the intense effort of hard skiing with winter interval training. An awareness of the sensations of stress and pain will leave you knowing how hard you can push on race day, when you are going under, and when you're in control.

Other than actual competition, interval training is one of the best objective gauges of your level of conditioning. After running a particular interval in November, do the same workout in later weeks. You should be able to ski more repetitions with less strain and need less time to recover. These factors will prove that your conditioning has improved. As TEZ moves up, you will have to increase the terrain, intensity, and pace of your interval workouts. Keep track of your kilometer-per-minute pace as a guide in planning your training. Improvements in your reactions to interval training, as recorded in your training log, are also a strong indication that you are at a peak or approaching one.

Formal intervals are controlled by intensity, terrain, the clock and the pulse rate. A typical on-snow interval involves a short section of trail which offers specific types of terrain. The athlete skis the section of trail repeatedly and is timed. He takes a recovery period between each effort. The number of repetitions is determined by an increase in the racer's time skiing and/or the time it takes him to recover from the effort.

As the racing season approaches, greater intensity should be added to your training through intervals. Early in November concentrate on endurance training, then add intensity—first through aerobic and then through anaerobic intervals. Some people shy away from doing intervals and tempo training near competition because they have the false idea that these workouts are only successful if they completely exhaust you. Intervals and tempo work need not be negative training sessions.

Intervals, and tempo training, get the skier ready for racing but are certainly not the same as racing. Only racing is racing—interval training is simply preparation for competition. Also, don't confuse natural intervals with formal interval training. Natural intervals are a part of endurance training and do not provide the controlled aerobic and anaerobic benefits derived from formal interval training.

Aerobic Intervals. To review, aerobic intervals are designed to improve the body's peripheral circulation efficiency; the transfer of oxygen to the muscles and the muscles' ability to use that oxygen. The athlete trains at a pulse rate in the upper limits of his training effect zone. His oxygen intake equals his oxygen usage.

An on-snow aerobic interval involves skiing a loop of 3–10 minutes over moderate terrain. You may need to slow your pace on uphills to keep within the training effect zone. After skiing the loop, take a break until your pulse is down to 120 beats a minute. The recovery period may last two minutes or less, during which you might ski easily and do stretching exercises. You may want to put on a jacket to keep warm. After recover, repeat the loop and recovery period. The workout continues until the time it takes to ski the loop or recover increases markedly.

Anaerobic Intervals. Through short, intense work periods, anaerobic intervals improve the body's central cardiovascular system so the heart pumps more blood (and oxygen) faster. During this type of interval, the pulse rate is at or above the athlete's anaerobic threshold; oxygen usage is greater than the oxygen intake so the body functions in a state of oxygen debt.

To reach this state, the athlete skis 30 seconds to 3 minutes at race pace or above, pushing his heart beat to 80% of maximum or higher. He rests between efforts until the pulse rate is down to 100 beats per minute. The number of repetitions is controlled by increases in either recovery time or skiing time. Complete recovery comes with rest after the workout.

Anaerobic workouts may be accomplished in several ways and over a variety of terrain. They are conducive to intersquad mini-races, provided the conditioning level of each individual is carefully monitored. Each skier's condition must be reassessed as the workout continues. Compensation for less-proficient skiers may be made through a handicap system in which these racers may ski less distance than the better skiers. Also, when some skiers tire, their workout is ended while others continue with regrouped teams.

Suggested Anaerobic Interval Workouts

1. Timed sections over variable terrain.
2. Timed sections using varied technique. Determine whether it's faster to double pole or single stick over a specific section. Then scramble as fast as possible without regard to technique and compare the time to when the section is skied with emphasis on good technique. Pay attention to how each technique affects the body—which is more tiring, which muscles are affected, etc.
3. Ski relay intervals around a short loop with three or four skiers on each team. No timing is needed because the number of people on each team and the length of the interval determine the recovery period. Double tracks are necessary.
4. Red Rover relays are successful with large groups of skiers broken down into 2–4 teams. Two or three people face the other half of their team across a section of track. Each skier races to tag a teammate at the other end of the track. Again, the recovery period is deter-

mined by the number of skiers on each team and the length of the section of track, so no timing is required.

5. Two people race each other over a specified section of a double-tracked course; no timing is needed. The skiers might alternate between skiing a fast lap and a moderately paced lap.

6. Accelerator intervals are when the skier starts the interval at a very easy pace and accelerates until he is above race pace. When his technique falls apart or when he has lost control, he returns to the start for a recovery period. The workout is controlled by pulse rate recovery time.

7. For a short and very intense workout, plan to overload the skier. Ski a loop or specific section of track very fast for a certain period of time. The recovery period between efforts is predetermined to be too short for full recovery. Do a series of repetitions until the athlete is totally winded, have an extended rest period, then another series of intense intervals.

Frequency of Intervals. Although it's physically possible for well-conditioned athletes to ski intervals daily, I don't recommend it. An interval workout should be followed with a day of relatively easy endurance training. The frequency and type of interval training is an individual decision based on the skier's needs in preparing himself for competition. It's often difficult for the athlete to know what type and how much interval training he needs, and coaching is helpful in setting up a program. Some athletes need more intervals than others, some skiers thrive on them, and others hate them; but intervals are a necessary part of a racer's training program.

The coach or the self-coached athlete must carefully evaluate individual needs in determining a schedule of intervals. What type of training does the athlete need? What does he think he needs? How does he respond physically and mentally to the different types of intervals? Some athletes may need more endurance work while others need more speed and tempo training. The diet of intervals should be varied; no one wants a steady diet of anaerobic hill intervals, nor should he have only aerobic intervals on the flats.

Again, the best way to evaluate an athlete's status and needs is through evaluating the times and reactions to interval training he has recorded in his log. Not only are the logs encouraging as your conditioning level improves, but they are necessary to follow the raise of your training effect zone so adjustments are made to increase the intensity of your training.

As a final reminder, don't forget to warm up and warm down during interval training. Keep warm during recovery periods. Also, a relaxing sauna after a workout does wonders for a tired body.

Tempo Training

Tempo training is designed to increase your skiing pace as part of your final preparations for competition. The primary concern in tempo training is to ski as fast as possible over a specified distance, paying only secondary concern to technique. Tempo training is basically a short race or a series of short intervals.

Tempo workouts become increasingly important as the racing season approaches. Tempo training is also important during the season to keep up your skiing pace. The goal of tempo training is to increase velocity, which is stride length combined with quickness of movement. There are two accepted methods of tempo training: the Norwegian method and the American method.

Norwegian tempo training is a series of medium-length intervals followed by an extended recovery period. The athlete skis at race pace or above for 3–7 minutes, rests for a period three times longer than the interval, then repeats until his body has had enough. There is no emphasis on pulse rate recovery and the skier will usually run two or three intervals. For example, you ski a five-minute loop at race pace. Then you put on your jacket and ski easily and stretch for 15 minutes before skiing another fast interval.

The American method of tempo training is one repetition of skiing at or above race pace for distances just under race length. For women, this means skiing 10–15 minutes and 20–25 minutes for men. The workout is timed and the skier simply skis as fast as possible. Tempo training should be scheduled progressively three to four weeks before an important meet. For women, the first week would involve one tempo mini-race of 10 minutes. A minute or so would be added each week until you have a 15-minute high-speed workout the week before the event. Men would build their time similarly toward 25 minutes.

If snow hasn't arrived and it's time to get ready for racing, remember that tempo training and interval workouts may be accomplished on roller skis. The methods and principles are the same whether you're on snow or not. The goal is to put the pedal to the metal—ski fast!

MONTH-BY-MONTH WINTER TRAINING GUIDELINES
November

November is TTV month: transition, technique, and volume. Snow is either falling or will soon fall, so you must be ready for the transition from dryland to on-snow training. It isn't likely that you'll be racing this month, so you can accumulate nonpressured kilometers and concentrate on tuning up your technique, whether on snow or roller skis.

Ideally, November is the heaviest month of the year in terms of hours spent training and kilometers covered. National team members have the best opportunity to reach a training high in November because they will be on snow. For the rest of us, November is the time to reach a dryland training peak in which we adapt our muscles to skiing through highly specific activities so we'll be ready to step on skis when the snow flies. There is little time for anything but roller skiing; every workout must involve activity that will ensure an easy transition to snow.

Endurance training is as much as 85% of your November effort. The emphasis is particularly heavy the first 2–3 weeks of the month, whether you're on snow or roller skis. Toward the end of the month in anticipation of December races, high-intensity workouts become a bigger part of your program. Where you might have had one interval workout a week early in the month, intervals and tempo training progress to about 20% of your training time during the last 10 to 12 days of November. Your endurance training pace increases throughout the month.

Work on technique. Elite racers and skiers who trained with specificity during the off-season will likely have their technique under control by November. Everyone should concentrate on making and repeating good technical moves while roller and/or snow skiing. Develop muscle memory through the repetition of good technique. Get on film early in November, study the film, and work to correct technical mistakes quickly. Late in November and once or twice in between if possible, get on film again to evaluate your technique.

Your November training should include strength and flexibility work. If you're on snow, shift to a muscle maintenance program. If you expect to be skiing in two or three weeks, concentrate on strength exercises with specificity, such as the lats bar, the Exer-Genie, the roller board, sit-ups, and back extensors. If you don't anticipate being on snow for a month, continue with your full off-season strength program. Three sessions of 45–60 minutes each week are in order.

To plan a November training program, use the activity percentage figures (Table 11, p. 83). Remember that interval and tempo training will average 15% of your monthly training time but will be increased progressively through the month as endurance training decreases somewhat.

Your early November program should include a weekly dose of intervals with each repetition between three and seven minutes in length. As December and the racing season approach, two interval workouts and one tempo workout per week are in order. The goal is to ski faster in both your endurance and speed workouts as competition gets closer.

Schedule intervals on the days of the week and the time of the day when races are likely to be held. This will get your body and mind in tune and on schedule for the effort of racing. Racing is a weekend happening, as a rule, so plan one workout on Saturday or Sunday and the other during the middle of the week. The mid-week interval should be fairly long and aerobic (at the high end of your training effect zone a low race pace), while the weekend interval should be anaerobic (at race pace or above over a shorter distance). Interval workouts should be followed by a day of easy distance work.

Carefully read how your body is reacting to the increased load of being on snow and interval training. Timed intervals are a good indicator. Remember, the increased workload makes flexibility work an even more important part of your daily regimen. Stretching will help you recover and get ready for the next day's training.

By late November, it's time to change the percentages of your weekly training activity a bit. Endurance work remains the prime concern, but it might be reduced to 75% while increasing interval and tempo work to 25% of your training time. This applies to both on-snow and dryland training.

The final week in November should include some time trials, which actually translate into tempo work, although they are also a gauge of how you're doing in relation to your teammates.

December

December is a transition month from training to racing. The competition season begins whether the skier is ready or not. Skiers love to race, but they're afraid to find out whether their preparations have been weak. Fortunately, December is normally not a heavy month for racing, so the transition is comfortably gradual. The typical competitor will have 4–6 races on his calendar.

Integrate your training program into your racing schedule. This is a big concern for international competitors because every race seems critical. Most other skiers can view December races as secondary to their training. Of course they want to start the season off with good results, but training still takes priority over racing because they are gearing up for important competitions in January and February. With just one or two races a week, planning for the month is fairly simple and there is plenty of time for training.

December is one of the last chances to fill your gas tank, so it's important to get in as much training as possible. Your volume will be down from the heavy regimen of November, but higher than the rest of the winter when racing and traveling will leave less time for training. Kilometers for women during December will range between 225 and 340 and between 300 and 500 kilometers for men. A good high school skier will be able to handle the low range of volume, while the high levels would be the goal of a well-ranked national competitor. International skiers would be covering even more distance in December—600 to 750 km for men and 425 to perhaps 600 for women.

Plan your month based on your race schedule and the training activity percentage guidelines (10% racing, 70% endurance training, 20% intervals and tempo training). Each week will include volumes of 55–100 km for women and 75–165 for men. In planning and recording your activities in your training log, be accurate. For example, kilometers spent in warm up and warm down for races and intervals are actually endurance training.

Endurance work should involve increasingly difficult terrain. Set up measured trails for training and record the pace you ski each kilometer. By the end of the month, your pace should improve as you adjust to the increasing effort and improve in conditioning. This improvement, even if only a few seconds a kilometer, will mean a great deal in your race results.

One problem all racers face in December is erratic weather and snow conditions. If you know the principles of training, you will productively adjust your training plans when a scheduled race or on-snow training session is cancelled. For example, if a race is called off because of no snow, replace it with an interval workout or other timed, racing-type situations, whether you're on snow or roller skis. A good athlete can adjust and keep his program moving forward despite the weather.

A Typical December Week. Let's say you had a race Sunday and will have another one next Sunday. On Sunday night and Monday, evaluate your body's reaction to competing. Depending on how you feel and what training you did the previous week, **Monday** will either be a day off or an endurance session over fairly gentle terrain. Women will ski 5–15 km and men will ski 10–25 km. End the day with your muscle maintenance and flexibility program.

Tuesday will be the hardest workout of the week. Plan an interval workout. Women will warm up and down for 2–5 km and ski 3–5 km of intervals. Men will have 3–7 km of warm up and warm down and ski 4–6 km of intervals. Relate the workout to any problems you had in the race on Sunday; if you had problems double poling, concentrate on that in training. Each interval repetition should be timed and you might ski each with a different technique to work on problems you had in racing. The workout should be hard, but not to the point of total exhaustion.

Wednesday is another endurance day. Ski twice the distance of the race coming up Sunday. Be overly conscious of making good technical moves during this workout.

On **Thursday,** return to intervals but don't plan a workout as hard as Tuesday's. Women will warm up and down 3–5 km and ski 2–4 km in intervals. Men will warm up and down 3–7 km and cover 3–5 km in intervals. The emphasis is speed and quickness, not exhaustion, because you don't want to be tired for Sunday. If you're at the race site, run intervals over sections of the course where you might have difficulty. Otherwise, use terrain that will demand training in the weakest area of your technique.

Friday is another distance day with women covering 7.5–15 km and men going 10–25 km. Work in the low to mid-range of your training effect zone so you feel comfortable with the effort.

The day before the race should involve an easy workout of 5–10 km for women and

10–15 km for men. The ideal plan for **Saturday** would be to ski around Sunday's race course and plan strategy: which hills to attack, where to switch tracks, where to begin your sprint to the finish. If a particular section of the course presents technique problems such as skating or a quick transition from a downhill to a herringbone, ski the section several times. If you're not at the race site, work on any technical difficulties you've been having. End the day with some good stretching and prepare your equipment for the race.

Most December races are short, so you should plan to have plenty of time and energy to ski the whole course **Sunday** as your warm up for the race. This effort shouldn't tire even the beginning racer. If you run out of time, check out at least some of the course, particularly the start and finish area, and study the course maps.

This typical week will be altered depending on the number of races in the week and your reaction to competition and training. Evaluate your recovery from racing to determine if you need a day off or can put in a few extra kilometers of endurance training during the week. Working toward a peak for later in the season requires careful monitoring of your physiological condition in December.

January

The number of January competitions for the average racer will double from his December schedule. You might race 8–12 times during the month, possibly as much as three times a week. Plan your race schedule for a gradual buildup of competition with, say, two races in the first week of January and three races in later weeks.

January marks the time of the year when you begin to be more concerned about resting than training. Because 30% of your monthly volume is spent racing, conditioning starts to take care of itself to a certain extent. Your endurance volume is down to 60% of your volume, and interval and tempo training are back to 10%. Meanwhile, the muscle maintenance and flexibility programs become even more important to keep you in readiness for competition.

A Typical January Week—Classified Racer. The classified racer is likely to have a week in late January which involves competition on Wednesday, Friday, and Sunday. Citizen and school racers might follow a similar race schedule, although their training would be a bit lighter than the more active classified racers.

Monday would be a day for light skiing followed by stretching and muscle maintenance. **Tuesday,** unless you are traveling, would be another day of easy skiing. A good plan would be to ski around Wednesday's race course, consider strategy and, do a few light sprints of 25–45 seconds. Concentrate on quickness.

After the race **Wednesday** (and after every race) warm down by skiing easily for 15–25 minutes. This warm down is important in cleansing the body of fatigue, maintaining a peak, and preparing for the next race. Stretching is another important part of your post-race regimen.

Thursday is similar to Tuesday—light sprints, course study, and strategy planning. **Friday** is race day, and **Saturday** is another day for light sprints and course check in anticipation of **Sunday's** race. **Monday** and **Tuesday,** depending on how your body has reacted to the racing, will be either days off or days for very light skiing.

If your racing schedule is particularly heavy, it's important to get plenty of rest. For example, if you have five or six races in a two-week period, I would advise you to spend the third week taking it easy. You might have two days off, put in a couple of days of endurance training, and schedule one race on the weekend. Rest and a good diet will keep you racing well during this critical time of the year. If you are in a peak or approaching one, don't push it. It's a common mistake to press and over train when you feel really good. Be cool, be smart, and stay in control.

Advice for Marathon and Cit Racers

Marathon and citizen race circuits typically begin in late January, but don't wait until then to start competing. All racers simply must be competing throughout January. Enter the events on the classified racers' calendar. Short races against intense competition will help the citizen and marathoner pick up their racing pace, allowing them to be more relaxed when they move to their own level of racing.

A second good program for the marathoner seeking more speed is based on improving his pace from the season before. Figure out your minute-per-kilometer pace in last year's marathons. Let's say the pace was 6 min/km. Establish a loop 10–20 km long. Over a two-week period, increase your workouts to the longer distance. Ski the workout twice a week if you have a weekend race or three times if you don't have a race that week.

During the workouts, ski the first kilometer or two at an easy pace as a warmup. Then, alternating kilometers, ski at a pace of 5.00 or 5.15 min/km for 1 km, then at a pace of 6.15 or 6.30 for the next kilometer. Continue alternating the pace until you near the end of the distance, then use the final two or three kilometers for an easy warm down. The distance you ski is gradually increased up to 20 km over a two-week period.

This program is a good three-week preparation period for a marathon. The first two weeks are spent with the pace workout with easy distance workouts on alternating days. The final week before a marathon should involve easy distance work, one good interval workout, and rest.

Citizen racers not interested in marathon distances may utilize this same pace training program by figuring their average race pace from the previous year and planning progressive workouts from 10–15 km.

A Typical January Week—Marathon Racer. With proper training and post-race recovery, citizens can race marathons weekly during the height of the marathon circuit in late January and February. Let's take a typical week when you have a marathon on Sunday and another on the following Saturday. After the **Sunday** race, avoid traveling. Eat a bit of food, drink fluids, shower or at least change clothes, and walk for 20–30 minutes. Then take a nap for 2–3 hours. Get up and eat a good meal of light foods. Do some light stretching and maybe take another walk; your system has to be active to remove the lactate built up in your muscles. Let the whole system relax and go to bed.

Monday might be a travel day. No strenuous workouts should be planned—maybe a walk or some easy skiing and more stretching. Also, pack in the food to replenish your body. **Tuesday** is much the same—nothing strenuous, perhaps ski for 10–15 km and do your muscle maintenance. **Wednesday** calls for some very light sprints or aerobic intervals, but no repetitions over three or four minutes. **Thursday** would be an easy 15–20 km ski followed by muscle maintenance. Ski easily again on **Friday** and check the course for Saturday's race. Review the start and finish areas, as they are particularly important for strategy, and go over sections of the course that cause concern.

This type of weekly race and recovery program allows the conditioned skier to compete in marathons throughout the season. A poorly conditioned athlete might have trouble recovering from week to week, but he would be surprised how good he feels if he takes proper care of himself.

February

February is the heaviest month of racing in North America. It is also the focal point of the season around the world, although March is actually the busiest month of racing in Europe. Your weekly schedule will vary a great deal in February depending on how many times you're racing and over what distances. The coach or self-coached racer must carefully plan this part of the season so the skier knows what's coming up and when he can anticipate rest days and training days. It's disastrous to operate on a day-to-day basis in February. The activity percentage guidelines indicate that 40% of the month's volume will come in racing, 50% in endurance training, and 10% in interval and tempo training.

In establishing your February schedule, try to work in a good day of training as often as possible. It isn't likely that an active racer will have more than one day a week to train, but it's important that he works in a good training session now and then between his racing and traveling.

March

March is often the most exciting month of the racing year. Because most of the season's major competitions are over, the skier can go overboard in accumulating racing kilometers.

Juha Mieto was a prime example in 1980. After winning two silver medals at the Olympics, he had a racing bib on an incredible number of times during the spring. The Finn raced in a total of 61 events over the season. Between March 15 and April 25 he had only three days when he wasn't competing. Plus he traveled a great deal. Although many of the races are planned in close proximity to each other, one night Juha raced at 6:00, hopped in his car and drove 1,000 km during the night to be at a 9:00 A.M. race the next day. There was obviously quite a bit of financial incentive behind Mieto's hectic racing schedule, but the late season is the time when skiers can feel free to pursue the type of schedule which would be crazy any other time of the year.

At 6'5" and 220 lbs, Finland's Juha Mieto is so big his number has to be pinned on because the bib won't fit him. He's a giant of a competitor, shown here in the 1979 Pre-Olympics.

Chase down competition and extend your season by racing as often as you can in March and April. The school and citizen racer should enter classified events in addition to their own races, while the classified skier should seek out cit races to augment his schedule. Sixty percent of your monthly volume should be covered in races.

When you're not racing, get in the tracks and ski. Racing takes care of your tempo and interval work, so the rest of your monthly volume comes in endurance training. It's a good time to work on technique and accumulate kilometers. Continued flexiblity and muscle maintenance programs will aid your March efforts.

With so much racing, your main concern in March is to stay healthy and rested. Check your body signs and take a day or two off when needed. But don't overreact—just because you had a bad race or feel tired doesn't mean you still can't be accomplishing a lot on the race course. March is a great time to learn how much racing your body can handle. You never improve unless you extend yourself. Don't worry about bad races; get ready for the next ones.

There are a couple of ways to approach spring races. One is to take advantage of the opportunity to race without pressure, which allows you to concentrate on technicial problems that troubled you during the season. Straighten out these problems for next season. March is also a good time to experiment on technique; try new equipment and test new waxing theories.

Another approach to March competition is to push yourself and race as hard as you can in every event you enter. Maybe you want to beat a guy who stomped you by a minute in a February race. Or maybe you want to improve your national seeding points by posting some hot results in high-point races. You can race at full bore without worrying about anything but the finish line.

April

The season ends April 1 in the minds of all too many racers. I disagree. Don't put your skis away! There are plenty of places to ski in North America, and there's much to be learned and enjoyed from spring skiing. As our sport becomes more sophisticated, there will be increasing opportunities to race in April.

There are four activities on the racer's April schedule: racing, touring, making the transition to dryland training, and planning for the next season.

Staying on snow is one of the best things the racer can do in April. If you can't find a race, take a lot of tours. Because cross-country racers spend about 90% of their skiing time in tracks, many of them never really learn to relax on their skis. The more relaxed you are on your skis, the faster you'll be able to race. One of the best ways to learn to relax comes from having to react quickly to changes of terrain and to obstacles that pop up at you while bushwhacking through the woods.

April is the time to be trying wild things on skis. Head into the woods and work to handle whatever comes up—avoiding trees, jumping brooks, skating around rocks, coping with different kinds of snow as you move from sun to shade. You'll be making so many saves you'll think you're a hockey goalie. By trying things you've never dared attempt, you learn to handle your body and your skis, improve your kinesthetic sense, overcome fear, and learn to react without taking time to think.

Besides, spring skiing is just plain fun and a great way to end the season after working hard and focusing only on racing all winter. One bit of advice: use an old pair of rock skis

On a spring fling, don't let a few bushes slow you down. Learn to make moves that will improve your skiing next winter.

and aluminum poles you don't mind abusing. This kind of skiing can be hard on equipment.

Cover the k's in the spring. Learn about turning, skating, maneuvering on one ski and handling downhills. Another way to get in some downhill training is to go Alpine skiing. Take a few lessons if you're inexperienced. The balance and confidence with speed you'll gain will pay dividends next season.

Most importantly, end your ski season on a high note. Have fun, relax, and enjoy your sport. Then take a break and begin planning for next winter and your off-season training program.

4

CROSS-COUNTRY EQUIPMENT

The Revolution, Its Benefits, and Its Demands

Those of us involved in cross-country skiing prior to 1974 often revel with amazement at the progress made in all facets of equipment from skis to underwear in a brief period during the mid-1970s. An equipment revolution swept our sport, relegating to the ski museums the goo of pine tar on wood skis, the clumsy bamboo and aluminum poles, the cumbersome boots and bindings, and the bulky, uncomfortable ski outfits. Today's ski equipment features the radical improvements incorporated during the '70s which, combined with continuing refinements, have had an almost incalculable effect on our sport.

Modern gear allows the competitor to cover the distance with an efficiency and comfort impossible before the equipment revolution. However, today's equipment is complicated and demanding. The racer must know his gear, how it works, and how to take care of it to obtain the maximum benefit it offers. The racer's concern for his equipment will be reflected in better race results.

THE EQUIPMENT REVOLUTION

The equipment revolution began in 1974 at the World Nordic Championships in Falun, Sweden, where Austrian Alpine ski manufacturers Kneissl and Fischer introduced fiberglass cross-country racing skis. When nine of the first dozen finishers in the opening men's 30-km race, including winner Thomas Magnusson of Sweden, wore the synthetic skis, violent shocks reverberated throughout the world of Nordic skiing. A stampede ensued as racers scrambled to obtain fiberglass skis and ski companies strained furiously to catch up to the revolution created by Kneissl and Fischer.

Kneissl must take the greatest measure of credit for the ski revolution because the ski it introduced in 1974 was radically different in material and design than any ski ever before used in cross-country competition. The Kneissl was double cambered and had a foam core. The camber peaked in the middle of the ski and was so stiff that the kicker wax was off the snow during the glide phase. The ski was very lightweight, had no sidecut, and was thicker and narrower than the traditional wood ski. These factors, along with the P-Tex base, made the Kneissl ski considerably faster than wooden skis.

There has been amazing progress in ski design since 1974. On the left is the wooden Landsem ski used by Martha Rockwell when she placed her record 10th in the 1974 World Championships. The two skis on the right reflect the modern designs developed since 1974. Note the tip variations and narrow profile of the fiberglass skis.

Kneissl dropped the bomb at Falun and the fallout is still being felt. Fiberglass skis opened a whole new world for all skiers, not just racers. The only thing in common between the wood skis before 1974 and the synthetic skis during and after that season was that both turned up at one end and had grooves in the base. As refinements were made, even the profiles of the tips of fiberglass skis were altered and skis were produced with no grooves, multiple grooves, and partial grooves. Cross-country skis had been made of wood for hundreds of years. After the revolution in 1974, everyone from racers to beginning skiers became aware that wood was dead. During the 1975 competitive season in Europe, all the racers were on fiberglass skis. By 1976, no wooden skis appeared in major North American competitions and they were rapidly becoming a rarity in citizen races. The ski revolution was over in two short years.

Just as the fiberglass ski came to the fore, a revolution in poles began. In 1975 Exel-Silenta of Finland introduced a pole featuring new designs and materials in the shaft, basket, grip, handle and strap. The major breakthrough in the Exel pole was its shaft of tapered graphite. The carbon fiber material is extremely light but stiff, so the full energy generated by the arm while poling travels down the shaft, delivering a more efficient push on the snow. The butterfly basket is also light and efficient and solves the problem of the pole slipping out of the snow in hill climbing and double poling. The tip of the pole is short and sharp so it goes to work immediately. The lightweight grip and improved strap design combine with the light shaft and base to decrease recovery time from each movement and improve poling pace, matching the increased speed of the fiberglass skis. The graphite poles were an immediate success and every serious racer was using them within a year.

Within that same year, the cross-country world was also rocked by a boot/binding revolution. For the 1976 Olympics, Adidas of France designed new footgear that threw leather boots and 75-mm bindings out the racer's window. The Adidas boot upper was made primarily of nylon and the sole was of Hytrel, a DuPont plastic. The sole extended beyond the toe about an inch and a half, and this nub was inserted into a 38-mm-wide binding and locked down. The benefits of this system, and others quickly developed in response to Adidas, were immediately apparent. The narrowness of the boot and binding enhanced speed by reducing friction against the walls of the track. The system was incredibly lightweight, saving energy. With the nub of the boot firmly attached to the binding and a very flexible boot, the skier had a greater range of motion in both kicking and gliding. Most importantly, the system provided much needed control over the fiberglass skis. The heel of the boot had a notched groove which slipped onto a V-shaped heel plate. For the first time, skiers had lateral stability at high speeds and Alpine-type turns were possible.

While revolutions were shaking up equipment, a quieter explosion was taking place in racing clothing. The knickers, separate tops, and wool kneesocks were on their way out as competitors realized the benefits of full-length, one-piece uniforms. By 1978, virtually all top competitors were in lightweight, streamlined full uniforms of Lycra, a form-fitting material with four-way stretch. Equally streamlined underwear was developed to complement the uniforms and keep skiers warm and dry. Not only are the new racing clothes more colorful and attractive, but they are also faster than knicker outfits. The U.S. team proved in wind tunnel tests that a one-piece uniform, a form-fitting hat, and smooth gloves have 16% less drag at 30 mph than the bulky outfits worn by racers for preceding decades.

The final stages of the revolution came underfoot with developments in waxes, waxing methods, and waxless skis. The fiberglass skis forced the creation of new types of waxes; others from Alpine skiing were added to the cross-country skier's wax kit to build the most efficient ski surface on the P-Tex bases. For the first time in history, the Europeans weren't at an advantage over North American racers because the new skis and waxes put everyone on an equal footing as we began experimenting with and learning about the new skis and the waxing they required. Americans came to the fore in waxing after extensive research, investigation, and experimentation. We theorized that because of the angle of the knee and the dynamic body position, the major force during the kicking movement was transmitted two to three inches in front of the binding. Therefore, there was no reason to apply kicker wax behind the heel plate. The ideal pocket for kicking wax was centered on a point two to three inches in front of the binding and ran for an equal distance in front of and behind that point. With kicker wax restricted to this area, it is held off the snow by the ski's camber while the Alpine wax on the remainder of the base does its work during the glide phase of skiing.

Chart 9 illustrates the waxing areas of the modern cross-country ski. The binding is normally centered on the balance point, although some brands of skis vary. The chart provides an accurate picture of the relationship between the binding, heel plate and camber pocket or kicker wax zone.

CHART 9
Defining the Kicker Wax Zone

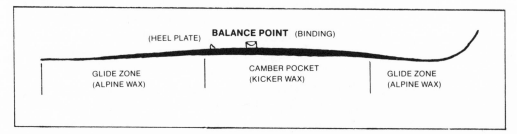

(HEEL PLATE) **BALANCE POINT** (BINDING)

GLIDE ZONE
(ALPINE WAX)

CAMBER POCKET
(KICKER WAX)

GLIDE ZONE
(ALPINE WAX)

As coaches and competitors experimented to master waxing fiberglass skis, advances made in waxless skis for tourers came to benefit racers—an interesting turnabout from the norm in equipment refinement. By 1976 several companies, led by Trak, had developed no-wax bases for high-performance racing skis which proved efficient in certain snow conditions. Although waxless skis have been used only a few times in major competition, we'll be seeing them more often as the base patterns continue to improve.

The years since 1974 have been exciting. The equipment revolution threw almost everything we'd known about our old gear into obsolescence and replaced it with a whole new world of information to be learned about skis, poles, boots, bindings, waxes and clothing. Continuing refinements demand that the dedicated racer undergo an ongoing

The old days. Note Martha Rockwell's round baskets, aluminum poles, 75 mm bindings, leather boots, wooden skis, and two-piece knicker outfit.

Today. Within four years, cross-country gear from skis to underwear had been completely revolutionized.

equipment education. Further, the equipment revolution and related developments have placed new physiological and technical demands on the skier.

Traditionally the Scandinavians dominated cross-country competition with their endurance and a technique noted for fluid strides and graceful motion. Then the Soviets stormed onto the winner's stands in the early 1970s with a technique that emphasized raw strength. Soviet success led to an increase in training volumes and strength work of all international racers. This move occurred about the same time and perhaps in reaction to the equipment revolution. As racers became more professional in their training and as they acquired more efficient equipment, they began to ski faster. Then track setting and maintenance improved and race courses changed in design; double sets of machine-set tracks were laid around smoother, faster courses.

The end result of all of this has left racers skiing faster and faster. Winning times in international events are on a constant decline because equipment and good waxing let the racers go faster, better training improves their speed and power, and course design and maintenance allow for faster skiing.

Cross-country competition is a better test of athletic ability now than it was before 1974. Endurance is not the only factor in modern racing. Competitors have to ski better technically, handle their equipment at high speeds over turns, bumps, uphills, and down-hills. Anyone without solid training, athletic skills, good technique, and knowledge of his equipment is at a handicap. The 1970s were a decade of great change in all aspects of cross-country skiing. The changes and continuing refinements add excitement to the chal-lenges facing the racer.

SKIS

Skis are the most important piece of equipment for the racer. You might be able to get away with less-than-the-best poles, boots, and bindings, but second-rate skis will be a definite disadvantage on the race course. Buy the best gear you can afford and the invest-ment will be well worth it. The old saying about getting what you pay for certainly holds true in ski equipment. A good ski will make you a better, faster skier, will require less maintenance, and will last seasons longer than a cheaper model.

The question I'm probably asked most often by skiers is what brand of ski I think is best. By and large, the top-end, high-performance models produced by the various ski manufacturers are just about equal in quality. All the firms have caught up with the tech-nology of fiberglass ski design and production. If you take skis from different companies that cost $160 and up, you'll find that each ski is comparable in quality of materials, design, and construction.

When looking for a good pair of racing skis, the most important factor to consider is not the brand but the particular skis and what you'll be using them for. You must know your technique, skiing style and strength, so you select skis suited to your characteristics as a racer. Then you must decide the purpose of the ski—racing or training—and if it will be used in soft powder snow, klister, or hard powder conditions. After narrowing down these factors, evaluate the characteristics of the ski: camber, sidecut, tip and tail flex, type of base, extent of the grooves. The pair should be truly a pair, not a mismatched set of skis.

Selecting a good pair of skis is one of the biggest challenges facing the skier. Is that pair of skis good for you? Will they work for your body weight? Are they right for your technique? Will they perform with the type of kick you generate? Are they designed for the snow conditions you'll confront? If you're spending $160 to $200 for a pair of skis, you'd better have the answers to these questions. Determining the answers takes know-how. Take your time selecting skis. If you're going to buy the best skis, don't just head into one store and grab a pair. Look around. Talk to people in the know. Borrow skis and try them out, or at least test them to get a feel for what you're looking for. Then tour the ski shops and talk to salespeople. Watch for sales and shop early so there's a good selection. Find a shop with knowledgeable clerks who are patient and will let you spend time testing numbers of skis.

Go into the shop with a procedure for picking a good pair of skis. Testing 10–30 pairs of skis can become confusing unless you have an organized system. You might want to take a notebook into the ski shop, have a numbering system by which you grade the characteristics of each ski, and keep track of the skis you've eliminated so you gradually narrow your selection down to the best pair of skis available. Again, take your time.

The best way to learn about selecting skis is to do it yourself. Develop a feel for the types of skis and how they flex. Know your needs and how you ski. Take up the challenge to learn everything you can about skis.

Skis for the Racer

The number of skis needed by the racer depends on the level of his racing and his pocketbook. National team members travel around the world toting up to 15 pairs of skis with them, each with a slightly different camber and flex pattern. On race day, they will wax two or three different pairs and test each to determine which pair most perfectly fits the particular snow conditions.

Most racers are in great shape if they have three pairs of skis, or perhaps four. The three would include a pair for soft powder conditions, one for hard powder, and one for klister/skare, granular snow. The fourth pair would be a waxless ski, but its use is so limited that I doubt the majority of racers need a waxless pair.

However, a racer can get by on a single pair of racing skis. I wouldn't advise this, but it's possible if the skis are carefully selected. In addition to considering your technique and ability when buying a single pair of skis, be aware of the type of snow conditions most prevalent in your area. In Colorado, you'd likely use a soft powder ski most of the season, while in the East a hard powder ski would be the best. If conditions vary from the norm in your area or it you travel to different types of conditions, you will have to adjust the wax and the length of the kicker wax you apply.

A good way to build your stock of skis is to buy them gradually over the years. Because fiberglass skis will last up to five or six years of racing if they are well maintained, you can buy a different type of ski every year or so without straining your budget all at once.

Ski Characteristics

When selecting a pair of skis, there are seven main factors to consider—compatibility of the two skis, camber, sidecut, tips, tails, base and grooves. These characteristics are built into the skis at the factory and will vary a great deal. Not only do the materials, design and manufacturing processes vary from brand to brand, but each individual ski has its own characteristics.

Compatibility. Just because two skis stand together on the rack in the ski shop and have the same serial number doesn't necessarily indicate they are a good pair. Modern skis are made individually, and numerous processes are involved. One ski might end up with a touch more resin than another, or maybe a little bit more fiberglass, or perhaps it stays in the mold for 15 minutes longer. These types of things will affect the characteristics of the individual ski.

Camber. The primary difference between the three main types of skis is in the camber, the curvature built into the ski which supports your weight and determines the ski's flexibility. The old wooden skis had a smooth, parabolic camber. When Kneissl came out with its fiberglass ski in 1974, the most significant characteristic in the ski was that it had double camber. About 90% of today's fiberglass skis have this feature. The curvature of a double-cambered ski is parametric, meaning that it has a definite, almost inflexible spot at

CHART 10
Double vs. Single Cambered Skis (exaggerated representation)

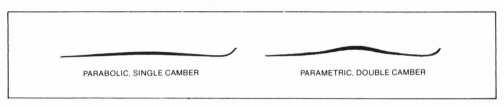

PARABOLIC, SINGLE CAMBER   PARAMETRIC, DOUBLE CAMBER

its high point (Chart 10). The double-cambered ski cannot be completely flattened out. The energy generated in the kick will flatten the ski enough for the wax to be in contact with the snow. Otherwise, the kicker wax is off the snow, enhancing the speed of the glide.

The double camber will vary. It can be located in the very center of the ski, or ahead of or behind the midpoint. The placement is determined by each company's philosophy about the best location for this zone. The camber can also be stiff or soft, depending on the type of snow for which it has been designed. Thus, a soft powder ski will have a softer camber while a granular snow ski will be stiffer.

Sidecut. Wooden skis had a sidecut, which meant that the tips and tails were slightly wider than the middle of the ski. The design, construction, and materials used in fiberglass skis eliminated the need for a sidecut, thus enhancing speed and improving contact with the ski track. Although there are some models of fiberglass skis with a minimal sidecut, virtually all modern skis are the same width throughout. They are also considerably narrower than the wooden skis.

Tips. With the development of the fiberglass ski came the opportunity to experiment with tip design. Refinements are still being made and a variety of tip configurations are available. The significant factor in these refinements is that the profile of the tip is lower and often much narrower than the tips on wood skis. Although it seems that the lower tip is designed to decrease wind resistance, it is actually planned to reduce the mass of the tip. When skiing over bumps and undulations, a tip with a lighter mass will vibrate less. This means you have a quieter ski which stays in contact with the snow and is, therefore, faster.

An increasing number of brands of skis feature what is called a boat shape or javelin tip. The tip (or prow, to explain the boat analogy) is considerably narrower as it curves upward from the point it leaves the snow. The tip on the most radical javelin cuts measures 30 mm, as compared to the 44- to 45-mm width of the rest of the ski. One purpose of the javelin tip is to limit the tip's contact with the rail or sidewall of the track in long radius turns, enhancing speed. The tip is said to be particularly fast in wet conditions because of reduced friction against the snow. A modified javelin tip is best in other conditions.

There are several variations in tip profiles. Some javelin tips continue their narrower width further down the ski than others. Some brands offer tips with very low profiles or squared-off tips.

Flex patterns in tips also vary between skis. The stiffer the tip, the easier the ski is to turn but the slower it will be. The tip should flex in a long, smooth curve for even distribution of your weight on the ski. Tips should also splay a bit, which means they will lift off the snow under pressure and easily conform to undulations in the track so there is

A sample of the variety of ski tips available includes the Kneissl in the center, currently considered a standard tip because it has no decrease in sidecut. On the right is a narrow, radical javelin tip profile made by Peltonen, which led in the javelin design. The Elan on the left features a modified javelin tip.

CHART 11
Adidas Keel Bases

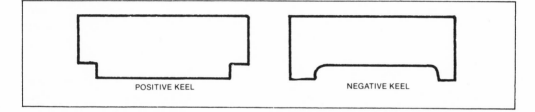

less resistance against the snow and the ski is faster. The ski tip is still being tested and refined and I'm certain we'll see more variations.

Tails. Tails should be slightly shoveled or upturned at the end of the ski, which provides smoother contact with the snow and avoids having the tail dig into the snow if you slip backwards. Hanging tails, which were typical of older skis, should be avoided because they cause friction against the snow.

Flexibility in the tail is a prime consideration in skis. A good ski will have a long, smooth radius when pressure is applied to the tail (and the tip) so weight is evenly distributed. A tail that is too stiff or has an uneven flex pattern will allow the energy generated when the ski is compressed to end up in one point or hard spot of the ski. Hard spots will slow the ski and can cause directional problems.

Bases. Most of today's skis have a P-Tex 2000 base which best absorbs and holds wax and enhances speed. The surface was borrowed from Alpine skis. There are variations to P-Tex which are a function of its density or hardness. Some skis use the certain densities of P-Tex for specific snow conditions. Other materials, such as Teflon, have also been used on bases, but the majority of racing skis available to the public use P-Tex 2000.

Some experimentation has been done with base configurations, as well. Most notably, Adidas has introduced a keel configuration (Chart 11). A positive keel is said to provide the

This selection of skis indicates the variety of bases available on modern skis. From left to right are a Fischer no-wax mohair, a Trak Fishscale, a Peltonen varied groove (three grooves in the tail and a single groove from the camber pocket to the tip), an Elan with no groove in the camber pocket, and a Fischer Crown waxless base.

skier with a stronger kick in certain conditions. The negative keel is for use in wet snow conditions when you want to keep your kicker wax off the snow as much as possible. Neither base has a groove. The keel base has yet to gain wide acceptance among competitors but is an example of the type of refinement and testing underway.

Grooves. Perhaps the area of most experimentation is in the groove of the base. The groove is designed to provide stability to the ski. It doesn't appear that the ski companies have yet determined exactly how the groove does its job because various brands sport wide grooves, narrow grooves, routed grooves, molded grooves, multiple grooves and no grooves. I believe a single groove that is discontinued in the camber pocket is most efficient. Because the ski is double cambered, a groove underfoot has limited contact with the snow and seems useless in terms of stability because the ski is already stable while kicking. Further, the lack of a groove increases the area for kicker wax significantly, so the length of the kicker can be reduced to allow for more glide area. I've tested skis with no grooves in the camber pocket and found them to be very efficient and fast. However, they are not widely available because many companies mold in grooves, which eliminates the possibility of discontinuing the groove underfoot.

Tests for Selecting Skis

When buying skis, you're investing a sizable amount of money—from $160 to over $200—so you should spend some time studying the options. What follows is a series of nine tests I advise skiers to use when selecting a pair of new skis (see pp. 115-117).

In conducting these tests, keep in mind that you are trying to determine how the skis will function on snow. How will they compress when you're riding them on a downhill? What will happen to them when you push them through a turn? What will one ski do when you have your full weight on it during a skate turn or herringbone? How will the skis react to the various demands you'll put on them while skiing? The tests should help you find answers to these questions and select the best pair of skis for your needs.

Warp Test. The first test for the skis you're examining is to check for warp, concavity or convexity. Hold a pair of skis together, base-to-base. If they don't rest against each other smoothly and are twisted or warped, eliminate them from consideration. If you can see daylight when looking through where the tips and tails touch, eliminate the pair because the bases are convex or concave.

Warping is less common today because less and less wood is being used in the cores of racing skis. It's more likely that the base will be concave or convex because the ski might have been scraped or sanded a bit too much at the factory.

Pair Test. The second test is to check that each ski of a pair is compatible. Find a flat surface and lay the skis down side by side, bases down. Look across the tops of the skis to be certain they are the same camber height, particularly as they curve away from the midpoint. If one ski is higher than the other, it likely has a stronger camber. If the camber is unequal between two skis, they are not a pair and should be rejected.

Sidecut. With the skis lying base down on a flat surface, pull them together tight. Since racing skis have no sidecut, they should line up perfectly with the side walls in contact the whole length of the skis except the tips. Test that both sides of each ski line up cleanly with the other ski. If they don't come together, one ski might have a side camber warp. This could be due to manufacture in a faulty mold. Reject any pairs that don't line up perfectly.

Camber Type Test. If you're looking for a single-cambered ski for soft powder conditions, hold the pair base to base and squeeze. If you can squeeze the camber pocket so that the bases touch, you have a single-cambered ski. If you can't get the bases to touch at the middle of the ski, you have a double-cambered ski for hard powder or granular snow.

A second way to test for type of camber is to take one ski, lean the base of the tip against your shoulder, put a leg around the ski at the camber pocket, and try to put a reverse bend in the ski. If the ski curves smoothly, it's single cambered. If it curves, but has a slight bump in the camber pocket, it's double cambered.

Hard Spot Test. When you clamp a pair of skis together, base-to-base, eye the skis forward from the mid-point to the tip and back to the tail. If the skis pop open anywhere you've got what is known as a hard spot, which means you have a slow ski. If the skis clamp together evenly, you know that they will evenly accept the pressure of being stepped on during the kick phase while skiing.

Tip Splay Test. With the ski bases held together at the balance point, check for tip splay. When the skis are squeezed together, I like to see the tip open up a bit or splay. This means you've got a flexible tip which will raise up a bit when sitting on the snow, thereby enhancing speed. A flexible tip won't turn as well as a stiff tip because it doesn't have the resistance to hold you during the turn and will want to slip out a bit. You can compensate for this with skillful use of the boot/binding systems and good technique. I like a flexible tip because it's faster and glides better, outweighing the benefits of having a stiff tip for turning.

Flex Direction Test. With the skis clamped together at the midpoint, pull one tip away from the other. If the free ski moves toward the ski being pulled, reject it because it will put too much pressure on the snow when compressed by body weight while skiing. Test each tip to be sure both stay in line under pressure. Turn the skis around and test the tails the same way. If the free tail moves toward the one being pulled, reject it. Just as with the tips, the tail has a hard spot and will press into the snow with your body weight, causing drag.

Tip and Tail Flex. The first step in this test is to be certain the tip of the ski has a softer flex than the tail. Hold the skis base-to-base and tip-to-tail. When clamping them together, the tail of each ski should overpower the tip on the other ski—there will be a slight curvature of the tail toward the tip. Then clamp the skis together tip-to-tip to determine if each tip flex is equal to the other and each tail flex is equal. There should be no curve or pressure from one tip or tail on the other. If there is a curve, the skis should be rejected.

To determine the extent of the tip flexibility, don't just grab a tip and pull it back as so many people do. Hold your hand against the base of the tip and press on the middle of the ski to simulate how the tip will react against snow. As you push, you want the tip to flex in a smooth, long radius so your weight will be distributed evenly on the ski. Much of your weight will be supported by the middle of the ski and the rest is distributed gradually and evenly, decreasing toward the tip. If the flex is too long or too soft, the vast majority of your weight will be on the center of the ski, slowing your glide. If the tip flex is too short and too stiff, you have a hard spot and a lot of energy will be transmitted to that spot, making the ski slow. The goal is a smooth, even flex down the length of the tip so your weight and energy forces will be evenly distributed.

To test the tail flex, stabilize the tail on the floor and press the middle of the ski. Again, you are looking for a smooth, long arc which will allow even weight and energy distribution.

If you ski on skis which are too stiff, the energy required to step on the ski and kick will make the ski want to leave the track; it will shoot out to the right or left. The energy you've used to depress the ski has gone out to the tip and tail areas, not to the center. Further, skis that are too stiff won't undulate over the snow smoothly and will shoot off to one side or the other, particularly when you're on an edge while turning.

Camber Tests. By this stage of your testing, you should have eliminated a number of pairs of skis and have one pile of skis that have passed all the tests. The final test will determine skis appropriate for your weight and the snow conditions in which you expect to use the skis, based on camber.

There are three tests used to check camber. This does not include the hit-and-miss method of simply squeezing the skis together at the camber pocket. This method is unreliable because it's impossible to determine if the strength in your hands is equal to your weight.

The most common camber test is known as the paper test. Find a perfectly flat surface (not an old wooden floor) and lie the skis down about track width apart, four to six inches. Stand on the skis where the bindings will be located. Evenly distribute your weight by slightly bending your knees and looking straight ahead, not down. Then have someone slide a sheet of paper under your feet. Because you want your kicking wax off the snow as your weight is evenly distributed during downhills and double poling at high speeds, the paper must be able to fit between the camber pocket and the floor.

Next, determine the extent of the camber. Your weight is obviously a factor in determining what type of camber you need, but you also must consider how strong a kick you have. A strong kicker will want a stiffer ski with a longer pocket, and vice versa. Therefore, the figures listed below for each type of ski may be changed a bit to meet the individual's needs based on his skiing style.

If you're looking for a ski to use in granular snow (klister/skare) conditions, you should be able to move the paper 12–18 inches forward and back of the balance point. (If the balance point isn't marked on the ski, balance the ski on a metal scraper to determine the point.) This means the camber pocket is 24–36 inches long. For hard powder skis, the pocket should be 6–11 inches on either side of the balance point. For women, the pocket for both granular and hard powder skis will be an inch or two shorter. With soft powder skis, you should just be able to slide the paper under foot up to 5 inches. Keep in mind when you're waxing your skis that the length of the kicker wax will be shorter because all your weight will be on one ski while kicking—it won't be evenly distributed on each ski as in this test. The amount you can move the paper under the ski when all your weight is on the one ski is your optimal kicker length. The energy of the kicking movement will pressure the camber pocket (and wax) into contact with the snow.

In order to avoid the inaccuracies caused by an imperfectly flat surface in the paper test, I designed a simple device to test camber. Take a 1 × 6-inch board about 30 inches long supported by 2 × 4s. On top of the 1 × 6, I've nailed thin guides 45 mm apart and cut a hole to accommodate a binding. By placing a pair of skis on this device and standing on them, I can more accurately accomplish the objectives of the paper test in determining whether the skis are hard power (6–11 inches), soft powder (little or no distance), or granular snow (12–18 inches) skis for my weight. Instead of paper, which may vary in thickness, I use a standardized metal feeler gauge of 0.012 inch inserted between the skis to determine the length of the camber pocket.

More and more shops are offering another device to test camber. A $60–$70 clamping gauge works on the same principle as the paper test, but the clamp provides the pressure. The gauge is adjusted to your weight and clamped on the skis. Then you run paper or a feeler gauge between the skis to determine the camber pocket length. A chart provided with the clamp will tell you if the ski fits your camber needs.

Three factors must be considered in determining proper ski length: your height, weight, and ski ability. As a guideline, a ski should reach the palm of your raised hand. If you're heavy or have the ability, you will want a longer ski. A longer ski is faster because there is more area for even weight distribution through the camber.

Warp test. Eye the skis to be certain they rest against each other smoothly.

The pair test. I'm forcing the difference in the camber on this pair of skis to indicate a potential problem—one ski might have a stiffer camber than the other and the two are not compatible.

Sidecut test. By holding the skis tightly together in the sidecut test, you determine if their sidecut is even. If so, the skis will have clean contact the entire length (except at the tips).

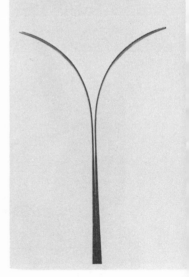

Camber type test. To determine the type of camber, exert pressure on the camber pocket and eye the base to observe whether the curve of the camber is parabolic (single camber) or parametric (double camber).

Hard spot test. In checking for hard spots, eye the bases to be certain they clamp together evenly and don't pop open anywhere other than at the camber pocket. Also watch for a straight line of closure, indicating that each ski has the same stiffness.

Tip splay test. By clamping the skis together at the camber pocket, check for tip splay. The air space down in the shovel area indicates a tip splay that will allow the skis to undulate through terrain without much resistance so the skis will be faster. Tip splay is an asset, although it was considered a flaw at one time.

Flex direction test, tips. To check for tip flex direction, clamp the skis together at the balance point and pull away one tip. If the other stays in place, it has a good flex.

Flex direction test, tails. If the free tail moves toward the tail being pulled, it has a hard spot and, therefore, will be slow.

Flex test, tip and tail. A good pair of skis has a slightly stronger flex in the tail than in the tip. In holding the skis tip-to-tail, the tail should overpower the tip somewhat.

Tip flex test. In testing for tip flex, watch for a curve with a long, smooth radius.

Tail flex test. The tail should flex in a long, smooth curve when it is under pressure.

Camber length test. My assistant runs a feeler gauge between the skis to measure the length of the camber pocket.

To make the final determination between two pair of skis, check for minor flaws in construction and cosmetics. Look closely at the finish, the paint job, the sanding of the bottom, the tips and the tails. Make certain the base is solidly bonded with the ski. Examine the grooves for proper alignment. These factors should help you decide on the best pair of skis.

Ski Maintenance

It's been my observation that one quick way to tell an elite racer from an average racer is by taking a look at the condition of his skis. Invariably, the top competitor's skis are in good shape while the other racer's skis are covered with knicks, scratches, and gouges and obviously haven't been properly maintained. For a skier to go through the sweat and strain of training and then show up at a race with skis that aren't in shape for good skiing is beyond my comprehension.

On the other hand, elite skiers spend an incredible amount of time working on their skis. Even though they have access to dozens of pairs of skis, they spend hours and hours repairing every little knick and gouge, keeping each ski waxed and simply caring for their equipment. I believe this concern is an indication of the athlete's dedication to his sport.

To protect the bases of your skis, a good coat of Alpine wax should *always* cover the glide zones. This prevents the bottoms from oxidizing and drying out and keeps the bases free of dirt. It's particularly important to iron in a coat of Alpine wax before you travel with your skis. During the season, I keep my camber pocket clean between skiing and coat even this area with alpine wax to store my skis in the off-season. Waxing is an on-going process for all skis; they should never be without wax.

Breakage is only a minor problem with today's fiberglass skis. If they are mistreated—taken over a bump the wrong way—or if maintenance is ignored, they can break. They are fragile in the tip and tail areas, but, compared with wooden skis, breakage is minimal and fiberglass skis give the skier a good return on his dollar.

Skis can delaminate and sidewalls are susceptible to damage, so it's important to seal up knicks and scratches on the top, bottom and sides of skis to prevent any moisture from seeping into the ski. If moisture gets in and is allowed to sit there or, worse yet, freeze, your skis will be irreparably damaged. Anytime you have a knick or gouge, quickly fill it with paint, if it's minor, or epoxy. Carry epoxy, white glue, P-Tex candles, or polyplastic mending strips, clamps, and a fiberglass kit in your wax kit so you can make repairs as necessary.

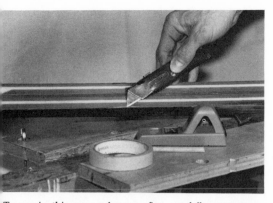

To repair this gouge damage, first carefully remove any dirt and wax in the gouge and then clean with solvent.

Place masking tape on the edge where the ski is gouged. This will stop the P-Tex from dripping over the edge and allow it to build up in the damaged area.

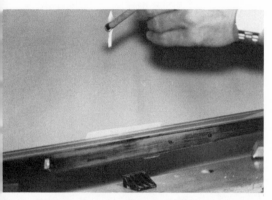

Light a P-Tex candle and let the material drip onto the gouge. Hold the candle away from the ski so the P-Tex won't be too hot when it touches the base.

With a mini-plane, smooth and square up the edge and base of the ski where you've dripped the P-Tex. Then use a metal scraper or sandpaper as a final step in smoothing the repaired area.

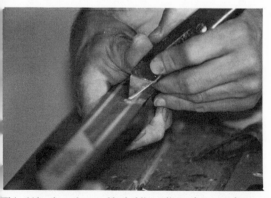

This ski has been damaged by holding a lit torch to one place too long, causing the P-Tex to bubble. With a sharp knife, cut away and remove the bubbled P-Tex and a bit of the surrounding area. Cut carefully and avoid damaging the fiberglass layer directly under the P-Tex.

After removing the bubbled P-Tex, you can fill the hole by using a P-Tex candle or iron in a Toko Polystrip. The Polystrip melts under less heat than P-Tex so there is less chance of damaging the rest of the base. The strip can be melted in with an electric iron or a torch-heated iron as shown here. If there is excess buildup of the repair material, smooth it with a mini-plane. The final step in this repair job is to work the area with a metal scraper or sandpaper.

Reprepping Skis

A good way to add longevity to the life of your ski is to reprep it twice a year: once in mid-season and again before you put your skis away for the summer. If you fail to reprep in the spring, be certain to do it before the next ski season starts.

Reprepping removes any dirt that's accumulated on the base and in the pores of the P-Tex and also reopens pores which may have been closed by the use of torches and irons in waxing. The first step is to completely clean the ski base. Scrape all the wax off and then take a torch and rag to remove additional wax off the entire base. Take a liberal amount of wax remover solvent and rub it all over the skis. Let the liquid sit on the ski for 30–45 seconds to ensure penetration into the pores. If it evaporates, add more remover.

Now take a wire brush and give the entire base a good hard scrubbing. This will bring up the P-Tex ruff so you open all the pores in the base and remove all the dirt. You should see a residue of dirt on the ski, which you wipe away with a clean rag or Fiberlene. Apply another liberal coat of wax remover and work it around the base. If you didn't raise the P-Tex ruff before, wirebrush the base again hard—you can't really damage the base. If you're nervous about this, test the effects of brushing on a section of the tip that isn't on the snow. After raising the ruff, wipe the base with a clean cloth. You may want to apply wax remover again if this last brushing accumulated more dirt residue.

Wipe the ski dry and clean of dirt. By now, the ski should look very much like it did when you first bought it. At this point, the ski is ready to be prepped and waxed according to the process described for new skis in the chapter on waxing.

Maintenance of Waxless Skis

The glide zones, sidewalls, and tops of no-wax skis should be waxed and maintained just as other skis. The kick zone requires a bit different care. The patterned bases which have the kick zone routed or pressed into the base will be cleaned with wax remover, with careful attention to removing dirt and grit from the small indentations in the pattern.

Silicone is the secret to treating mohair kicker zones. The more mohair is used, the more it gets matted down. Spraying it with silicone and then brushing up the fibers will help retain the mohair's kick. Mohair often picks up wax and dirt from the ski tracks, especially in the spring when other skiers are using klisters. Clean the mohair with wax remover and then spray with silicone.

BOOTS AND BINDINGS

The racer originally had only two basic choices in selecting a boot/binding system from the time Adidas came on the scene in 1976 until 1978. In addition to the Adidas 38-mm binding, the Scandinavian firms developed the Nordic Norm, a 50-mm system with inter-changeable boots and bindings. Since 1978, new systems have been developed and continuing refinements are being made to the 38-mm and 50-mm boot/bindings.

In 1978 Dynafit, a Fischer subsidiary, developed its own unique system. The binding is different from others currently available because it is based on notching devices which firmly hold the boot in the binding. The shape and closure systems are not compatible with other systems. The boot is unique in that it has an aluminum plate in the sole which allows for full forward flexibility but is stable sideways. This plate is said to add stability and control where the boot overlaps the ski.

Salomon has spent a number of years developing its own boot/binding system. The toe of the boot and the binding are double hinged, which is said to allow the ski to stay in contact with the snow longer during the kick so the skier can have a longer kick. The double hinge also alleviates tension on the foot at the end of the kick. The sole of the boot has a V-shaped groove under the ball of the foot which slips into a ridge attached to the ski for immediate control of the ski. This system is to be available on the American market in 1982.

Trak has developed a system for controlling the ski which involves two ridges under the ball of the foot and one on the heel. This Trakker system seems to work quite well and the boot is compatible with all 50-mm bindings. The Trakker and Salomon systems should also be beneficial in controlling roller skis.

Adidas must be credited with the concept of combining the boot and binding to improve stability, durability, function, and control. Minor refinements have been made since 1976, particularly the development of a binding which features forward pull. The binding continually pulls the boot into the binding, enhancing the relationship between the boot sole and binding sidewall to provide added control over the ski.

The choices in boot/binding systems will likely increase as new developments are made. You can't go wrong with any of the racing bindings because they all function quite well. There are some pros and cons to each system, so your choice might come down to personal taste. Just remember that there is no compatibility between the various systems, so stick to one for all your skis and roller skis.

When selecting a boot/binding system, I'd advise you to study the options and determine how each system works. One factor to look for in selecting a 50-mm binding is finding one which has forward pull, similar to the Adidas 38 mm. Then try on boots. Find one that

In the center is the 75-mm boot/binding combination used by all racers until the 1976 Olympics. On the left is the Adidas 38-mm binding and a modern synthetic boot. On the right is a 50-mm Racing Norm system including a Trak boot and a Bergan binding.

fits well and will function well for your style of skiing and go with that system. Virtually all the racing boots on the market have a 7-mm thick sole of DuPont Hytrel. The upper on racing boots is most often nylon, with some leather support. Gortex is being used more frequently now and is more waterproof and possibly warmer.

The serious racer will need at least two pairs of boots. He might use one for training and save the other for racing. If he's out skiing twice in one day, it will be difficult to have one pair dry for both sessions. The average racer might get away with one pair of boots, but the more he skis, the sooner the boots will wear out and need replacement. A good pair of boots should last a couple of seasons.

I think the continuing developments in boot/binding systems are very exciting. Some argue that features like the extended ridge underfoot of Salomon and Trak are overkill, but I don't think you can ever have too much control on your skis, just too little. One factor which has traditionally held back the beginning skier was the lack of control when turning, snowplowing and trying to stop. The new boot/binding systems have solved this problem for the tourer and have made the racer's job of getting around the course much easier and more efficient.

Maintenance and Race Prep

I'm always surprised by the number of people who spend a lot of time working on their skis, but ignore checking their other equipment for signs of wear and tear. A thorough check of your boots and bindings is very important before a race.

To care for your boots, I advise spraying them with silicone to help keep them waterproof. Check your shoelaces, particularly before a race, to be certain they aren't worn or aren't ripping out the lacing holes. Examine the sole of the boot for cracks or other indications of weakness. The toe area is particularly susceptible to damage and separation because of the pressure it undergoes in the binding while skiing. If you have a 50-mm pin binding, check to be certain the holes in the boot sole haven't worn and will retain firm contact with the binding. A good cobbler may be able to mend tears in the nylon and repair some sole damage. Otherwise, it's time to get new boots.

Routinely check the condition of your bindings. Ignoring a crack or a weakness the night before a race could mean disaster out on the course. If you have a bale binding, the pivot point may eventually weaken and need to be replaced. If the pins which hold the boot in 50-mm bindings become loose, remove the binding and use epoxy to stabilize the pins from below and above. With all bindings, check the closure mechanism to be certain it isn't worn, cracked, or in the process of breaking. Next, check to see that all the screws on the binding are tight. If not, reglue them. Also check for cracks around the screw holes and be certain the heel plate is attached to the ski firmly. A cracked binding cannot be fixed.

Mounting Bindings

The first thing to do with a new set of bindings is to study them. Think about how they work, see how they fit with the boots and heel plates, and carefully read the mounting directions provided by the manufacturer. Then check your skis as to the type of construction and the instructions on the skis as to binding placement and mounting. Some types of skis require a special process or gluing material for binding mounting. Know what you're working with and have all the necessary tools and materials on hand before you proceed.

Unfortunately, it's easy to make a mistake mounting bindings. You can drill holes too large or in the wrong place, fail to center the bindings or misjudge screw placement. If you misdrill a hole, plug it with wood or a good amount of epoxy. Let it dry and then redrill. But these types of mistakes can be avoided if you carefully follow instructions and use the proper tools.

Let's talk about the things you need for mounting. Almost all modern bindings are attached with Posi-head screws, which are better than Phillips head screws because the head doesn't strip and screws can be removed more easily. They require a Posi-driver screwdriver. The screws are secured into the ski with glue. If you plan to remove your bindings often for travel, use a white glue such as Elmer's. Otherwise, I recommend using epoxy, unless the ski manufacturer recommends something else. Other things you'll need for mounting are a drill and drill bits, a ruler, metal scraper, a wood block, hammer and center punch or nail, in addition to a work bench.

A tool available for the simplest method of binding mounting is what's known as a jig. This device serves as a guide for placing the screw holes and makes the job a lot easier and less prone to mistakes. Jigs are compatible to the holes on most bindings, and they center the drill bit when you're drilling a hole. Jigs are fairly expensive and not necessary to mounting bindings.

The first step in mounting is finding the balance point on the ski. Use your metal scraper held under the ski to find the point where the ski is in balance and draw a line across the top of the ski marking that point. Even if the skis come marked with a balance point, check for accuracy. Lay the pair of skis side-by-side to determine if the balance points are at the same point. If not, split the difference and draw a straight line across each ski at the common balance point. Each brand of binding will provide directions as to where to place the binding in relation to the balance point. Follow the directions and mark the place for the front screw hole, perfectly centered on the ski.

Punch a shallow hole where the front screw hole is marked. Use a nail or awl smaller than the binding screw to punch a hole that will guide the drill bit. Select a bit which is smaller in diameter than the threads of the screw. (When holding the bit in front of the screw, the threads of the screw, but not the shank, should be visible.) Either use a bit with a pre-set collar depth or wrap a piece of tape around the bit so you don't drill too deeply into the ski. Then drill the front screw hole.

Next, use the head of your screwdriver to ream the top of the hole a bit to avoid pressure on the top plate of the ski and prevent it from splitting. Put the binding in place and screw in the front screw. Get a boot and close it into the binding. Center the heel of the boot on the ski, adjusting the binding so it is perfectly centered. Carefully remove the boot without altering the binding's position.

Mark, punch, ream, and drill one of the back binding holes, then screw in the screw. Place the boot back into the binding to be certain the binding is still centered. If for some reason it's off center, you have one chance left—remove the back screw, center the binding, and place the other back screw in position. Fill the mistaken hole with wood and/or epoxy and let it dry overnight before proceeding. If you took pains to align the first two holes, locating and drilling the third will be simple.

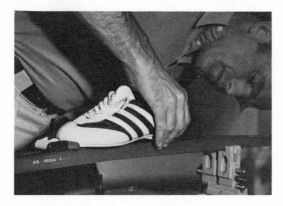

After inserting the first binding screw, use a boot to center the binding on the ski.

Remove the three screws and fill each hole with white glue, epoxy, or whatever the manufacturer recommended. Be certain the glue fills the entire hole by poking around with a nail. Replace each screw and wipe off excess glue. After attaching the heel plate, turn the ski over so the glue will run down the screws as it dries overnight.

Put the boot back in the binding and determine the proper place for the heel plate. Be certain the plate is centered; nothing is more distracting than having your boot mis-strike the heel plate every stride. Some heel plates are attached with small nails and others with a single screw and a nail. When nailing, set a block of wood under the heel plate to stabilize the ski when hammering or place the area directly in a vise.

To remove bindings for travel or transfer to another ski, first try to free the screws with the Posi-driver. If the screws are in tight with glue or epoxy, place a block of wood under the binding, set the screw driver in the slots, and hit it firmly with a hammer. Hopefully, this will break the bond and make it possible to remove the screw. If not, try heating the tip of the screwdriver with a torch and then hold it on the screw while the screw absorbs the heat. After a couple of times, the heat should break the bond. In desperation, you can take the torch directly to the screw. Be careful because the torch is likely to melt plastic bindings.

POLES

The main benefits of graphite poles are their light weight and stiff shafts, which mean they are more efficient. They directly transfer the athlete's energy from his arms to the snow during the poling motion.

Refinements in poles are continuing, particularly in basket configuration, grips and straps. The half basket offers a significant advantage because it lets the racer maintain the same pivot axis throughout the poling motion. Round baskets are a disadvantage because the pole is forced out of the snow as the forward angle decreases.

Some pole companies offer a variety of interchangeable baskets each specially designed to work best in a specific type of snow (hard packed, soft powder). Considering which type of basket will be best for the snow conditions should be a part of the serious competitor's race preparation. Give yourself every advantage on the race course.

This is a selection of the types of baskets available on modern racing poles. All feature the half or butterfly basket design and are used in a variety of snow conditions. The black device on the second pole from the left is an adapter designed for soft snow conditions.

Grips and straps have been improved. Many companies are using synthetic materials rather than leather, and experiments continue with the strap arrangement. Some poles offer a strap that comes over the center of your hand, which is claimed to provide a better power distribution. Well-made straps give you control over the pole through the end of the follow through. You never lose contact with the pole, even when your hand relaxes, and it's almost impossible to lose the pole if you hit something along the trail.

When selecting poles, length must be a prime consideration. The latest trend has been to go to long poles, but I think many racers have gone too far and created a major barrier in accomplishing good technique. A longer pole will give you a stronger push, but too long a pole will keep you upright, which means your poling action is less efficient because you end up pushing less off the pole and having an improper swing trajectory.

The formula currently being used to determine pole length is to take your body height in inches, multiply it by 2.54 to determine your centimeter height, and then subtract 35 cm. This is a good guideline but might vary a couple of centimeters, depending on your arm length, leg length, and other factors. Some national team members carry two or three different lengths of poles: shorter poles for hilly courses and longer poles for flatter courses.

When buying shafts, try to buy them as near to the length you need as possible. You probably shouldn't cut more than five or six centimeters off the shafts because it could affect the balance. Also, many brands require that the shafts be cut from the bottom; if you cut too much off, the basket won't fit properly. The handle is difficult to remove and replace from other poles requiring cuts from the top of the shaft.

Care must be taken in dealing with graphite poles. If they're banged around a lot, the carbon fibers may be crushed or cut which will cause fatigue in the shaft. I never use my good poles for summer training but save them for skiing and take care to pack them well and treat them with a bit of respect.

Before a race, go over your poles from grips to tips, looking for areas of fatigue, breaks or cracks in the shaft, baskets, and straps. If the shaft shows fatigue marks, you can reinforce the area with fiberglass tape or wet wrap it with fiberglass.However, I'd relegate any such repaired poles to training and use properly balanced, solid shafts for racing.

I always carry extra baskets and straps in my wax kit when I travel in case of breakage. The new baskets don't break often, but fatigue or cracks can occur in very cold weather.

Don't wait to check on these areas of the pole until the last minute because many ski shops don't carry replacement parts. Stock up before the season starts so you don't get caught with a broken basket or strap and no replacement parts before a race.

CLOTHING FOR SKIERS

As I commented earlier, there's no such thing as bad weather, just bad clothes. Skiers must be particularly attentive to their clothing. Not only do we face extremely cold weather during the season, but we have to deal with warm temperatures and inclement weather during our off-season training. Fortunately, the materials available today have made it possible to dress comfortably in all kinds of weather.

The new materials—nylons, Lycras, Gortex, polypropylene, double knits—offer welcomed advantages to the skier. They are better insulators, more durable, better looking, easier to clean and maintain, lighter, stretchy, and form-fitting. The software is water resistant and can breathe. We're no longer trapped in a cotton turtleneck while moisture builds up, making us cold, draining our energy, and leaving us skiing less efficiently. Now we have clothes which draw the moisture away, keep us warm, and don't waste our energy. The outfits are comfortable because they feature four-way stretch, which provides a good fit while being flexible enough to allow unrestricted movement. They are lightweight so we don't waste energy and can layer up on cold days without being bulky. When we get in from training, we can wash these clothes out and know they'll be clean and dry in the morning. They won't shrink and the fibers don't become matted, so they'll stay warm.

In taking a close look at the types of ski clothing available, let's start with the basics— underwear. Polypropylene is the best material for long underwear because of its wicking effect: it takes sweat away from the body where it can evaporate, thereby keeping the body warm and dry. It is also form-fitting and comfortable. Researchers have found polypropylene so useful they encourage skiers to sew it into their hats to provide a layer between the wet hat and the head to control energy and heat loss.

Long underwear is an essential part of the skier's clothing because it's so important to keep the extremities, particularly the legs, warm. Many skiers have extra linings built into the front of their uniforms to protect their legs and other extremities. Also, windshields are available in some underwear or may be sewn in to protect the crotch area in men and the chest area in women. This added protection is a blessing on a cold, windy day.

Next comes the uniform. I think before long almost all skiers will be in one-piece, full-length outfits because they are so functional. The one-piece uniforms are a streamlined shell. Warmth and protection from the elements come mostly from underwear. There are, as I said, uniforms with double linings for particularly cold days. Today's uniforms are stretchy enough to allow for layers of long underwear underneath on cold days.

In selecting warmup pants, I look for ones with a full-length zipper so I don't have to remove my skis to take them off. Tops never seem to have enough pockets to carry all the paraphernalia you need before a race. There must be a balance in a warmup suit that allows you to ski in it without restricted movements while still being warm enough to do the job. A hood attached to the warmup top will come in handy, as will a rain suit for added protection.

Hats should conform to the shape of your head. The big, thick wool hats with big tassles are out. Most racers prefer lightweight hats that are sleek. You can line them with poly-

This type of streamlined, comfortable uniform has made our sport more colorful and our skiers more aerodynamic.

A typical warmup suit is loose enough to allow for layers of clothing underneath but fits well enough to function while skiing.

propylene for additional warmth. In distance races, skiers often have an extra hat in the fanny pack or pick one up from a friend along the way.

Gloves are essential. When your extremities get cold, your ability to concentrate on the race lessens. Gloves are preferable to mittens because, like a race car driver's feel for the steering wheel, the skier likes to have a feel for his poles. Mittens are helpful to wear over your gloves to keep warm before a race, but you don't see many people racing in them. You do see skiers in cheap work gloves and so forth, which is a mistake. They have no insulation and, once wet, will quickly freeze your hands. Use leather gloves to keep your hands dry. A good pair will have Velcro or some other system for adjustments around the wrist to avoid constriction. Be certain they are long enough so there is no gap between the glove and your uniform cuff. On fairly warm days, I use gloves with holes in the back of the hand and fingers for ventilation and slippage. On cold days, I've had good luck with liners of the space blanket material. The material is very thin, warm, and woven so it breathes.

To keep feet warm and dry, particularly in long races, I wear overboots. Again, cold extremities affect concentration, so I do everything in my power to keep my feet warm the whole distance. This added protection should be as streamlined as possible, which is why many skiers still cut a hole in the toe of a pair of wool socks and slip them over their ski boots. There are a variety of booties on the market, but good ones are often hard to find. Rubber booties are useful in extremely wet conditions, but they lack durability.

Other tricks for protection in extreme cold include face masks, ear muffs, goggles, and skin lubricants. Face masks cup around your nose and mouth, forming a pocket where the air circulates and warms up before it gets to your lungs. Medical experts say it's impossible to freeze your lungs, but face masks will make the cold air less painful and could prevent a cold or pneumonia.

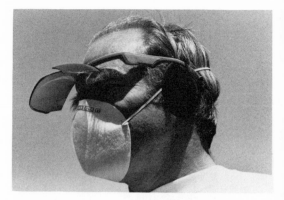

On the right is a typical overboot, which I recommend that racers wear in distance events to protect the feet from the cold and wet. Note how the uniform is worn over both the overboot and the ski boot to streamline the foot.

Gear for very cold weather includes a face mask, goggles that may be raised or lowered, and ear muffs.

Ear muffs are worn by many skiers to protect their ears from frostbite because hats are prone to slip during training and racing and leave parts of your ears exposed. I wear ear muffs almost all the time, even on days when it's warm enough to ski without a hat. Unfortunately, ear muffs are hard to find in the U.S.

Goggles are being used more on snowy days to keep the flakes out of racers' eyes and on cold days to protect your face and eyes. Good ones don't fog up and are particularly useful for people who wear contact lenses. If goggles don't work, I advise skiers to use some type of skin lubricant or petroleum jelly, such as Vaseline or SkinLube. This protects your face and makes you feel much warmer, especially early in a race before you're good and warmed up. Skiers who wear contacts often grease up around their eyes because the vessels around the eye are close to the skin and cold makes them constrict, allowing contacts to slip around or pop out.

Not only have the new developments in fabrics had a benficial effect on ski clothes, but they've improved gear for off-season training. The jogging boom and the new designs in running and other outdoor clothing has made training clothes for the skier much better. Clothes don't chafe your skin, dry faster, stay cleaner, and are more comfortable. Design improvements such as a built-in liner in men's shorts eliminating the need for a jock strap and jogging bras for women make life a lot easier when training.

The skier in training doesn't require anything extraordinary in the way of clothes. The main concern is dressing properly for the weather and having clothes and shoes that fit well. The serious skier trains in all sorts of inclement weather, so he needs to have clothes to protect his body. Shorts and tops should be light, comfortable, and water resistant. They will dry almost as fast as you sweat so you're not clammy. A rain suit that allows you to move freely is a must, as is a wind suit on cold, windy days. The new materials allow such suits to be small and light enough to fit in a fanny pack so the skier is prepared if the weather changes on a long roller ski or ski hike.

In the fall, adequate clothing is particularly important. Use the layer principle—wear layers of lightweight clothing that can be removed or added and easily carried in a fanny pack. The polypropylene underwear is great on a cold training day. The athlete has to keep his extremities and prime movers (the back and legs) warm in order to have a successful workout.

Shoes and socks are probably the most important pieces of training gear. Buy shoes for fit, not price or looks. The variety of good running shoes available is almost endless. A good pair will absorb energy to dampen the effects of pounding each time the foot strikes the ground. The shoes should be lightweight and have deep treads to avoid slips and falls and improve traction. Because most training injuries begin in the feet and legs and end up in the back, a good pair of shoes is vital.

A good pair of socks will further protect your feet and avoid painful, irritating blisters. If you wear loose, baggy socks, they'll slide around and cause blisters. Get socks that fit. Layering two pair of socks will stop blisters from appearing because any slippage will be between the socks, not between the skin of your feet and the socks.

I find all the new ski and training clothing very exciting. Currently racers are setting the trends in ski wear, but, as our sport grows more sophisticated, all levels of skiers will take advantage of the well designed, solidly constructed clothing available.

PACKING UP FOR WINTER TRAVEL

The racer has to protect his ski equipment whether he's traveling to a race in Europe or to one across the state. Without overloading, bring all the ski gear you might need and pack it carefully.

Every skier should have a ski bag to protect his skis while they're riding on top of a car or in an airplane. Bags come in a wide assortment of capacities, from those that will hold a single pair of skis to those holding 10–15 pair with compartments for poles, boots, and other gear. Determine your needs, but get a ski bag.

In packing the ski bag, strap the skis together firmly at both ends to protect the bases. Pad the tips and tails of your skis with clothing or something to guard these fragile areas from breakage. If you're taking a major trip involving several plane changes, remove the bindings and pack the skis base-to-top to further protect from breakage. If you pack your bag properly, you'll be surprised how much will fit in.

Carbon and glass fiber poles require more protection than aluminum shafted poles. A good method I discovered for packing poles is to go to the lumberyard and buy PVC plastic piping. Tubes two inches in diameter may fit into your ski bag easier, but are wide enough to protect only the shafts of one pair of poles. I get four-inch tubing for my pole carrier because it accommodates three pairs of poles including baskets. The pipe should be about two inches longer than your poles. Your pole carrier will travel best in your ski bag.

Plan ahead in packing your wax kit for a trip. Based on the duration of the trip and the expected snow conditions, stock up on wax. If I have some canisters of wax in my kit that are pretty well used up, I replace them. Then I check to be certain I have enough ski cleaner, spare parts, tools, and matches so I don't get caught short-handed at some out-of-the-way race site.

Kits are available from most wax companies. Another good place to find a variety of sizes of kits is at fishing supply stores; tackle boxes are great wax kits. Keep in mind that the items can be found in small sizes and containers. The following is a list of equipment found in a large wax kit. Short trips or personal preference will eliminate some items on this optimal list.

Here are four different sizes of wax kits to fit individual or team needs on the road.

Contents of an Optimal Wax Kit

Alpine wax	files	clamps or vice grips
kicker wax	thermometers	Posi-drive screwdriver
saucepan	fanny pack	pliers
brushes (Alpine & klister)	apron	Swiss army knife
electric iron	Fiberlene or clean rags	extra baskets & straps
25-foot extension cord	ski cleaner/wax remover	extra bindings & heel plates
torch and torch iron	fiberglass tape	notepad, pens, & pencils
3 synthetic corks	Epoxy and white glue	pipe cutter
wire brush	mending strips—polyplastic,	screws, nails
metal scraper	P-Tex	matches
plastic scrapers	fiberglass repair kit	waxing charts

TRAINING EQUIPMENT

While we're talking about equipment, I'll point out some considerations in selecting and maintaining some of your basic equipment for off-season training—roller skis, poles, and roller boards.

Roller Skis. When selecting roller skis from the several brands available, the most important consideration is to get the lightest brand you can find. There are skis that weigh as little as four or five pounds, which is close enough to the weight of snow skis to allow the athlete to properly work on ski technique.

Speed is another important factor. Find roller skis that move at about the same speed per kilometer as snow skis. Some brands are definitely better than others.

Check to see if your roller skis roll perfectly straight. New or abused skis often don't. All the models have adjustable wheels so directional variations can be made. Find a flat surface and simply shove the ski down it so it rolls 10–15 feet. If it veers in one direction, loosen or tighten the nuts or adjust the front wheel stay to get the ski to go straight.

Roller skis can cost up to $180, so it's worth your while to take proper care of them. After skiing on dirty roads or in the rain, you could have a bearing freeze up on you unless you maintain the skis. As a general procedure, a good dose of WD-40 spray after each workout will clean accumulated dirt, lubricate the bearings, and stop rust. Once a month, take the wheels off and give the unit a good cleaning. Because of the dirt on the roads, roller skis should get the same amount of care, if not more, than snow skis. Check with the manufacturer's instructions for specific maintenance procedures.

The evolution in roller skis led to today's light-weight, short, highly functional model in the foreground. The center ski was developed in the mid-1970s and featured an aluminum shaft and plastic hubcaps—both of which were improvements over the long, heavy, wooden roller ski of previous years, shown in the back of the photo.

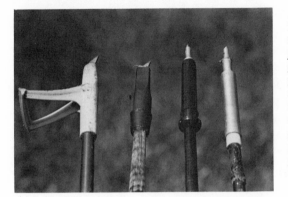

This is a selection of pole tips used in off-season training. The pole on the left has a modified butterfly basket and is used for ski running to prevent the pole from sticking too far into soft ground. All four pole tips may be used for roller skiing, but the ferrules on the three poles on the right were designed specifically for roller skiing. The second pole from the left has a carbide spike rather than a carbide point. The spike does a better job of digging into pavement than the points. The ferrule on the right features a shock absorber, which is beneficial although it's a bit heavy.

Use aluminum poles for roller skiing and ski hiking and ski running; save your graphite poles for racing. For roller skiing, it's essential to have angled carbide tips on the poles (standard on racing poles) so they can dig into the pavement. The carbide will remain sharp through quite a bit of use and may be sharpened when they become dull. A fast-moving grindstone is necessary to sharpen the tips because of the hardness of carbide. Such grinding will heat up the tips, so dip them in cold water or oil to cool them down and harden them up again. The success of a roller ski workout depends on sharp pole tips which allow you to ski properly.

The poles for roller skiing should be about the same height as your snow skiing poles, or perhaps a centimeter or two shorter if you have the new lower roller skis. There are special ferruls with carbide tips available without baskets for roller skiing training. Some of these have a built-in shock absorber. If you have problems with blisters on your hands when roller skiing, sharpen the pole tips and wear gloves.

Roller Board. To build a roller board, head to the lumberyard. You'll need one 4 × 8-foot sheet of ¾-inch plywood, two 14-foot 2 × 4s, four nonswivel dolly wheels, 10 feet of nylon mountaineering rope, and two grommets. With the plywood sheet, construct the plane of the roller board by cutting one strip 8 feet long and another 4 feet long. Each strip should be 12–14 inches wide. Connect the two with 12-foot lengths of 2 × 4 so you have a 12-foot plane supported on each edge with 2 × 4s. With the excess 2 × 4, make cross-struts at the top and bottom of the plane and another strut where the two plywood pieces join for extra strength. Cut the remaining plywood into two guides and nail them to the top of the board, parallel and 10 inches apart to serve as runners for the sled. The last of the plywood will be used for the sled, which measures 28–30 inches in length and 12–14 inches wide.

Nail another 2 × 4, four inches wider than the board, to the top at one end. Hook the rope to this cross-member. The rope should have holes melded in each end for grommets, which will be attached to ski pole straps. The straps should be fairly wide to prevent them from cutting into your hands. Mount the four dolly wheels close to each corner of the plywood sled board. The wheels should be 10 inches apart to fit inside the runners. I like to cover the sled with a piece of carpet or other padding so it's more comfortable.

In terms of maintenance, oil the wheels routinely and check to be certain the runners and other parts of the roller board are secure.

The selection and maintenance of your equipment will in large part determine the success of a workout and of a race. Your gear is the link which brings your efforts together in harmony with the elements. The condition of your equipment and clothing is a reflection of your attitude and dedication to your sport.

The committed racer selects the best equipment he can afford and spends hours caring for it. He recognizes how vital his equipment is to his success in the tracks and does everything he can to be certain that his skis, boots, bindings, poles, and clothes are completely prepared to meet his demands. Further, he reads about equipment, studies it, and listens to experts so he is constantly increasing his knowledge of how to obtain the maximum benefits from his gear. His concern for equipment is reflected in his race results.

5

RACING TECHNIQUE

The Final Form

A good skier makes cross-country technique look easy. He moves rhythmically across the snow with smooth, flowing strides. His style appears natural and his movements simple. However, cross-country technique is complicated and takes a great deal of effort to learn and perfect.

When the skier and coach sit down to analyze ski technique they soon discover that it is as subtle as the undulating terrain of a cross-country course. Each move of each technique is imperceptibly but consciously performed for ultimate efficiency and speed. Because of its complexity and subtlety, it's difficult to evaluate and explain the final forms of cross-country technique and even more difficult to perform them.

The dominant view of the cross-country skier is the diagonal stride. The skier must master this technique and the two methods of double poling, hill running, numerous downhill positions, various ways to take corners, and other maneuvers including the snowplow, the herringbone, skating, and the transition from one technique to another. Further, the ever-increasing speeds resulting from equipment, course changes, and sports medicine input have made cross-country technique even more difficult to assimilate mentally and physically.

The racer must work to perform each move correctly while under physiological strain. The more fatigued he becomes toward the end of a race, the more important it is to concentrate, evaluate the terrain, and ski technically well. Fear is a factor, even in this seemingly gentle sport, and must be overcome. Not only must the racer deal with downhills and corners while moving at high speeds, but the dynamic position involved in the diagonal stride and double poling can create a fear of falling on one's face. Anxiety often results in inefficient, incorrect technique. Bad habits are easy to come by and rectifying them can be as hard as perfecting the final form.

Although it appears otherwise, cross-country skiing is not truly a sport of natural movements. Learning correct technique and making improvements as new techniques evolve is a challenging mental process that must be translated into physiological movements. The concept of technique is difficult to present clearly to athletes, but, fortunately, recent biomechanical studies of skiing have clarified proper technique and enabled skiers to better understand the movements of the final form as it has evolved.

In watching good skiers over the years, I have been able to recognize any one of many athletes from great distances. The casual observer might assume the differences between skiers are a function of each using a different technique. It is important for the coach and the skier to differentiate between technique and style. To be technically proficient, every skier must work within certain ranges of movement, certain angles, and certain planes. The apparent differences between two good skiers is a matter of style, which is a function of body type or physical makeup and of natural abilities such as balance, reaction time, and coordination. The fact that each skier is built differently results in subtle differences in style. A skier with relatively long legs and short arms, for example, is bound to have a style distinct from another skier with shorter legs. In analyzing technique, we must be able to separate technical moves from the individual's style.

When I analyze technique, I look primarily at two areas of the body: the arms and the body position. The most significant technical indicator is what the athlete is doing with his arms. If his arms aren't in the right trajectory pattern—aren't following the proper range of motion—the rest of his technique will be incorrect. If the arms aren't exerting and relieving forces at the proper times, the upper body prevents the lower body from making the proper movements. Remember, cross-country skiing is dynamic, not static. The body is constantly in motion, and action in one part of the body will affect the movements of the other parts.

In working to perfect skiing technique, the racer should take advantage of all the learning aids available. Because of the complexity of the movements, one can't expect to master them without the assistance of a coach, knowledge of correct form, a solid level of physical conditioning, and visual aids such as videotape, Polarvision, and mental imagery. You must have a perception of both correct technique and how *you* move on skis.

The Europeans, particularly the Scandinavians, have an advantage over North American skiers because they are constantly exposed to good ski technique through the media. Cross-country races are televised regularly in Scandinavia and, through watching good racers, skiers have a solid image of proper technique. Because children are great imitators, young Swedes and Finns and Norwegians are skiing with good technique at an early age at least in part because of the media coverage the sport receives in their countries.

Until cross-country skiing receives this type of coverage in North America, we must depend on other visual aids. Back in 1972, we began using videotape in working with the U.S. team members on their techniques and found it to be tremendously beneficial. Polarvision, a more recent development, gives the skier an even better opportunity to see himself and others ski. For on-the-spot viewing of technique, the U.S. team uses a Polaroid camera developed for golf that shoots a sequence of eight shots and develops them within seconds so the skier can have a concrete image of what he's doing during training. Watching ski movies is another good aid in developing an image of proper techniques.

If you have no access to these visual aids, use a mirror to develop an image of the movements of skiing. In front of a full-length mirror, go through the motions of skiing so you develop a concept of the planes and angles involved in skiing, so you know where your hands should be and what it feels like when your body position is correct. Then, when you go out and ski, you'll be aware if your hands are in the wrong position and you'll be better able to make technical corrections.

It is imperative that you develop a mental image of what you want to look like on skis based on a knowledge of good technique. Developing a perception of yourself skiing properly is not a simple task. You can look at tons of pictures and talk about this and that aspect of technique without actually assimilating the information to your skiing.

Too many competitors only pay lip-service to technique, instead of making a conscientious effort to grapple with it and develop a self-image. One skier who didn't fall into this lip-service syndrome is Olympian Jim Galanes. Heading into the 1980 season, he made a determined effort to improve his technique. At every opportunity, he would sit down in front of Polarvision and study films of himself and others skiing. He'd pick each skier apart to figure out what was right and what was wrong. This process developed his image of what was correct technique. Jim's strong results in 1980 are an indication of the gains he made technically through this effort, as well as his improved physiological base.

Don't assume that you are free of technical problems even if you reach high competitive levels. The best racers have bad habits and make inappropriate technical moves. Technique evaluation, improvement, and correction is an ongoing process requiring a concentrated effort. Technique can't be ignored in racing or during winter training. Even if you're under stress in an interval workout, it's to your benefit to concentrate on making the correct movements while skiing. The same holds true in summer training. Technique work is actually easier then than in the winter because you don't have to worry about your wax; kick is 100%, so you gain confidence in your technique.

Many skiers go through the summer without coaching supervision or much thought of applying good technique to their roller skiing, hill running, Exer-Genie, and other workouts. It's important to work with a coach throughout the year and to employ the same aids of winter technique work to your summer training. Use videotape or Polarvision and visual imagery to improve your technique during summer training. During the summer of 1979, I worked with Kate Freeman and she made a serious effort to improve her technique. She developed a self-image and muscle memory that made her technically a much better skier when she stepped on snow.

In this chapter I'll present an explanation of the final form of cross-country technique: the diagonal stride, double poling, uphill techniques, downhill techniques, taking corners, and various other maneuvers necessary to be an efficient and technically proficient skier. The technical information is based on movements that have proven successful in competition and are backed up by the latest in sports medicine and biomechanical research. The goal is to provide concrete information on and understanding of the various aspects of cross-country technique so you can take this information and know how to translate it into moves that will make you a more successful, efficient skier. The discussion is based primarily on the accompanying illustrations. Although physical characteristics determine a person's skiing style, the body angles, range of motion, arm tragectories, and leg movements that are illustrated apply to every skier.

THE BIOMECHANICS OF CROSS-COUNTRY TECHNIQUE

For the first time in history, Americans are able to approach cross-country technique with an overview based on concrete, scientific information on how the body is propelled down the tracks. Recent biomechanical and sports medicine research has developed facts that have unified the approach to technique.

Sports scientists began seriously researching cross-country technique in the United States in the mid-1970s when Ken Sparks, a physiologist at the University of Colorado, evaluated high-speed films of the U.S. team members. In 1979 a grant from the U.S. Olympic Committee provided the funds for analysis of international skiers by Chuck Dillman, a biomechanics expert at the University of Illinois, and his research team. Their scientific findings have provided American skiers with an in-depth and wide-ranging biomechanical overview of the technique of our sport.

During the 1979 Pre-Olympics and 1980 Games at Lake Placid, high-speed cameras were set up at various points on the men's 15-km and women's 5-km courses. The movements of various groups of skiers were scrutinized to determine which aspects of the technique of successful racers differed from those of less successful competitors. Although coaches and skiers had a good grasp on what takes place while skiing well, the biomechanical research confirmed much of what was known and substantiated technical theories to the benefit of skiers everywhere. Dillman's research was expanded by the U.S. team's sports medicine experts, led by Dr. Bob Arnot, in formulating concrete information on what technique is most efficient, why, and what is required of the body to perform it.

Research Conclusions

The extensive research on ski technique and physical requirements determined numerous facts that have been implemented into coaching and instructional methods in the United States. For American skiers, perhaps the most significant factor determined from the films of the Pre-Olympics related to velocity, or the speed of movement of the skier down the track. Velocity is a result of power and may be determined scientifically by multiplying the skier's stride length by his stride rate.

Research demonstrated that there is only a minimal difference in stride rate between the successful skier and the skier who finishes at the bottom of the result lists. All international-class skiers will average a diagonal stride rate of 1.6 strides per second. Therefore, the difference was related primarily to length of stride. Researchers found that stride length is a function of strength.

With this information in mind, the U.S. team was put through a series of tests by the team's sports medicine people. The testing indicated that American skiers lacked full coordination between their upper and lower bodies. Also, they were generally weak in their use of their upper body strength, often expending too much energy vertically rather than propelling themselves down the track. In other words, a lack of total body coordination and ineffective use of upper body strength left most U.S. skiers with a shorter stride and a less dynamic body position than the successful European racers. These findings led to modifications in training programs (more specific total body activities, such as running with poles) and in technique (emphasis on the dynamic position, complete arm extension, and the immediate thrust of the arm upon pole implantation).

Biomechanics, Conditioning, and Style

Biomechanical studies confirmed that the skier must adapt his body to skiing to be successful. A person who has not conditioned his body for skiing might be able to take a few strides technically well, but he will not be able to continue for long with speed nor handle any variations from a perfectly groomed course.

Endurance is necessary to continue the movements over extended periods and strength is necessary to perform them properly with power. The well-conditioned athlete is in a positive state to function because he can control his movements and has a kinesthetic sense. He's not afraid that he'll fall on his face while skiing because he is strong enough to control his movements and relaxed enough to perform them with ease.

Skiing involves continuous motion. Without specific strengths and endurance, you will be unable to complete the necessary full range of motion. Although your stride rate may remain high, your stride length will be limited, thus reducing your velocity down the tracks.

The body must be conditioned into skiing shape, which is possible no matter what your physical makeup. An interesting aspect of our sport is that no particular body size has emerged to dominate competition. There is an amazing range of builds that have been successul in cross-country. Compare the jockey-type body of Sweden's 5'6", 135-pound Sven-Ake Lundback with the 6'6", 220-pound frame of Finn Juha Mieto, who looks like a basketball player. Both skiers have been highly successful because they have adapted their bodies to skiing through mental effort, physical energy, and intense training.

IMAGERY

As discussed in Chapter 2, part of the skier's job is mental training. U.S. skiers have found that imagery or visualization is a highly effective way to translate proper technique from the brain to the body. While in a relaxed, quiet state, you create mental pictures of what you want your body to look like while skiing and training for skiing on snow and on land. Start by picturing what your technique currently looks like and then improve the picture by imagining yourself executing technically correct moves. In this way, you will visualize what you've learned to be correct technical form and will help train your body to make the moves you've visualized. In essence, mental imagery develops your kinesthetic sense of what each part of your body is doing so you can make each part move properly.

Imagery is particularly important to beginning skiers who most likely have a difficult time of looking at photos and translating these images to their skiing. By creating a mental image of yourself making the moves in the photos, you've taken yourself one step closer to assimilating proper technique and being able to make those moves yourself. You teach your brain (which, in turn, teaches your body) what planes to be moving in, where your arms should be, when to time your kick, etc.

Imagery is useful not only in developing good technique but in correcting bad habits and assimilating new techniques as technique evolves. If you've been overreaching during your double pole for two or three years, it will be difficult to break the habit because of the muscle memory you've developed. You must take time and effort to concentrate on correcting this habit, and the place to start is developing a mental image of double poling without overreaching. While skiing, you translate this image to your body.

Of course it's vital that you know exactly what the proper technique looks like when using mental imagery. Study films, read books, watch good skiers, study photographs, listen to coaches, and use videotapes or Polarvision. Take time to learn what good technique looks like, apply mental imagery, and concentrate on assimilating that technique while you ski. In time your mental image will be translated to muscle memory and you'll have an improved, efficient, technically proficient form.

AMERICAN TECHNIQUE VS. THE FINAL FORM

Before getting into the specifics of the various aspects of cross-country technique, it's appropriate to point out a few factors that have influenced the development of technique in the United States and compare them with what the biomechanical studies have determined as the final, or most efficient, form.

In the years since 1969, I've noticed that Americans are not yet natural skiers. The sport is young in North America, and few people have covered thousands of kilometers on skis at a young age developing their technique. We don't have constant exposure to the best skiers in the world via television or even first-hand at competitions because there are few major international races on this continent. We simply don't have a background of technical expertise.

Therefore, when a North American takes up cross-country skiing, his technical input is dependent on his local coach, other local skiers, and whatever books and movies are available, many of which are out-of-date or otherwise illustrate incorrect technique. It's interesting to travel around the country or observe skiers from different regions at meets like the national championships. The careful observer can discern style differences in a skier from Alaska as compared with one from the East or the Rocky Mountains. The style of the dominant local coach is often imitated, giving skiers from each region a unique, stereotypical appearance.

Despite the regional style idiosyncrasies of American skiers, what I consider the American technique has evolved. Generally, the technique is fairly efficient, but one major problem stands out, leaving the majority of American skiers just short of achieving the final form. This problem will be perpetuated until we stop, recognize and define it. By identifying the problem common among even our best skiers, we can correct it and move toward the final form.

The American technique skier has little extension in his right arm beyond his hip in the follow-through of his poling motion. This causes a continuum of problems. One is that the limited extension curtails his upper body's forward motion; his center of gravity is prevented from moving up and over his right foot and his body is too upright. With his weight behind, his hips are behind his knee, which forces the left leg to return to the snow too quickly. With the left ski coming down too soon, he loses some of the energy of the gliding (right) ski with the decreased stride length.

The final form skier is more efficient due to his arm trajectory. Because both his front arm and his back arm are fully extended in this phase of the diagonal, he is able to raise his body into a more forward position. This increases the angle behind the right knee, bringing the lower right leg perpendicular over the snow while his left leg can extend more upright. These reactions to fully extended arms allow him to continue a faster forward glide because there is less pressure from his body weight to his skis against the snow.

All the energy generated by the final form skier in his kick and pole thrust is channeled into maximum stride length. By being more forward, he can effectively begin poling with his left arm; his weight is forward, the energy force can be punched down from the top of the pole, and he can continue to drive the pole. The other skier is behind in his poling action; he can't immediately activate his poling because he isn't in a position to have his weight quickly on top of the left pole.

The difference between the technique of the American and final form is small. By simply extending the follow-through of his poling motion, a skier can become much more energy efficient. The proper arm trajectory would change the whole scope of his body position and improve his ability to pole strongly, his stride length, and his speed of glide.

I imagine many American skiers could relate their form at least partially to this technical problem. Because the diagonal stride is the prime movement of cross-country technique, it's important that each skier master the final form. By recognizing problems, analyzing proper form, and working to correct even minor technical errors, skiers will gain more glide out of the energy spent on each stride.

THE DIAGONAL STRIDE

The diagonal stride is unique to cross-country skiing. Not only is it beautiful, graceful, and exciting, but the diagonal stride is the primary method used by the skier to propel himself across the snow. It is also the most difficult cross-country technique to master.

Although the diagonal appears simple because of the fluid, graceful motion of a good skier, it actually requires a great amount of energy and athletic ability to accomplish the intricacies of the movements. Perfecting the final form of the diagonal stride is the culmination of the skier's physiological conditioning, athletic abilities; mental application, and technical expertise. In pulling these factors together, the athlete is utilizing technical advancements that have evolved over years of skiing to perfect the ultimate movement in cross-country skiing.

The American technique. Note the angle created by the arm position compared with the other photo.

The correct position for the free glide portion of the diagonal stride.

Because the greatest percentage of a skier's time is spent in the diagonal stride, it must be mastered. The flowing stride must not be contrived; it is a learned movement. Form a mental image of the perfect stride and repeat it again and again and again until the movement feels natural. Skill, energy, and awareness of all parts of the body are required to perform the sequence of movements that will provide velocity to propel the body rapidly and efficiently across the snow.

Analysis of the Diagonal Stride

Keep in mind that the movements in this photo sequence are neither static nor independent; each movement is affected by the others and each movement also causes others.

The position in A is commonly called poling while standing, which is actually a misnomer because it implies a lack of motion. The goal of the movement is to keep the gliding (right) ski moving while poling with the left arm. The main concerns here are the placement and angle of the pole and body position.

In photo A, the skier has just planted his pole in the snow and is very conscious of the poling movement. He planted the pole just in front of the opposite, or right, foot, and it is close to being perpendicular to the ground. (The old school of thought was that the pole should be planted exactly opposite the gliding foot, but this prevents full forward movement of the body and also limits the amount of force the skier is able to generate down the pole. His body will have moved past the pole before he is able to push on it.) The left arm is at a slight angle at the elbow, which is a strong working position.

This movement of the diagonal stride is a question of timing the pole plant so it feels like the skier is punching a hole in the snow with the basket just in front of the gliding foot. He immediately puts downward pressure on the pole, which causes the body to compress a bit and begin angling forward. The body is still fairly upright. The right lower leg is perpendicular to the snow with the hips slightly back, but moving forward. This forward movement of the body thrusts increasing energy into the pole while allowing the right ski to maintain its glide. The right arm, meanwhile, has begun its move down from full extension and is in a recovery phase.

In photo B the trunk of the body has definitely changed position, becoming more rounded and slightly more compressed. This transfers energy from the body to aid the poling motion. Poling is not simply an arm exercise, but involves strength from the abdominal and upper back muscles as well as the triceps. Note that the angle of the left arm is the same as in photo A because the arm is levered to retain full thrust on the pole.

Also note that the lower right, gliding leg is perpendicular to the snow. This keeps pressure off the ski so it provides maximum glide. The left arm is now forward of the body and moving into the angle it will use for poling. The right ski is still gliding forward due to the poling force of the left arm.

Poling while kicking was once referred to as knee drop or leg compression (C). The angle behind the right knee has decreased somewhat as the skier starts to compress over the right ski. The feet are coming together as the right leg begins its switch from the gliding leg to the kicking leg. It is at this point that the right leg will stop for an instant as it takes on its new role. Although the skier is still poling with his angled left arm, the main velocity from that motion has been achieved.

In photo D, the skier has begun the kick off his right leg by pushing off the ball of his right foot. The weight transfer from the right to left ski is underway as the left ski moves forward and becomes the gliding ski. The angle of the right knee should now be opening as the kick is being completed while the left is beginning to rise to a perpendicular position for the glide. The poling motion of the left arm is almost complete and the arm, although not visible in the photo, is totally straight as it begins its follow-through to full extension.

The skier in photo *E* is in a position of initial free glide. Both poles are out of the snow and the momentum just generated from the kick of the right leg and the poling of the left arm propels him along the track. This is the culmination of the energy used to pole and kick.

In this initial free glide position, the right ski is beginning to lift off the snow. As the right arm reaches toward its poling position, the left arm is fully extended. This allows the body to rise up, the lower left leg to become more upright, and the upper left leg to rise, releasing the pressure on the gliding ski. The friction of the left ski against the snow is minimized, allowing for maximum glide.

The final position is the ultimate of the diagonal stride—a full free glide. The skier is dynamic and fully extended in readiness to plant his right pole and continue the powerful momentum he gained on the last kick. His left leg is perpendicular to the snow, and the angle behind the knee is open so he is taking full advantage of the free glide he has created. Any technical errors at this point will decrease the speed of the free glide and shorten stride length.

A. Diagonal stride, poling while standing.

B. Diagonal stride, initial compression.

C. Diagonal stride, poling while squatting.

D. Diagonal stride, the kick.

E. *Diagonal stride, initial free glide position.*

F. *Diagonal stride, full free glide position.*

G. *Diagonal stride, front view.*

Look at this series again and observe the movement of the right arm from the recovery phase up and to pole implantation. As the right arm comes down from its full extension (*A*), it recovers and straightens in readiness for poling (*B* and *C*). In *D*, the elbow joint begins to have a slight angulation, which increases in *E* and *F*. When the skier actually plants the pole, the right arm will be angled like the left arm in *A*. The angulation will remain the same from the moment the pole hits the snow until it is straightened upon passing the hip. This elbow angulation is the leverage or source of power for the poling motion. The proper arm trajectory illustrated here allows the skier to bring the pole to the snow in a downward, punching movement with the pole angled forward. This position is one of power.

In *G*, we have a front view of the diagonal stride to further illustrate proper arm positions. This shot demonstrates the important arm and pole alignment during mid-stride. The skier is coming into a position of initial compression for the kick comparable to the side view in *B*.

Note the skier's left arm. The basket is placed in a good position allowing the arm and shoulder to begin work from over the pole. The elbow is slightly out from the body, which enhances the use of available strength in the poling motion. The right arm is relaxed and in good proximity to the right hip. The trajectory of the right arm is natural and will flow almost straight forward, not much inside the line of the shoulder. The goal is to keep both arms natural and in the power alleys or vertical planes of strongest movement.

As the skier moves along, his eyes are focused down the track, not directly in front of his skis. He has established a horizon that gives him a sense of balance and allows him to evaluate the approaching terrain and his current speed in time to make necessary adjustments in his speed and technique.

This sequence illustrating the diagonal stride represents a time span of about a half a second. (Biomechanical studies, you'll remember, indicated that racing stride rate averages 1.6 strides per second.) An amazing number of moves occur in a fraction of a second during the diagonal stride. To completely illustrate each movement would require about 200 or 300 photos.

Because of the speed and intricacies involved in the diagonal stride, it's vital that the skier has a solid mental concept of what is involved. It's unlikely that he will be fully conscious of each move as he makes it or that he can actually observe each move while watching another skier perform the diagonal stride. Therefore, you have to be mentally aware of what movements are involved and understand how they affect each other before you can hope to successfully perform all of them in a split second.

Common Problems in the Diagonal Stride

In addition to the lack of a full arm extension in the follow-through of the poling motion, there are many other problems that occur in the diagonal stride.

Dropping the Back Ski. In A the left leg has dropped to the snow before the skier has completed the free glide. He has just completed his kick with the left leg, and he should be gliding on his right ski until he's ready to pole with his left arm. You can tell that he's gotten ahead of himself here because he's dropped his back ski before he's taken full advantage of the free glide. Correct position would put him between the positions of free glide illustrated in the previous photo sequence, E and F.

Dropping the back ski too soon is a common occurrence due to poor balance. The skier drops his ski to stabilize his weight on both skis in order to maintain his balance. Skiers who are not relaxed with the dynamic forward position of the diagonal free glide will often resort to dropping their ski. Much of this is a psychological problem caused by the fear of falling forward or otherwise losing balance while in this forward, correct position.

The result of this problem is a loss of momentum in the free glide. Dropping the back ski is a braking motion and reduces the length of the glide. To avoid this pitfall, work to be aggressive by moving your hips up and forward over the ski and by making the proper arm movements in your forward motion. With time and practice, you'll gain the confidence in your ability that will allow you to be relaxed during the fully extended free glide of the diagonal stride.

Too Forward. The skier in B has a problem that is about the opposite of the problem of the skier in A. Both have a poor image of what the final form looks like, but the skier in B suffers more strongly. He knows the dynamic position is forward, but he has overdone it. He is overreaching and has lost the upright position of the free glide that allows him to take advantage of the energy he has developed because he moves too quickly into the poling position.

Leaning too far forward, in addition to having an improper image of the free glide, may be caused by having poles that are too short or by dropping the head to look at the snow just in front.

Forward lean of this nature is a waste of energy. Because the center of gravity is so far forward, the weight is ahead of the kicker wax zone, so the skier can't kick effectively and his skis will slip. Forward weight will also mean a slower gliding ski. Further, because of the body position, the skier's leg drive is hindered because his body is in the way. The kick will likely be late and lack power.

Before making any suggestions to a skier with too great a forward lean, I would first watch him ski to determine the cause of the problem. If he is not simply overreaching due to a bad concept of the free glide position, I would check his head position or see if he is too bent at the waist. Next, watch where his pole strikes the snow and if the trajectory of the motion is correct. If not correct, the poles may be too short or his body is not upright enough because he is using both his front and back arms improperly.

After determining the cause of the problem, I'd speak to the skier about it and explain his error and the proper positions. Through demonstration of the proper form and examination of photos and films of his incorrect form vs. correct form, the skier should develop a better mental image of where his body and arms should be during the free glide.

Wrist Flicking. Wrist flicking is not a major problem but a waste of time and energy. It's interesting that it is a regional phenomenon occurring as a result of mimicry.

Wrist flicking is letting go of the pole during the rear extension and raising the hand above the arm. Although it probably won't cause any serious problems, wrist flicking could affect the timing of the poling motion. It may be caused in the skier's effort to fully extend his rear arm. To correct it, think about raising the elbow of the rear arm in extension rather than the hand. Let the hand relax and recover during the extension.

Figure 8. The skier must keep in mind that whatever his arm does while in front of the body will affect its motion in the extension. Although the skier in D and E appears to have two different problems—crossing the body and a wide extension—both are related to and caused by each other.

In D the skier is crossing his body with his poling arm. He ends up doing a circular motion so his arm will pass by the side of his body. The other half of this circular motion, completing the figure 8, will come when he swings his arm from inside his body in front to behind his body. The arm will naturally flow too wide in compensation (E).

This figure-8 poling motion takes the energy out of the power alley of the arm trajectory. By deviating one way or the other from the vertical plane established by your shoulders, you waste energy. The pole is forced into an angle that is not parallel to your forward motion, so you aren't getting the maximum power from the energy used in poling. Further, the circular motion of the figure 8 wastes energy both in front and behind the body as you try to compensate for the awkwardness of your misaligned poles. The figure 8 could easily cause a twist in the body as part of this compensation.

To correct the figure-8 arm motion, concentrate on keeping your arms in the power alley. Your arms should always be the same plane as your shoulders. To check yourself, stick your thumbs out a bit as they pass your hips; you should touch your legs as the arms pass. You won't want to be doing this during a race, but starting out a training session by tagging your legs on each poling motion will give you a good idea that your body is in alignment and your arms are working in the power alley. Also, watch your hands to be certain they are straight in front of your shoulders as the pole is planted.

A. Dropping the back ski.

Too forward.

C. Wrist flicking.

Figure 8.

E. Figure 8.

UPHILL TECHNIQUE

Skiing uphill is the most physically demanding part of cross-country racing. Because uphill sections can force the racer into the stress of an anaerobic state, you should know how to ski them as well and efficiently as possible so the majority of your energy can be directed to covering the section with maximum speed rather than wasting it on mistimed, miscalculated, and inappropriate movements.

There are three basic forms of uphill technique: hill running, transition skiing (change-up), and herringboning.

Hill Running

Until recently, uphill technique was viewed simply as a modification of the diagonal stride. It was thought that the skier simply compressed the diagonal into shorter leg strides and arm movements. However, biomechanical studies have proven that uphill technique demands different leg movements and ankle angulation than the diagonal stride.

Because of the increased friction or resistance when skiing an uphill, there is no free glide phase in hill running technique—one pole or the other is always working in the snow. In further contrast to the diagonal stride, in hill running the forward ski comes to a stop upon full weighting and there must be an immediate rotation of the body over the ankle. There is no compression or change in the knee angle, as in the diagonal stride. The angle change comes at the ankle as the skier compensates for the stopped forward ski by rotating his body over the ski in order to continue his forward motion.

In A, the skier is in the stage of left arm pole implantation in which the right leg is at its most forward position. The pole basket was planted near the foot, its exact location being a function of the steepness of the hill; the steeper the hill, the further back the pole will necessarily be planted. The right ski is almost at a standstill, and the skier is beginning to rotate over his ankle in order to get into a powerful position to fully push down on the ski and kick. The emphasis here is on a downward push on the leg.

In this phase of the hill running stride, the right foot is a bit ahead of the right knee. The angle behind the knee is established, and it will remain the same through the kick. The change in angle will come at the ankle. With the knee angle stationary, the right leg will be pressed or rotated forward over the foot to give power to the kick. Immediately rotating over the ankle at this stage is the most efficient way to keep moving, or increase the stride length. Racing stride rate for hill running is 2.1 to 2.2 strides per second. This stride rate is common among racers; stride rate still differentiates the good and the elite racers. The best racers have the strength and technique to quickly roll over the ankle, thereby increasing stride length.

In B, the legs have come together and the left is beginning to move ahead as the skier begins the full kick off his right leg. There is no feeling of bounding because the skis are in close contact with the snow. The concern is to move with the terrain and not expend energy in vertical movements. The right arm is in a recovery stage and moving toward a good, forward reach.

If you were to trace the angle of the right knee in this photo and compare it with the angle in A and C, you'd find the angle almost exactly the same in all three positions. Again, the change in angle comes at the ankle as the skier rotates forward during the kick.

Prior to the findings of the biomechanical studies, it was assumed that the skier would execute a knee dip or slight compression down over the ski, reducing the angle behind his

A. *Hill running, pole implantation.*

B. *Hill running, beginning full kick.*

C. *Hill running, kick.*

D. *Hill running, kick completion.*

right knee, to ready himself for the kick. However, high-speed films have shown that his compression typical of the diagonal stride is not necessary in hill running. It wastes time and is not a part of the move to rotate over the ankle, which is the focus of the kick in hill running.

Phase *C* is very similar to stage *B* except that the legs are beginning to come apart as the kick of the right leg nears completion. Again note the angle of the right knee. Also, the shoulders are more rounded here than in *A* because the skier is now using his trunk muscles to aid in a strong poling motion, important in increasing stride length.

The kick phase of the right leg is completed in *E*, and the ski is raised off the snow as the skier prepares for rotation over the left ski. The left arm is in a stage of completed extension, the right pole has been planted, and the poling motion is underway. The skier will then rotate over his left ankle to carry his weight over the kicking ski. This allows him to complete the kick and extend the left leg while retaining good contact with the snow.

In this sequence, note that the body angulation has remained fairly stable throughout. The body never becomes upright, but the back is rounded. This enables the skier to get his weight on top of his pole and bring the trunk muscles into play in the poling motion.

Common Problems in Hill Running

Many of the technical problems common to the diagonal stride also plague the skier in hill running: dropping the back ski too soon, leaning too far forward, and crossing the body with the arms or the figure 8.

Crossing the Body. Crossing the body with the arms (letting them move inside the power alley, also called side-bending) is particularly serious in hill running because there is so little time to recover. By crossing the arm, the hip will be thrown out of its centered position over the track and the combination will cause further problems in timing. If the body gets out of position on an uphill, it takes time to correct it and momentum will be lost. The skier gets bogged down as his velocity decreases, and he'll be forced to herringbone in situations where the skier with good technique will be able to hill run.

Too Upright. The fear of falling foward is even more common in hill running than in the diagonal stride because of the body's more pronounced relationship to the ground in hill running. Another cause for a too-upright position is that the skier might believe he should be perpendicular to the snow at all times, which was a basis in hill running instruction in past years. Or he may be using poles that are too long, preventing him from getting into the proper forward position. A fourth cause of an upright stance is a misconception in his mental image of the proper position.

Too upright.

Too bent over.

High reach, head ducked.

The skier with this problem should be shown film or pictures of himself and of other skiers in the correct position so he can form a mental image of the proper technique. Hill running in a too-upright position is ineffective because it reduces the skier's stride length and also makes it hard for him to get his weight over the kicking ski, thus he winds up making a very inefficient and ineffective kicking and poling motion.

Too Bent Over. A pronounced body angulation can, again, be caused by a bad image of what the correct position is. Other causes would be overreaching with the arms or poles that are too short, allowing his arms to come through too far. Being bent over is inefficient. You will slip backwards because the body weight is too far in advance of the kicking leg.

High Reach, Ducked Head. If an arm reach is too high and the head is ducked, rather than looking up the tracks, the problem is caused by poles that are too long along with a desire to watch what the skis are doing rather than looking ahead. The position will result in a great deal of slipping and will inhibit the forward foot from getting into the correct position. The skier will have to compensate with knee compression, which is slow and inefficient. To cure this problem, decrease the length of your poles and concentrate on looking up and ahead to establish an horizon for improved balance.

Uphill Transitions

Transition skiing is a technique often misunderstood or ignored by beginning racers in North America. They assume that they either do a technique for the flats or an uphill technique and that there is nothing in between to transfer them from one to another without a loss of velocity or to get them up a slight hill with maximum efficiency. They don't appreciate that their technique has to be as subtle as the terrain and that there is a technique that efficiently moves them through the transition from terrain demanding the diagonal stride to that demanding hill running technique.

Uphill transitional skiing allows the racer to take advantage of the most efficient technique over various terrain—from the diagonal to hill running, from hill running to diagonal, from the diagonal into or out of the double pole and up gentle hills—while maintaining momentum and carrying optimum speed.

In years past, transitional skiing was known as the change-up because it was often used over a long, flat section to change the body position in order to relax muscles that had been in one position for a long period. Eventually, conditioning and technique levels improved to the point that the change-up was viewed as a waste of energy and time and it started to disappear from the racer's repertoire of technique. This loss is now viewed as detrimental because young skiers are not schooled in change-up technique, so they are unable to apply it to its current uses in transition skiing.

Current technique calls for the use of the diagonal stride as long as possible in a variety of terrain provided momentum or velocity is being continued. For example, in the approach to a gradual uphill, you initially will be getting 170 cm of glide out of every diagonal stride. As the incline increases, you get 150 cm glide. As the resistance of the uphill grows, your glide decreases to 100 cm, 80 cm, 50 cm, and finally 30 cm. At this point you are unable to retain the free glide position of the diagonal stride and you must make an adjustment.

This adjustment must be directed to maintaining momentum. To use an automobile analogy, you don't want to shift from the third gear of the diagonal stride or double pole immediately down to what may be viewed as the first gear of hill running because you'll lose momentum. Use transitional skiing as second gear.

The accompanying sequence of photographs demonstrates the use of transitional technique from a double poling situation up a gradual uphill. The same type of technique would be used in changing from diagonal stride to double pole, from diagonal stride to hill running, and vice versa in each case.

In the sequence, the skier is, in effect, rushing his poling in order to force the rest of his body to follow. His body is pulled into a forward position that accelerates the leg action into a hill running technique without actually moving to the stop action of hill running. This technique allows him to run up and over a small hill, to hold momentum over a longer hill to put off the necessity of herringboning, and to maintain momentum at the bottom of the hill. The trick to transition skiing is evaluating the terrain in relation to your speed.

In *A*, the skier is carrying a lot of speed into a gradual uphill out of a section of terrain where he double poled. While the left arm goes into a normal poling motion, the right arm is forced more forward than normal for either hill running or the diagonal stride. The right hand is elevated and cast (or trundled) forward. This forces a longer stride, enabling the skier to continue his momentum up the hill without losing velocity.

Photo *B* indicates the extent of the casting motion of the right arm. Note how the body

A. Transitional skiing, initial casting.

B. Transitional skiing, casting.

C. Transitional skiing, forward body position.

is forced forward in following the cast, which carries the momentum and encourages a long stride.

Photo C indicates the long stride forced by the casting of the pole. Because of the elongated pole placement, the poling in this stride will not be terribly forceful but puts the skier in position to be particularly powerful in the next poling motion.

In transitional skiing, the body is forced forward by the casting motion of the right arm, momentum is carried, and the skier is able to return to the diagonal stride without resorting to hill running technique to climb this gradual uphill. Another skier unable to master the timing of this maneuver would be forced to use hill running on a gradual uphill, costing him momentum, energy, and time.

Transitional ski technique requires practice to develop a feel for the terrain combined with the timing of the casting motion. Many skiers have mastered the motion only with one arm, but practice will make you proficient in casting with either arm so you can perform transition skiing properly no matter what the demands of the terrain.

The Herringbone

The herringbone is a technique used to negotiate hills that are too steep to allow hill running technique. Because herringboning is so different from other forms of skiing and because it is seemingly awkward, racers rarely practice this technique out of a feeling that it is not really a part of cross-country technique.

However, the herringbone is definitely a part of racing. All major courses involve some herringboning. The lower the level of competition, the more herringboning you'll see in a race because less proficient skiers resort to it more often than experts, who are likely to run up all but the steepest hills. The skier with herringbone expertise can always make time on less proficient skiers on steep hills, so it's important that this technique be practiced and perfected.

In the herringbone, the tips of the skis are spread apart, which allows the skier to establish a base for thrust off the inside edge of the ski as he steps down in an angulated body position. He poles with the arm opposite the foot under pressure, planting the poles behind the extended skis. Although the legs are spread, the body remains centered and forward. The head is up.

The prime consideration in herringboning is angulation. The knees, ankles, and hips are pressed forward. The knees angulate toward the middle of the trail, rolling the ankles so

Herringboning.

the body weight is on the edge of the skis. This allows the ski to dig into the snow, providing a platform for the forward thrust. This angulation is forced by reaching the arms forward, similar to the effect of the poling motion in hill running.

As you can see from the photo, the arms work in propelling the body forward. The technique depends on good arm-leg coordination. There is no appearance of vertical bounding, but of forward movement with the terrain. The herringbone is actually a running movement, and the skis are kept fairly close to the snow.

Common problems in herringboning include being too upright, which will hamper forward movement with any power. The skis should not be flat on the snow but angled so they dig firmly with each step. Until you are confident with the movements, you will likely tense up, affecting coordination. Through practice you will be relaxed and get a feeling for both how far each ski must be moved forward to avoid stepping on the other and for the proper spread of the skis, which will vary with the steepness of the hill.

If you feel your herringbone technique is good but the tails of your skis continue to strike each other, there's a good chance that the skis are too long for you. Herringbone is a good determination of proper ski length.

Modern trail maintenance has made the herringbone a bit less awkward. Uphill sections are often groomed so that tracks are removed and a small mound is built into the center of the course. This facilitates angling the knees and ankles and makes herringboning easier. Some people object to such grooming because they believe it is artificial, but I think it's no different than setting tracks for the diagonal stride or other aspects of good trail maintenance. Besides, if the mound isn't built in, it will develop naturally after several skiers herringbone up the hill.

DOUBLE POLE TECHNIQUE

Current double pole technique is broken down into two movements: the double pole with no kick and the double pole with a single kick. The mechanics of both motions are similar to those of the diagonal stride, except that the poling motion is performed simultaneously with both arms rather than alternating arms.

Double poling is used when the skier achieves a certain speed that calls for combined arm motion. This occurs on the flats, on gradual uphills, and on gradual downhills. Double poling without the kick is used at faster speeds on a gradual downhill, while double poling with a kick is used at the somewhat slower speeds on flats and gradual uphills.

To determine when to double pole, you must evaluate your speed. Velocity is the major consideration, not terrain, because the double pole may be used in all types of terrain if your speed is great enough. When your speed tells you it's time to change technique, shift gears efficiently. For example, on a gradual downhill you might want to use the casting movement of transition skiing to build speed as you switch from the diagonal stride to double pole with a kick. As your speed further increases, you'll double pole without the kick. As another example, you might be diagonal striding into a downhill. To build as much velocity as possible heading into the downhill tuck, you will double pole off the crest of the downhill for maximum thrust.

With the arrival of synthetic skis and improvements in course design and maintenance, double poling has become an increasingly prevalent part of skiing. The goal is to get from Point A to Point B as fast as possible. Because competitors can double pole more, this technique has been, in essence, forced on racers, which, in turn, forced them to improve their upper body strength because double poling is physically demanding in ways different than other ski movements.

In my estimation, the double pole is the easiest part of cross-country technique to learn. The beginning skier can easily get a feel for the movements involved on a gradual downhill during his first time on skis. A short teaching session will allow the beginner to accomplish the basic double pole on the flats. Further, the double pole is the easiest movement to accomplish on roller skis, so the beginner can get a good dryland workout by continuously double poling his first time out on roller skis. In fact, all many Scandinavians do on roller skis is double pole.

Although the basics of the double pole are fairly natural and easy to accomplish, the skier should be aware of current evolutions in the double pole technique. In recent years, efficient double pole was believed to compress the upper body during the poling follow-through to the point where the back was parallel with the snow. Skiers were asked to have a $90°$ hip angulation between their upper and lower body. However, such complete angulation of the hips is actually a time-consuming waste of energy and velocity. The time it takes to raise the body up from the $90°$ angle results in reduced speed, counteracting much of the velocity gained from this full angulation.

Today's double poling technique calls for the skier to keep his head up, preventing hip angulation of much more than $110°$ after he has made the initial poling action. The angle allows the skier to generate almost the same amount of velocity from the pressure of his upper body on his poles. By halting the angulation at this point, he is immediately able to raise his upper body into its recovery phase and quickly go into his next poling motion. By eliminating the compression, the skier is in a higher position but his velocity is at least the same, if not improved, because his poling is almost continuous.

Double Pole Without Kick

Double poling with no kick is used in stages of velocity between that when he is able to kick and that of the downhill tuck. In other words, the movement is used commonly on gradual downhills. The speed is such that there is no time to kick while poling, but not great enough to go into a tuck.

As the skier recovers from a double pole movement, he rapidly evaluates his speed to determine whether he should kick or not. If he feels that no kick is possible, he begins delivering his poles forward. His left foot is slightly ahead of his right, which serves to release some of the pressure off both skis to augment the glide. This phase of the double pole is comparable to the free glide phase of the diagonal stride. The skier is moving strictly by momentum; he is performing no movements that enhance his velocity.

As he prepares to plant his poles (A), his arms rise. He will drop his elbows a bit and lock them in a powerful working position (see double pole with kick series). His arm reach pulls his body forward to get its weight over the poles. The pole implant will be initiated by both the body and the arms with the body serving as the force for poling and the arms as rigid angulated levers.

The skier in B is in the middle of his poling action. His arms are angulated as powerful levers, and his hands are moving downward toward the knees. The body is compressed to a $110°$ angle at the hips. Note that there is no change in his leg position; the ankle and knee angles remain the same through the poling motion and the only angulation change is at the hips. The rigidity of the legs helps maintain velocity.

In *C*, notice that the hips have not dropped because this would neutralize the pushing force of the arms and upper body. As the arms passed the hips, they straightened out for the follow-through. The head is still up. The body is still angled forward but is rising as the arms follow through. The heels are in front of the hips, which accelerates the skis and increases glide.

The skier continues to raise his upper body in *D* as the poling motion enters the recovery phase. Again notice that the left foot is slightly in advance of the right, releasing pressure on the skis and helping the skier maintain his velocity as he prepares for his next poling motion.

A. Double pole without kick, initiating.

B. Double pole without kick, poling.

C. Double pole without kick, follow-through.

D. Double pole without kick, recovery.

Double Pole With Kick

The double pole with kick is used most commonly on flats and gradual uphills where the skier is carrying a good deal of speed. Many beginning skiers find it more natural to kick with just one leg, but they will find that, with practice, alternating the kicking leg will not only feel natural but will be more efficient.

The skier will be in a neutral position, having just recovered from a double pole. He has the choice between kicking or not kicking on his next double pole, and his decision is based on this current velocity. One foot will be slightly ahead of the other, which will carry his speed better and help him prepare to move into position for his kick.

In *A*, the skier has initiated the kick off his left leg and is driving his arms forward for pole implantation. He is moving his body weight up and over his poles. The angle of the right knee has decreased just a bit, and this slight compression rocks the body forward so the body will be in a position to aid the poling motion. The key here is to time the pole delivery and the kick simultaneously.

This is the most critical phase of the double pole *(B)*. The skier must commit himself to a forward, dynamic body position in which he feels he would pitch forward if his skis stopped suddenly. If he fails to get forward in this dynamic position, he will be unable to use his body as the force for the poling motion and poling will become simply an arm exercise.

The angle of the right knee has increased from that in *E* as the skier rolls his weight forward. This leg will remain fairly straight through the actual poling phase of the movement. As the poles move toward the snow, the upper body will start to compress downward and his left leg will begin to move forward.

Note that as the skier makes his final reach for pole implantation, the poles are just beyond the perpendicular. This would normally indicate a bit of overreach, but the snow conditions were very fast the day these photos were taken and the extent of the reach was necessary for timing and in order to have the poles perpendicular at the point of implantation.

In *C*, the skier has levered his arms for a strong poling motion by bending them at the elbow just before implantation. His upper body assists in the work of thrusting the poles downward and back because of its forward angulation at the hips. The left leg aids the compression by moving forward with some force. If the skier is lazy in driving this leg forward, the compression will be lazy. The upper body moves in reaction to the leg, and a fast forward leg drive will facilitate a fast poling motion.

The arms have passed by the hips in *D* and have straightened out as they go into the recovery phase of their trajectory. The skier has forced his recovery (left) leg ahead of the other, allowing him to release pressure on the right ski to enhance his speed as he glides down the track.

The arms are fully extended in completing the poling motion in *E*. This extension raises the body, an action that helps the skier overcome gravity without having to use the back muscles to lift the body. The left foot is slightly ahead of the right, and the right leg prepares to be the kicking leg for his next double pole.

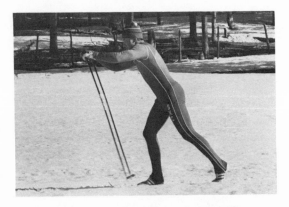

A. Double pole with kick, initiating kickoff.

B. Double pole with kick, forward position.

C. Double pole with kick, bending forward for leverage.

D. Double pole kick, arms straightening.

E. Double pole with kick, full extension.

Common Problems in Double Poling

Many skiers have poor double poling technique because of a fear of the dynamic position. Because they're concerned about falling when getting their body forward enough to assist in poling, double poling becomes an arm exercise. "Arming it," as this problem is called, doesn't create as much velocity and is also exhausting to the arms. By the end of the race, the skier is so tired that he has trouble both double poling and poling in the diagonal stride. Practice the double pole to gain confidence with the dynamic position in order to take advantage of the velocity gained by using the upper body as the force in poling.

Arms too Bent. Sometimes a skier may plant the poles well, but he doesn't get his body fully forward. He bends his arms too much at the elbows and pulls them back toward his body with his poling motion rather than pushing them down toward his knees in a strong, levered position. He loses the use of this upper body in aiding his poling motion and is therefore unable to gain the maximum benefit from his efforts.

Squatting. Squatting or scooching is the second most common problem in double poling. Instead of holding the angulation of his upper legs and knees, the skier compresses his lower body, dropping his hips and bending his knees. Again, this leaves the skier without the use of his upper body in poling. The skier should be made conscious of keeping

Arms too bent.

Squatting.

Overreaching and head ducking.

his legs slightly angulated and of only changing his angulation at the hips as he compresses onto his poles.

Overreaching. When a skier reaches too high, this is a waste of energy and is inefficient because he loses time while waiting for the poles to reach the snow. This is often caused by trying too hard to get forward and into a dynamic position. The skier should reevaluate his visual image of the correct double pole position.

Head Ducking. While overreaching, the skier may duck his head between his arms. Not only does he lose sight of the tracks ahead, but the ducking will cause poor timing of the double poling movements and cost him the use of his upper body in poling.

DOWNHILL TECHNIQUE

Downhill skiing refers to the technique and body positions employed by the skier when he reaches speeds that are too fast for poling. The basic technique is the tuck, which has several variations. Further, the skier needs to know downhill transition technique to move efficiently from a poling motion into a tuck and know prejumping technique to carry him over major undulations in the course. An additional downhill technique is the snowplow, which is used as a safety valve in dangerous situations and to slow the skier from excessive speed.

Downhill Tucks

The tuck has evolved through a great deal of experimentation and scientific research into what is the fastest, most aerodynamic position for the skier to assume on a downhill section of the track. Today's skiers are carrying amazing speeds on downhills as a result of research into the tuck, combined with improvements in equipment and course design. U.S. team members have been clocked at 40 mph on downhills and claim they have gone even faster in some situations.

The tuck is an important part of the racer's technique because it's a great way to gain easy time. The skier with confidence and an efficient tuck may gain seconds on a less skilled skier over a downhill section without any major physiological expenditure. The other skier will have to make up that time over the flats and uphills; he has to earn back the seconds that were basically a gift to the good downhiller.

In addition to providing speed, a good tuck position is the skier's physiological recovery period. The downhill is the only portion of a race where the skier is not hard at work poling over flats and up hills. Therefore, it's important that the skier have a tuck position that is comfortable so he can relax as much as possible when the terrain allows.

But the prime consideration in the tuck is speed. The U.S. Ski Team conducted a series of tests in the wind tunnel at Colorado State University to determine the most aerodynamically sound tuck position. Although there are many variations from what the Alpine skiers call the egg position, the tests determined that it created the least drag or wind resistance of any physically comfortable tuck. Four positions were tested: the maximum drag (standing upright with arms extended), the East German tuck, the Finnish tuck, and the U.S. tuck (egg position). The East German position created 52% less drag than the maximum drag position, the Finnish tuck has 59% less drag, and the U.S. tuck was the fastest position with 63% less drag.

The low egg tuck.

The resting tuck.

High tuck.

U.S. Egg Tuck. The ideal, low egg tuck is used by Alpine racers as well as cross-country skiers. The skier's back is parallel to the snow and rounded and his armpits are over his knees. In this low tuck, the skier's elbows are below his knees and the poles are no higher than his back. His hands hold the poles up in front near the face and are together, a V-shaped effect that will avoid the creation of any turbulence. His head is up and his weight is evenly distributed on his skis. This position will cause little wind resistance by the body as it moves down the slope.

On a straight downhill with no problems ahead, the skier can enhance the speed of this tuck by sitting back on his heels and pulling up on his toes. This will transfer the body weight to the alpine wax on the back of the skis and relieve pressure on the tips. Such a position is the ultimate for speed under most conditions.

Resting Tuck. The resting tuck, is a variation of the egg and is used for recovery and on long downhills. The only change is that the skier's elbows are resting on his knees. His weight is transferred to his lower legs through this solid, bone-to-bone framework. Although the position is a bit higher than the egg tuck, it is still aerodynamically efficient. It is used most of the time in downhill skiing, particularly in distance events. The longer the race, the more the resting tuck is used to save energy and allow the body to recover.

High Tuck. The high tuck is a variation of the egg with a raised body position. The

The balance tuck.

The squat tuck.

The East German tuck.

skier's back remains curved and parallel to the snow, his hands are still in good relationship to his face, his poles about the same height as his back, and, overall, he remains fairly aerodynamic.

The high tuck is used when the skier wants to take a look far down the track or if he anticipates a bit of trouble ahead, such as a corner or undulation.

Balance Tuck. This tuck is used when the skier is facing some trouble on the trail but doesn't want to lose his momentum by standing upright. He's kept his hands and weight forward and his back flat, which keeps him low, but has moved his hands down and out a bit to help maintain his balance. His legs are in a position to act as shock absorbers over undulations in the terrain. The skier hasn't panicked and stood up but has remained low and ready to handle anything.

Squat Tuck. The squat tuck is even more aerodynamic than the low egg tuck. The skier is squatting way back on his heels in a very low position. The squat tuck is used by skiers who are flexible enough to get in and out of this position quickly and easily. It is best used on long, easy downhills because the position doesn't readily allow fast position adjustment should a difficult situation require another tuck. Although the squat tuck is fast, it doesn't allow for good physiological recovery because the angles hamper good circulation to the lower body. It is not a relaxing position and creates muscle tension.

The Finnish tuck.

The panic tuck.

East German Tuck. The East Germans developed this tuck, and it actually isn't as aerodynamically unsound as it appears. Many East Germans and several U.S. Nordic combined skiers use this tuck with success. It's fairly relaxed, except the hands, and about as efficient as the high egg tuck. I find this tuck uncomfortable and stiff in terms of being able to react quickly to terrain changes.

Finnish Tuck. Although the Finns have used this tuck in competition, it is technically erroneous. This is a high tuck for recovery with the elbows resting on the knees. The fact that the skier has dropped his hands, thereby elevating his poles, means the tuck will create more turbulence than necessary. His hand position will continuously scoop air into his chest area, causing it to boil in front of him, and his elevated pole baskets will result in additional turbulence. By simply raising his hands toward his face, this skier would get a much better glide.

Panic Tuck. This skier is afraid of his speed or what's ahead on the track and has compensated by standing up and shifting his weight back, both of which are mistakes. He's cramped his arms back against his body, forcing his back upward and his weight back. The skier in this position is asking for more trouble than he's already in because the slightest undulation is likely to cause him to fall. His balance would be better if he'd lower his hands and keep them forward.

The downhill skier must be conscious of finding the fastest line through each section of track. Because the tracks are not set on fast downhills on many courses, the skier must select his own route. The straightest line is usually the fastest, so cut corners when possible to pick up speed. Practice downhill sections before the race and concentrate on finding the fastest route.

Getting into and staying in a good, aerodynamic tuck is one of the least demanding parts of cross-country skiing. It takes no more energy to use a good tuck than a bad one, and the benefits of a solid position certainly pay off in speed and glide. A bad tuck will decrease your speed, so you'll have to get back to work poling when you reach the flats a lot sooner than the guy with a good egg position.

A useful key to maintaining a good tuck position is noting your hands. Don't let them wander around. Lowered hands will raise the basket area of the poles and slow you down. Crossing the hands will force the poles out sideways. One of the worst things to do is let

A. *Downhill transition, dropping into crouch.*

B. *Downhill transition, tuck.*

your hands drop behind your hips, which will throw your weight back and leave you in a very tenuous position. If you're in a tough situation, keep your arms forward and your weight even or slightly forward and lower your hands for balance until you weather out the difficulty and can return to the low egg or resting tuck. The seconds you gain by staying low and aerodynamic as long as possible will save you strides on the next uphill and improve your results every time.

Downhill Transitions

When changing from a poling technique into a tuck, the timing, as in all transition skiing, is based on the speed you are carrying down the tracks. As you gain experience on skis, you'll have a feel for when you should go into a tuck. Most often, you will move into a tuck position from the double pole. The prime concern is to time the transition properly and move into the tuck with power and efficiency so you'll gain every possible inch of glide out of the downhill.

As the skier completes a double pole as a gradual downhill approaches, he evaluates his speed and decides if it's time to go into a tuck. As he begins his follow-through from the double pole, he knows that he's got the speed and prepares to go to a tuck. Rather than completing the follow-through from his double pole, he begins to drop into a crouch and gathers his poles back to his body (A). He then quickly pulls his hands together and angulates his body into the start of his tuck by bringing his back down parallel with the snow. Within the fraction of a second, he is down in his low egg tuck (B). He has made his transition without any false, momentum-hampering moves and is ready to get the most out of the downhill.

The Prejump

Because competitors are carrying more speed over downhills, prejumping is becoming a more common cross-country maneuver. Developed by Alpine racers, the prejump allows the body to serve as a shock absorber through sections of terrain that involve a compression or dip followed by an undulation or slight uphill. If you remain in a low tuck position through such a compression, you will be thrown in the air at the crest of the hill. Being airborne is slow because of increased wind resistance and can throw you off balance and cause a fall.

Preparation for prejump.

Prejump.

Timing the prejump properly is a function of the radius of the dip or compression and your speed. The shorter the compression and the steeper the rise, the faster the skier will have to make the maneuver.

The skier carries a good amount of speed off a long downhill and sees a rise ahead on the course. To prepare for this bump, he begins to lift out of his egg tuck. In the first photo, he has traveled through most of the compression while he continued to raise up into his high position. His legs are ready to serve as shock absorbers as he moves up the bump.

In the next photo, the skier nears the crest of the hill and begins to drop back into his low tuck. Because he has stood upright into the compression, he can absorb the bump by dropping back to his tuck on the uphill. As he completes his prejump and returns to his tuck position at the crest of the hill, he can ride on over the hill in complete control without becoming airborne. Of course, this takes practice and experience. The skier must learn to evaluate an upcoming compression so he can time his movements correctly. He must learn what type of undulations require a prejump so he's not caught unaware, winding up in the air and perhaps falling.

The Snowplow

Although good racers rarely need to resort to the snowplow, every skier should know how to use this maneuver. The snowplow slows the skier's speed in situations where the skier is not sure of himself and what is coming up on the trail. Good racers will use it when trail conditions are dangerous and when they need to slow down for a sharp corner.

The best place to learn and practice the snowplow is on a small Alpine-type slope with hard-packed snow. This allows the beginner to concentrate on performing the movement without fear of trees along the trail and undulations in the snow or concern about tearing up the tracks that have seen set.

The snowplow involves extending the tails of the skis while leaving the tips fairly close together. The extent of the plow will vary with the steepness of the hill or the skier's need to slow down. By angulating the ankles and knees inward toward the center of the track, the skier exerts pressure on the snow with the edges of his skis. This pressure brakes the skier's speed. To move straight down the slope, the skier keeps equal pressure on each ski and his weight centered and slightly forward. To execute a snowplow turn, the upper body

The snowplow.

and its weight is angulated over the ski opposite the direction of the turn. Thus, if he wants to turn left, he will weight and angulate over his right ski.

The snowplow has been made a much easier maneuver for cross-country skiers with the development of modern bindings. The grooved heel plates allow the skier to exert good lateral pressure, which was almost impossible with the free heel on older boot/binding systems. The skier now has much better control over his speed.

Some racers and coaches don't feel that the snowplow is truly a part of cross-country technique. I believe that it is, just as the herringbone is. Granted, the better racer will rarely need to use the snowplow. However, every racer eventually faces a situation where he needs to control his speed and the snowplow is a good braking maneuver.

A final comment on downhill technique. In the past, the downhill was viewed by competitors as only an opportunity to rest and recover for the next uphill. Today's top competitors know that the downhill is a demanding part of skiing. Seconds can be saved that will mean better results. Further, modern courses and equipment have made downhills increasingly fast, requiring better and better skill. The racer is now under the burden of skiing downhills—not just riding them out and resting, but going for speed and working for every inch of glide and every second of time on each downhill.

TECHNIQUE FOR CORNERS AND TURNS

The racer will encounter all types of corners he must negotiate with speed and efficiency during a competition. The key to a well-executed turn is being aggressive. Many skiers approach corners, particularly when they are traveling at high speed, with a little doubt, if not downright fear. They feel they can't make it. Such doubts carry over into the execution of the required maneuver.

Falling should never enter the racer's mind. Make a deal with yourself before each and every race that you simply are not going to fall no matter what's out there on the course. Decide that you'll do everything in your power to avoid a fall. In this frame of mind, you'll surprise yourself with what you can overcome and what you can accomplish. You may get yourself into some weird and perhaps tenuous positions, but you'll survive them handily if you've worked yourself into a confident, positive, and aggressive state of mind.

Skiing corners with aggressiveness is possible on modern courses because they are

A. Long radius turns, preparation.   *B. Long radius turns, rotating knee.*

double-tracked, cut to widths of 12–15 feet, and often banked and manicured. The old single tracks that snaked their way through the woods forced the skier to slow down and negotiate corners with a skate or step turn. Although these maneuvers are required sometimes on today's courses, the majority of the corners are designed so the racer can carry his speed through them. Instead of slowing down, the racer approaches the corner as if the track were straight, confident that he can retain his momentum, if not increase it.

Long Radius Turns

The long radius turn that allows the racer to continue his diagonal stride through the corner is the most common turn on modern courses. Tracks are set through the corner, and the racer must make only minor adjustments in his body position to negotiate the turn efficiently.

As the skier heads into the corner in A, centrifugal force is beginning to have an effect so he leans to the inside (his left) to compensate. In order to carry his speed through the turn, he must concentrate on stepping and driving on the forward ski with each stride. The arms will help keep the weight on the forward ski, whether it be the inside or outside ski.

In B, the skier is conscious of rotating his outside knee toward the turn to maintain his momentum and direction. Minor adjustments will need to be made as the tracks are skied by others. When they are set, the tracks will be flat, but, as more and more racers ski the corner, the tracks will become beveled; there will be a slight angle in the snow leaning from the top of the outside of each track down to the inside. The beveled snow will actually make it easier for the skier to maintain his balance through the corner without as much body lean or angulation and knee rotation. The skier has to evaluate the condition of the snow to determine how much body angulation will be necessary.

Coming through the corner, the skier makes good use of his outside arm and leg. He leans into the corner and his outside arm crosses his body a bit in order to get his pole in the most powerful position to help drive him around the corner. Although it's possible to take the arc of the corner while kicking off either ski, the outside ski will provide more power and the outside arm will serve as a stronger directional force.

The Reverse Shoulder

Cross-country skiers have picked up a defunct Alpine technique known as the reverse shoulder. This maneuver is a highly efficient way to negotiate a long radius turn when you're in a tuck and carrying fairly good speed.

The skier is in a tuck and approaches a long radius turn. Instead of going into a panic and standing up or snowplowing, the skier is confident that he can carry his speed through the corner by using the reverse shoulder.

As the skier enters the turn (A), he moves his hands toward the outside of the turn (to his right), causing his upper body to rotate in that direction. This feels abnormal because the shoulders are in the opposite (or reverse) position from where they would naturally flow.

In reversing his shoulders to the outside of the turn, the skier forces his knees and buttocks to the inside of the corner. Thus, the main portion of his body weight is inside to fight the centrifugal force that pulls him to the outside of the turn. As you can see in B, forcing his knees to the inside angulates his skis onto the sidewalls of the tracks. As more skiers take the corner, the tracks will become beveled.

With practice, you will develop a feel for the amount of effort required in pushing your hands away from the corner to accomplish the reverse shoulder over various types of corners. Determining factors will be your speed, the radius of the corner, and the amount of bevel in the track.

The reverse shoulder is a very useful maneuver to gain time around a corner because the skier stays low and compact. It may be used on corners with set tracks or on speed corners where the tracks have been obliterated by skiers or taken out by machine.

If you get into a corner using the reverse shoulder and find that you're carrying too much speed, use the maneuver known as the outrigger to control your speed. The skier retains his reverse shoulder position but steps out of the track with his inside ski. The inside ski will widen the base and gives the skier a better platform from which to operate. He doesn't have to resort to a full snowplow or stand upright to control his speed but can remain low and carry good momentum through the turn.

A. Reverse shoulder.

B. Reverse shoulder.

Step Turns

The step turn is the basic maneuver for handling corners in cross-country skiing. New techniques, such as the reverse shoulder, along with higher speeds and the prevalence of long radius turns has reduced the use of the step turn somewhat in recent years. However, the maneuver is still used in situations involving a change of direction in a confined area, such as a short radius turn.

In typical step turn, the skier approaches a fairly sharp corner in a tuck. He evaluates his speed and the track conditions to determine whether the corner will require a single step, a series of steps, or an Alpine turn to negotiate it most efficiently. By reading the track, he'll get a good clue as to what is the best method. In the photo, the tracks have been molded into a step turn by earlier skiers so the decision to use a single step is confirmed for the skier.

The key to a good step turn is a commitment to shift all the weight from ski to ski. Skiers who fail to do this and leave their weight balanced on both skis will find themselves in trouble; they'll be unable to negotiate the corner and likely wind up off the course in the woods.

In the photo, the skier is in the middle of his step turn. His outside or right ski has angled off the main track forming a platform from which he can drive around the turn. He has shifted all his weight to this outside ski, compressed his body down to push off the ski, and angulated his body by rolling his knee into the turn to combat the centrifugal forces. After skier use, the track will become beveled, facilitating his angulation and thrust off the outside ski. The skier is now ready to commit his weight to the inside or left ski.

As this shift of weight is underway, the skier is rounding the turn and transferring his weight to his left ski. This is a strong movement from his thrust off the platform formed by his angulated right ski as it digs into the snow. After shifting his weight to the inside ski, the skier will drive the freed right ski around and back into the track. The skier maintains a low position through this step turn, so he's ready to resume his full tuck or change into a poling motion, depending on his speed and the upcoming terrain.

Step turn.

A. High-speed turn.

B. High-speed turn.

High-Speed Turns

The high-speed turn separates the racer from the hacker. The confident skier will take the corner in the most efficient position possible, while the timid will panic, try to slow down, use poor technique, and wind up losing a great deal of time negotiating the corner.

The trick on a high-speed turn is to keep your feet moving. The minute you get nervous, you'll stop using your feet, which will get you into more trouble than taking the corner aggressively. Concentrate on your effort and the track ahead and ignore any doubts.

As the skier is coming off a downhill (A), he has to crank a short radius turn around the tree to his right. Notice three main factors that get him through the turn: the movement of his feet, his weight shift, and the position of his left pole.

In A, the skier is already about halfway through the high-speed skate turn. His left pole is tucked under his arm because he's confident in his ability and is intent on staying as aerodynamic as possible. If he were to question his balance, he could free the left arm which would make it a bit easier to keep his feet moving. His weight is on his outside ski and he is making a step movement with his inside (right) leg. He leans into the turn to maintain his balance. Because it's best to have his weight on his outside ski, he keeps his right ski up and angles it into the turn.

When it's time to get off the outside ski, the skier is certain to step firmly onto the inside ski and switch his weight there. He rides the right ski for a moment as he pushes off his outside ski and brings it around and into position (B). The outside ski is the main source of power in this turn, so it's important he generates as much energy from it as possible before stepping to the other ski. He remains low during this stepping motion, and his left pole is still tucked under his arm.

As the skier gets back into the set tracks, he continues pulling his outside ski into position while he glides on the inside ski. Meanwhile, he brings his arms into position for a strong double pole. He's charged through the corner and isn't letting a bit of momentum go to waste, but immediately capitalizing on his speed by poling.

When approaching a corner at high speeds, keep your feet moving, your weight shifting, and your body as low as possible and be aggressive!

A. *Alpine turn.*

B. *Alpine turn.*

C. *Alpine turn.*

D. *Alpine turn.*

Alpine Turns

The development of today's boot/binding systems, including the grooved heel plate, has probably benefited cross-country skiers most in the execution of Alpine turns. Because lateral thrust is possible with the new bindings, the Alpine turn has changed into more of a cross-country maneuver. In the old days, the skier would have to keep almost all his weight on the downhill ski to execute an Alpine turn. Now he can distribute the weight evenly between skis and also use the stepping motion while turning.

The design of the synthetic skis has also affected Alpine technique for cross-country skiers. Because the skis have no sidecut, it is necessary to keep an even weight distribution on both skis. This distribution actually makes it easier to turn the skis. The difficulty comes with the speeds generated in racing; the movements of the Alpine turn must be very quick. Although it's easier to make an Alpine turn at high speed, the speed too often creates fear and lack of confidence.

The best way to learn and practice the Alpine turn is on an open slope. Without trees and other obstacles to worry about, you can concentrate on properly executing the movements involved. As you gain confidence with your ability, try it out on the trail.

In *A*, the skier has just risen out of his tuck to unweight his skis in anticipation of a sharp corner. As he poles with his right arm, he lifts the right ski and steps it over in the direction of the turn.

After making the quick step to the right, the skier shifts his weight back (*B*) so it is evenly distributed on both skis. He uses his left, outside arm to help pull him around and then quickly steps his left ski parallel to the right and applies lateral heel force to the outside of the turn on his left ski.

With his weight in even distribution (*C*), the skier continues to pull himself through the turn by using his outside arm to lead his body direction and now exerts lateral heel force to both skis.

As the skier rounds the turn (*D*), his left arm is moving into position for a pole plant and the skier continues to angulate through the corner.

OTHER TECHNICAL MANEUVERS

As you gain expertise as a cross-country skier, you will develop a better feel for your skis and for what moves you can make to be most efficient in propelling yourself across the snow. This section will deal with some basic technical maneuvers that every skier should know how to execute. The expert may be able to refine these maneuvers to suit his own style and, with practice, will become more adept in applying them to various situations he encounters during competition.

Skating

Over the past decade, course maintenance has changed; today there are more sections where tracks are not set but left smooth so the skier can choose his own line and technique. A trackless section facilitates skating, an important aspect of cross-country technique that seems to be one of the least practiced and seldom perfected maneuvers among racers. Skiers seem to assume that because skating is so similar to the movements in the step turn they don't need to practice it. However, skating should not be ignored. The racer uses the skate to gain time in relay starts, in charging to the finish line, in taking sharp corners, and over any long, flat sections of the course.

In executing the skate, keep in mind that it is basically a continuous repetition of the step turn but is used mostly to move straight ahead. Therefore, the key is committing your

Skating without poles.

body weight from one ski to the other. There must be a conscious effort to transfer your weight completely onto one ski. Then you push off that ski from an angulated knee and ankle position and step quickly to the next ski. A second key to most types of skating is to time your double poling motion so that it occurs simultaneously with the drive off the weighted ski.

The technique may be compared to ice skating because the movements are so rapid that pole usage is inefficient. The skier simply skates with his legs and uses his arms only in a swinging motion to aid in his forward propulsion and balance.

In sections where there is a track, the skier seeking more speed will combine skating with double poling. He'll keep one ski in the track and use the other to skate and alternate the skating with the double pole. The important thing is to time the double poling so it occurs simultaneously with the drive off the weighted ski. In other situations, it's fastest to leave the tracks altogether.

Skating is used in many situations by the racer. Because of the platform built for each forward thrust, skating is more powerful and therefore faster in some circumstances than the double pole or diagonal. The skier can gain valuable seconds by skating and may be able to catch a competitor at the finish by utilizing a practiced and powerful skating maneuver. The skate is also useful if your kicking wax is ineffective.

Changing Parallel Tracks

In today's double- or multiple-tracked courses, racers switch from track to track for a number of reasons. One would be to keep in the best line or route toward the finish. Changing tracks can also be a tactical ploy to shake another skier who is shadowing you. By switching tracks when he least expects it, you might surprise him enough to lose him. Similarly, following someone, then switching tracks and charging by him, could prevent the other skier from pursuing you. The skier must know how to change tracks efficiently so

A. Changing parallel tracks.

B. Changing parallel tracks.

C. Changing parallel tracks.

he can follow the best line, go for the best snow and track and negotiate around other racers on the course.

The main concern when planning a track change is to do it in a place and with movements that will at least maintain your momentum, if not increase it. Don't change tracks without planning because you can get hung up between tracks, lose all your speed, and have to struggle to get in the other track. Switch tracks when the snow conditions won't interfere and when you are carrying enough speed to make the move.

Changing tracks is similar to the skating motion. In A, the skier has good momentum and has been double poling. To initiate the switch, he goes into a low body position and transfers all his weight to his right ski. He'll platform off this ski and double pole to drive across the tracks.

The skier has directed his left ski across to the other track in B and has transferred his weight to that leg, which helps keep his momentum going. In C, his left ski rides beyond the outside track, allowing him the maneuvering space to bring his right ski into the inside track. As he gets the right foot in the track, he transfers his weight to this ski and then pulls the left ski into its track. Meanwhile, the skier has been getting his arms and body in position for a double pole.

Handling Intersections

The racer is likely to find himself facing an intersection of tracks out on the course. The intersection may not be smooth as two loops junction or lap tracks converge. The skier must be able to keep in the proper track without losing any momentum, coming off one loop and making nearly a right-angle turn onto the next loop of the course. He prepares for this intersection of tracks by planning the timing of his step turn. In A he has kept his momentum going by gliding on his left ski and letting it cross the tracks to establish a platform. Meanwhile, he brings his right ski into position for a strong forward drive down the track.

A. Intersection track change.

B. Intersection track change.

The skier transfers his weight onto his right ski as he drives off the platform of his left, poling with his right arm. In *B*, the skier has completed his weight transfer to the right ski and is gliding on it while initiating a poling movement with his left arm and driving his left ski around. He then thrusts that left ski forward and kicks off his right.

The sequence indicates that it is certainly possible to make what appears to be an awkward corner without any loss of velocity. This type of maneuver is very efficient, but requires practice. Good execution of an intersection corner is proof that the skier is smart in planning ahead, timing his moves, and mastering proper weight transfer and other aspects of this maneuver.

Tacking

Tacking is a strategic maneuver that allows the racer to take best advantage of the terrain and snow conditions on an uphill. There are several occasions when tacking is useful, and the smart racer will have determined tacking situations during his prerace course inspection.

If the slope is angled into a sidehill, the skier can best keep his skis flat on the snow (for full wax use) by angling across the tracks. If the uphill is followed by a corner, the skier may wish to switch tracks on the hill to be in the best line for cutting that corner. The hill might be too steep for hill running, but he can avoid resorting to the herringbone by taking it at more of an angle so he can platform his skis to best keep momentum.

As the skier gets bogged down on an uphill, his momentum is hampered by its steepness. He begins to rectify this by initiating a tacking maneuver. He weights his right ski and drives off it as he lifts his left ski out of the track and across the slope. In the photo, the skier has kicked off the left ski and shifted his weight back to the right. He continues across the slope, at which point he will either make a step turn to his right back across the slope or step into the tracks, depending on his momentum.

Tacking involves hill running technique, with step turns added as the skier changes direction. It is simply one more maneuver the good racer will have in his skiing repertoire.

In watching skiers over the years, it's been obvious that the winners are those racers who are never satisfied with their technique. The competitors who finish on the back pages of the result lists accept the basics of technique and don't master the various movements or the other maneuvers of cross-country skiing.

In a close race, the winner will be the skier who uses sophisticated maneuvers aggres-

Tacking.

sively. The losers are off in the trees with broken skis because they were over their heads in a critical situation and didn't have the technical expertise to handle the course. The only way to be an aggressive, confident skier is *practice*. A tense body will never perform correctly. The skier must be relaxed and confident. The old saying that practice makes perfect certainly applies to ski technique.

Many skiers assume that training is simply for physiological conditioning. Technique work must be a factor in your training throughout the year, winter and summer. Physical and technical training are not separate activities. Keep in mind that skiing over the same section of a course to practice a certain maneuver, to select the best line, or to determine the most efficient technique will benefit your conditioning level as you improve your technical skills.

One of the skier's biggest jobs is course evaluation. He must be able to judge which technique will be fastest over each variation in the terrain. Good judgment, just like good technique, is a function of practice and more practice. Experience counts.

Technical expertise is not only physical, but mental. You can't perfect your technique unless you have a mental image of perfect technique. Imagery is an essential part of mastering technique. It's also fundamental in mastering a course. Take time to imagine yourself skiing a difficult section of the course, just as you take time to form a mental image of yourself making that faultless diagonal stride. Practice in your head and perfect it on the course.

The mind is a powerful tool. Talk yourself into being aggressive in both training and racing. Practice that aggressiveness to perfect your technique.

6

THE RACING SEASON

Strategy and Tactics

A distressing syndrome seems to prevail among American cross-country skiers: a fear of racing. They spend seven to eight months training and getting physically and technically ready to race. Then, when the competition season comes in December, they're not mentally prepared to compete. They are destroyed if their preparations haven't been perfect or if they have one disappointing result.

Don't get caught up in this fear-of-racing syndrome. When December comes, it's time to put on that bib and race, ready or not. If your preparation hasn't gone exactly the way you'd planned, too bad. It's racing season, and you're as ready as you're going to be. Don't throw away all those off-season training hours by sitting out available races. Get to the starting line and go for it! Then, don't let a bad race or two ruin your season. You learn by overdoing, not underdoing, so pick yourself up and get racing.

Just like conditioning, your involvement in competition should be progressive from month to month and from year to year. The beginning racer can't expect to jump in and have 40 starts in his first season; he must increase the number of races he enters from one season to the next. Further, he should gradually increase the number of races entered in each month during the season so he works up from a few short races in December to a high in March. Work into the races slowly; you don't want your first race in December to be a 30 km, but short events where you can work on speed and adjust to the physiological and psychological loads of competition.

The emphasis in early season races should not be on winning or doing well. December races are learning events. Concentrate on skiing technically well, getting a feeling for competition, and establishing a pattern of racing that will serve you well as you work to peak for major competition later in the season. Learn to evaluate the upcoming competition and approach it with realistic goals. Some races will be used for tempo training, others for technique work, and others just as a warmup for the season.

December races are also an evaluator of your program. The goal isn't necessarily winning but seeing where you stand. Results and your reaction to competition will indicate the tone of your training in preparation for the main part of the season—if you need more tempo and interval work or if you should spend the next two or three weeks emphasizing endurance training. If you come out of early season races not skiing up to your goals, you can adjust your program in time to improve for the important January and February events. But you have to start racing early in December in order to have time for any necessary adjustments.

LEVELS OF COMPETITION

Cross-country racing certainly made great gains during the 1970s in North America, but existing programs will be augmented and new ones developed as our sport grows and becomes more sophisticated. The most exciting area of growth in our sport has been the boom of citizen racing. In 1980 there were nearly 100 cit races scheduled in the East alone, and 5,000 people entered the American Birkebeiner at Telemark. There were more racer starts in 1979 than the total starts during the 1960s and early 1970s.

Citizen racing offers something for everyone. There are a variety of types of racing from short jogs to two-day, 100-km marathons. Family participation is encouraged and most events are divided by age-group classes rather than on ability, so Grandpa has as good a chance of winning a medal in his class as does his granddaughter in another class. Usually everyone gets a little something just for finishing. The emphasis is on having fun and enjoying the sport and the outdoors.

As the ability and expertise of the cit racer improves, he has the option of entering other levels of competition. Marathon races appeal to thousands of average skiers. In 1979 the U.S. Ski Association formed the Great American Ski Chase, a series of marathons organized around the country. The Chase has generated much interest from skiers, the media, and commercial sponsors and has added more dimension to marathon racing. Each race has its own personality, and all share a minimum distance of 50 km, good organization, and the opportunity for the top skiers in each age class to be named to the honorary U.S. Marathon Ski Team at the end of each season. A goal of the Chase is to have skiers travel to all, or a good number, of the races to enhance their competitive experience in a variety of events at a variety of locations.

Cit racers wishing to add international racing to their experience have the option of competing on the World Loppet League. This circuit includes world-famous marathons in the countries of Middle Europe, Scandinavia, Canada, and at the American Birkebeiner. A valuable experience, the WLL offers special medals to skiers who complete all races on the circuit.

From my personal experience racing in the American Birkebeiner, I can tell you that nothing matches the excitement of standing at the start with 5,000 other racers at a marathon. Covering the 55-km course to the cheers of the huge crowds is really something. One finisher commented that racing a marathon is like being born, living your life, and dying all in one day. You certainly get your money's worth from the entry fee because marathons are a happening offering more racing experience in one day than you'll likely get elsewhere during the entire winter.

As cross-country continues to grow, clubs will naturally align themselves with the commercial touring centers popping up all over the country. It would be a consistent outgrowth of the cit racing boom and build the appeal of the touring center. The centers should learn from well-planned Alpine ski areas to separate touring and racing trails and realize the promotional values of hosting competitions, cooperating with club programs, and building their market by providing good instruction and coaching for all levels of skiers.

In the meantime, our most encouraging program for the future of Nordic skiing lies in the Bill Koch League. I'm pleased to say that Al Merrill and I had a part in developing this league in the late 1960s and that our Olympic medalist Bill Koch lent his name and continuing interest to it in 1976. The BKL is designed to introduce boys and girls 13 years and younger to Nordic skiing. The youth are given a positive introduction to cross-country, jumping, and Nordic combined by qualified instructors. The products of the BKL will emerge in greater numbers in the coming years and give our country a strong base of competitors for the first time in history.

In the past few years, moves have been made to develop a program for skiers coming out of the Koch League. A Junior Olympics is held annually for kids 13–18 years old. Unfortunately, there is currently no strong program to carry on this progression as skiers reach the age of 18. Granted, there is some competition for skiers in schools and colleges, but few viable, year-round programs involve large numbers of skiers and carry them on to senior competition. This area is where the development of strong club organizations will fill a gap in organized skiing in the U.S.

Any skier who is working to reach his potential on the race course is wise to seek the guidance of a coach. More and more skiers are recognizing this and seeking a coach to provide shape and direction to their programs. The concerned racer needs a coach to evaluate his training and racing programs, provide advice and concrete direction, and, most importantly, to provide objective input and continuity to the racer.

Most elite European racers have a club coach who guides them throughout their career, in addition to coaching from the national team staff. This type of coaching situation is being encouraged by the U.S. Ski Team; more and more national team skiers are establishing a relationship with local coaches to assist in the planning and execution of their programs. It's best to work with coaches in your area so you have the opportunity for at least weekly contact. The personal contact is important in any coach-athlete relationship.

Many skiers are self-coached. Until you can find a good coach, you'll have to be your own coach. Training logs are vital to the self-coached racer in order to organize and monitor a program. If you're self-coached, talk to everyone you can about the sport and read everything relating to training and competition, including books on other sports, weightlifting, physiology, and sports medicine.

Self-coaching presents problems to the athlete. He lacks a source for an objective evaluation of his program and his progress. He has no one to aid him in dealing with logistical problems including waxing, traveling, and training. He can't rely on the experience and knowledge offered by a good coach. Self-coaching means the athlete's learning process and progress in his sport will take longer than that of the coached racer.

Coaching is increasingly important as the racer moves up the ladder into classified competition. This level of racing involves the best competitors in the country, and success in the classified ranks leads to berths on the U.S. Ski Team. Top-level racers are ranked by the National Point List, a system established in the late 1970s to compare performances of our best skiers throughout the country. The system was developed so that a racer in Alaska can objectively compare himself with a racer in the East, even though they never compete against each other face to face.

The National Point List is updated four times a year. Racers are given points, depending on their performance and the caliber of the field in each race they enter. Their three highest points are averaged to determine national ranking. The point list is used in seeding competitors at races (establishing the running order) and in selecting various teams: Olympic, junior national, divisional squads, etc. The point system has created excitement and enthusiasm among classified racers because they can compare themselves with their peers and with top members of the national team.

Classified racers belong to a division of the U.S. Ski Association and participate in USSA-sanctioned events. USSA membership guarantees that classified events will be run according to FIS (International Ski Federation) competition rules. Races for classified women include distances 5–20 km and relays, while men race relays and distances 10–50 km. Good performances in divisional classified races lead to berths on teams at national junior, senior, and veteran championships. These championships are held each winter and feature the best competitors in the nation in their various categories. The national championships are often one of the few opportunities in the season where divisional racers compete against the entire U.S. team.

Classified racing has long been the backbone of competition in the U.S. Recently, citizen racing has taken the lead in terms of the numbers of skiers participating, but classified competition remains the top of the racing pyramid. More and more skiers and athletes from other sports are advancing their way through the system. The U.S. is finally developing levels of racing from the Bill Koch League up through various types of competition so that skiers with ability and dedication can truly reach their potential by gradually moving up through the ranks to the elite group of national competitors.

RACING STRATEGY

Strategy is a military term defined as the planning and directing of operations for battle. Cross-country racing can be viewed as a battle against the variables, other competitors, and yourself—the battle of getting the most out of yourself on the race course. To win the battle, you must be organized and prepared; you must have a strategy. When I enter a race, my strategy is to know everything I can about the race. I find out as much as I can about the course, the race organization, and the logistics of the competition. I know the rules of racing and have prepared by body, my equipment, and my brain to be in perfect readiness for competition.

Americans, from my observation at races over the years, don't give enough attention to strategy. Race strategy brings to fruition all the efforts in training, preparing equipment, and waxing skis so that every advantage is possible.

Prerace Logistics

Prerace strategy actually involves the first hour spent training and the first day spent planning for the season. It's a 12-month effort for the serious racer in which he works and strains and plans to reach his potential as a ski racer.

During the winter, strategy starts with the race schedule. Enter the races, fill out the forms accurately, enclose the race fee, and send it off to the race organizer. This is a basic step that signals your determination to compete. Now it's time to plan your attack. The time between entering a race and your starting time is when you focus on your strategy for the race so that you are fine tuned and ready to charge out on the course with direction and purpose.

Make your travel plans, be certain to pack all the necessary gear, and have a checklist as you pack to be sure you haven't forgotten something vital. Know when and where the race is and arrive on time. For major events, arrive at the race site the day before the competition so you can totally familiarize yourself with the race organization and course. This means getting reservations at a local motel or finding some other type of accommodation.

When you arrive at the race site, locate the registration area. Sign up for the race, find out where the official bulletin board is so you can follow the official messages as they are posted, ask if there are any changes in the schedule, and determine the waxing facilities. Be certain to pick up a course map, find out the size of the field, the starting procedure and starting intervals, what kind of timing will be used, and where the start/finish area is. Find out about coaches' and seeding meetings and picking up your racing bib. Talk to local skiers who have been over the course to find out about the snow conditions, the lay of the course, and particular problems to watch for. They might be able to tell you a good waxing combination and other factors that will help you.

Then find a good place to wax your skis in preparation for inspecting the course. If the wax room is inadequate, find another place with access to electricity. Course inspection is a good time to test wax for the race. If you're with a group, this will be easier because each skier can try a particular combination. Take your fanny pack along with wax and scrapers so you can adjust the wax out on the course. Compare notes with the other racers in your group and with other skiers after you've tested the wax during course inspection.

Course Maps. Knowing the course is the best way to avoid major problems (getting lost) and minor setbacks (taking a corner wrong). If you know the course, you are free to concentrate on your race. I've watched and helped organize many ski races, and there are always skiers who miss their start, ski off the course, fail to have their skis marked, or blow the finish because they haven't been professional in their prerace strategy. The smart athlete knows the course and therefore has a decided advantage over the lazy racer who simply shows up at the start area on race day.

Begin your course inspection by reading the race information provided by the organizers and studying the course maps. Attend or get a report on the coaches' meeting to be certain you understand the course and starting procedures.

The course maps and course profiles are extremely helpful to the athlete and coach alike in planning race strategy. Not only will they tell you where feeding stations are in a distance event, but they will aid your coach in planning timing and support stations and give you a good idea of what you'll face during the race.

The first thing to look for on the trail map is the total climb on the course—the total of the verticals on each uphill. The FIS has a maximum of 600 meters of climb for a men's 10 km, for example; so if you have a course with 575 m of total climb, you know right away that it will be tough racing. The second measurement on a good course map will be the maximum climb, or the vertical of the longest single uphill. The FIS limits this to 100 m for men and 75 m for women. The third measurement is called height difference, the vertical difference between the lowest and highest points on the course. If the figure is great (over 200 m), the course will have long, tough uphills. If the difference is slight, you'll have short, quick, rolling hills.

The course profile on the map will tell you where the biggest climbs are, where you'll be able to recover, and where you can push. If the toughest climbs are early in the race, you should have a more extensive warmup than normal so your body is ready.

The profile and the map let you know what to expect where. If there's a steep downhill on the profile, for example, the map will tell you whether there's a straight runout at the bottom or a curve so you can predetermine an appropriate speed. Also, the height differential will tell you where to test wax. If there's a significant difference, it's likely that snow conditions will change between the low and high points. You should test at both places, come up with an adequate compromise, or carry wax in a fanny pack or have a waxing station out on the course to adjust your wax during the race.

The map will tell you if you'll ski the loop more than once, if there are a couple of loops off the start area, and which particular trail is the race course so you'll know what way to go at the intersection of several trails. Feed and first aid stations will be marked on the map, and you and your coach should determine where he'll be for additional feeds and for interval times.

Course Inspection. After studying the map, head out to inspect the course. Take your fanny pack with extra waxes to test and a pad of paper and a pen. Because cross-country courses are becoming more and more difficult, smart racers take notes during course inspection to remind them of the specifics of the course. Just before a steep downhill, for example, there might be a kilometer marker, tree, or something else you can note so when you see it during the race you'll know what's coming up on the course. During the race you'll be alert to the downhill, so you will change your pace or switch tracks to carry your speed through the downhill.

The first step in your course inspection is to find the start and finish area. Evaluate the best way to start and which track to head for, based on the type of race and whether it's a mass, dual, or single start. If you'll be skiing more than once through the area to catch various loops, determine the best way to negotiate the lap area. Then determine the best approach to the finish line. This type of evaluation will prevent you from hesitating during the race and will allow you to focus on skiing.

Head out on the course. During inspection, work with your coach and teammates to discuss strategy, waxing, and race tactics. Ski along easily, stopping to take notes. You may

Here is a typical feeding situation. I'm passing a drink to Tim Caldwell, who's being followed by Doug Peterson during the 1980 U.S. Nationals at Mont Ste. Anne in Quebec. When feeding on the move, keep your eyes on the bottle or cup being handed you. A missed feed can hurt you both physiologically and psychologically.

want to ski over particularly difficult sections a few times to practice and determine the best technique and line to get you through the area.

If there are a double set of tracks, be aware of where you'll want to switch from one to another. You should determine this before the race, based on the most efficient way to take the course. You may decide that the inside track on a downhill is fastest and that it will be best to take a corner from the outside track to set yourself up for the next corner. You want to be able to change tracks with smooth skill and good power so you don't lose momentum. Test places where you can best time your track switches.

Next, concern yourself with the skill areas: uphills, downhills, and high-speed turns. There are several ways to take uphills, depending on the steepness and condition of the track. Don't simply assume that you have to herringbone an uphill. You may want to single stick from the right-hand track and angle up to the left track in a tacking maneuver. This will keep your skis flatter so your wax has more contact with the snow. If you have a late starting number, you might not have a choice between striding or herringboning up a hill because the earlier racers have wiped out the tracks by herringboning. Try tacking or, if you're lucky, the earlier racers will have herringboned up only one side of the trail, leaving a set of tracks for those who want to stride up. If the hill will easily accommodate a single poling technique, check to see which track has the better angle and better snow, letting you ski a flatter ski.

On downhills, you want to be aware of which track will be faster and best lead you to the next corner or uphill. One track might be set more firmly in the snow, which will give you better control. Practice running the steeper downhills a few times, especially ones involving corners.

When you are going around the race course, keep in mind the sequence of hills and rest areas. Plan where you can push hard and go anaerobic and have a good downhill after for recovery. Think about what you'll do if you encounter other skiers on a particular section of the course—can you blow them away or should you wait for the next hill?

As a final consideration, determine where you should start your final sprint to the finish. Ideally, this final effort will be long enough that you'll reach the finish line totally exhausted.

Course inspection and careful evaluation of your options in covering the course can make the difference in your race results. A few seconds gained here and another few gained there could add up to quite an advantage by the finish line. With a course strategy firmly in mind, you'll be better able to concentrate on racing and tactical situations that arise.

Rules. I would suggest that racers obtain an FIS rule book and be aware of what is expected of them as competitors and what is expected of the race organizers. The serious racer should study all of the rules so he doesn't make a costly mistake during a race.

If track conditions are marginal, race organizers may limit the time the course may be used for training and inspection. Check the official bulletin board for such notices, because you can be disqualified from the competition if you're out on the course during non-training hours.

Each racer must enter the marking pen near the start area with his bib on and have his skis marked. If you fail to have your skis marked, you'll be disqualified.

The official starting signal includes an attention warning 10 seconds before the start and then "five–four–three–two–one–go." With electric timing, you may leave three seconds before the go signal. In the starting gate, your feet should be behind the starting line and the front of your skis and poles ahead of the starting wand. If you're late, you can start at any time, provided you don't interfere with another racer. Tell the starter what you're doing but don't block other competitors. If you start early and are called back, you must return and cross the starting line again.

If there is a question or a protest, don't stand around and argue about it. Go run your race and wait until after the race to file a protest if you feel it's necessary. You won't get any official ruling at the start.

The competitor is required to follow the marked course from start to finish and pass through all the controls. The course markings must be clear throughout the course so the competitor is never in doubt about where the course goes. Sometimes race organizers fail to mark the course clearly. Other times, the racer under the stress of oxygen debt will easily be confused by obvious markings. The racer should be aware of any potentially confusing areas from course inspection and have them clarified by race officials before the start.

The racer must ski the entire course under his own propulsion. You can't have someone push you on an uphill or have someone ski beside you setting a pace. You may change both poles during the race, but you have to finish on at least one of the marked skis you started on. If you need to rewax along the course, someone may provide you with the necessary tools, but he must not touch your equipment or aid you in waxing.

If you are overtaken by another racer, you must leave the track on his first demand, even if the course is double tracked.

Your time is marked at the moment one foot crosses the finish line. Some skiers try to break the eye of electric timing with their poles, but officials are aware of this and correct the time to when the racer's foot hits the beam.

After the official results have been posted on the official bulletin board, you have up to two hours to file a protest. Before doing so on a timing error, ask a race official to do a check of your time. If you decide to lodge a protest, you must submit it to the race officials in writing and pay a deposit (usually $15–$20). The organizers will keep the money if you lose the protest; otherwise, you'll get the deposit back after the jury meets to hear your protest. Be organized if you protest. Know what racers were around you when the incident occurred and gather information so you can accurately recreate the incident for the jury.

The Night Before

The racer has several chores to take care of the night before a competition: equipment preparation, mental preparation, and rest.

Go over the gear you'll be using in the race. Make certain that you've got your bib and that your uniform is ready to go. Then examine your skis, poles, boots, and bindings. Repair any knicks or weak areas. Are your baskets and grips attached to your poles firmly? Are your binding and heel plate screws tight? Are your boot laces sturdy? Your skis will get special attention. Check the tip and tail areas for separation or cracks. Go over the bases and repair any rough spots.

If you're at the race site, watch the weather forecast. If conditions are stable, you can apply your Alpine wax the night before the race. This will put you one step ahead on race day so you can be calmer and better prepared in the morning. I don't like putting on kicker waxes, even binder, the night before the race because their temperature range is much narrower than Alpine wax and they have a tendency to dry out. This isn't a problem with

Alpine wax. If conditions do change, you can always make adjustments to your Alpine wax or start all over if need be.

After preparing your skis, put them in a place where they will be protected from picking up dirt and being knocked around. Store them in a warm place overnight to ensure good penetration of the Alpine wax.

Check your wax kit to be certain everything you'll need for your final waxing is in order and ready to go. If the race is long or conditions are expected to be variable, organize a fanny pack to wear during the race. It will weigh less than a pound and won't affect your skiing but could avert problems during the race.

Once your equipment is checked and ready for the race, relax. Pull out the notes you've taken on the course and the trail map and review the strategy you've planned. Go over the course in your head and memorize problem sections and details of corners, uphills, and other tough sections. Use mental imagery; visualize yourself taking every corner, every downhill, and every uphill perfectly. Think about making every technical move better than you ever have before. Then get a good night's sleep. If you're a bit nervous and don't sleep well, don't worry. It's not the night before the race that counts, but the sleep you've gotten two nights before.

Race Day

If you weren't at the race site the day before the race, the activities described previously will need to be compressed into the two or three hours before your starting time. Arrive at the race site in plenty of time to inspect the course and test wax. Based on weather reports, you should arrive with a pair of skis waxed and just about ready to go, except kicker wax adjustments.

Upon arrival, find the registration area, sign in, and get your bib. If registration isn't open, find out when it will be and head out to the course—don't wait around but take advantage of the available time. Get a map, check the official bulletin board, find a good waxing location, and head to the start/finish area.

A temperature board should be posted near the start area, which will tell you the air and snow temperature at the high point of the course and at the start area. This will give you a clue as to what wax to be testing and how much variation in snow conditions there will be over the course. Changes in the temperature will be posted routinely, so keep checking the temperature board for indications that you'll have to adjust your wax.

The most important thing is for you to stay in control of yourself. Don't panic. You won't need to if you've taken time to find out about the race procedures and have com-

More and more racers are wearing small fanny packs like this in marathons and other distance races. This pack includes extra wax, a small cork, a scraper, tape, and a feed bottle. Optional items are toilet paper, a razor blade, Bandaids, a dry hat, Swiss army knife, extra binding, and screws.

pleted your prerace strategy. Stay on your toes, concentrate on your upcoming effort, and take care of yourself. If you have a couple of free hours before your start time, don't let nervous energy sap your strength and concentration. Relax and focus only on your race. Go over the course again in your head; don't waste energy watching another race.

Don't depend on your coach or fellow racers for things that you can take care of yourself. If your coach gets caught out on the course testing wax, you have to be prepared to organize yourself and get to the start on time. Get your own bib, wax your own skis (giving them time to cool after hot waxing), and head out on the course.

Ski hard enough to get an indication of how the wax will work during the race. Don't use the start/finish area for wax testing because it won't be indicative of the conditions on the course. At a minimum, ski a couple kilometers from the start and then a couple from the finish to test the wax. The more of the course you ski, the better indication you'll have of your wax. Try not to panic about your wax. Have confidence in your skills and your coach's skills. Make minor adjustments, if necessary, but don't get panicky and add another coat of kicker wax at the start area simply out of nerves and lack of confidence.

After your course inspection, come back to the start area and make your final preparations. Your body has to be warmed up, and it's important to time this properly so you're warm just before your start time. You want to have time to recover before starting, but not more than three to eight minutes. Then, when you head out of the starting gate, your body can take the shock of the physiological strain. If you're not properly warmed up, you take a chance of injury and going under during the first 5–10 minutes of the race.

A good warmup will open the pathways of your cardiovascular system so your muscles are ready to go to work. Ski until you're in a good sweat and breathing fairly hard. Return to the start area and do some stretching while you recover. Be certain to fully stretch those muscles that will be used in the race so they will immediately be able to go comfortably through the full range of motion when you leave the starting gate.

Many junior and cit racers don't warm up properly because they're afraid to waste energy. This is a mistake. The small amount of energy required in a prerace warmup will definitely enhance your performance.

While you're warming up or recovering, go over your race strategy. Visualize how you will ski the race, where you will press yourself, which hills you'll attack, how you'll handle downhills. The course, feeding stations, timing stations, and other aspects will be ingrained in your memory. You are confident that you'll handle all parts of the race well and will come in with a good time because you're completely prepared.

Stretching before training or racing is a must. The skier has to be loose and warmed up before exerting himself physically. This series of photos demonstrates some typical stretching exercises.

Prerace stretching.

Prerace stretching.

Prerace stretching.

Prerace stretching.

Prerace stretching.

Prerace stretching.

As your start time approaches, get your bib on and have your skis marked. Pay attention to the starting procedures as other skiers take off. Keep stretching and stay loose. Just before your start time, remove your warmups. Check your watch in the starting gate so you can time your race for your own information and as a backup for a possible protest. Have a good race!

Postrace Strategy

As you finish your race, check your watch to determine your time. Be aware of who finished in front of you and behind you so that you can be certain you get a fair shake in the results. Protect yourself in case a problem or protest occurs because of a timing malfunction or some other error.

Put on your warmups and get something to drink. An electrolyte-type drink at warm temperature is best. Don't gulp down large quantities because your system isn't ready to handle it. Your body certainly isn't able to handle much in the way of solid food immediately after the exertion of a race.

Once you feel in control again, begin your warmdown. You might want to change to dry clothes before heading out for an easy ski over three or four kilometers. Go back indoors and do some stretching. This warmdown will help your body recover and be ready to go again for the next workout or race.

Your warmdown is a good time to think about the race you've just completed. Evaluate your performance. Did you make some mistakes that can be avoided in the next race? Pat yourself on the back if you skied a good race. Think about how well you skied that downhill and how well you handled that tactical situation so you'll remember those moves next time. Later, record these reactions in your competition log.

Unless you have no choice, stay at the race site, preferably overnight, particularly after long-distance races or if you've had several competitions in the past week. Take a nap, eat a light meal, get some light exercise. A sauna or massage will make you feel great and expedite your recovery.

Then work on your skis. Clean off the dirty wax to protect the bases, hot wax them, and put them safely in your ski bag. This is a good plan even if you have to take off after the race and will only take 10 or 15 minutes. Afterward, attend the award ceremonies whether you've won a prize or not as a small vote of thanks for all the work and expense the organizers have gone to in hosting the race.

RACING TACTICS

Tactics, like strategy, is a military term relating to combat. It is defined as the procedures used to accomplish a specific goal. In cross-country skiing, tactics are what you use to complete the race course in the fastest possible time.

Tactics are involved to some extent no matter what the level of competition. Many citizen racers and marathoners insist they don't enter events to race, just to finish, but every race is a race whether you finish first or 900th. You'll be out on the course and someone beside you will pass you on the uphills and then you'll catch him on the downhills. As you approach the finish, you're going to want to beat that guy across the line. You end up racing, and you should know how to use some tactical ploys in order to come out ahead.

Tactics are involved from the beginning to the end of the race. How will you leave the starting gate? What do you do about the hundreds of other people in a mass start or the other guy in a dual start? What happens when you overtake another racer or when someone overtakes you? How do you cope with bad wax? What about feeding in long races? What are the advantages of interval timing during the race? How do you get psyched up for the race and during the race in order to put forth your best effort throughout? These are some of the tactical questions the racer must be able to answer to be successful in competition.

Race Psychology

There have been numbers of studies on the psychology of sport champions because ultimate success is a function of the brain. Bill Koch will tell you that top-level competition is 90% mental—the athlete's ability to deal with pain, his confidence in his ability to perform the task well, his ability to deal with the other competitors, and his ability to concentrate intensely throughout the event.

Psychologists have determined several factors common to champion athletes. The prime factor is self-confidence. Based on their training, their past success, and external and internal influences, they know they will win. Their mental imagery of an upcoming competition is always positive; they see themselves performing well and have no fear of failure.

Confidence means that the athlete will remain physiologically effective under stress. A lack of confidence will create tension and nervousness, which hamper muscle function and impair peripheral vision. The champion continues to perform well in difficult, stressful situations because he has confidence that his abilities will ultimately lead to success.

Champions are competitive and goal-oriented. They view life as a contest and are hungry to take up the challenge. They have a will to win that comes through training and the influence of other people. They are never satisfied; one victory makes them starved for more.

This leads to an ability to concentrate intensely during competition. Champions are unflappable—mentally tough, as the coaches say. They don't think about anything but winning by making that stride perfectly, taking that corner perfectly—concentrating positively on every aspect of the course and the competition. The mental toughness allows them to be flexible and able to adjust to unexpected situations without losing their concentration.

True champions all seem to share these attributes, and when they reach the pinnacle, their job is even harder. It's much more difficult to be No. 1 than to get there because of the incredible pressure facing the successful athlete. External pressure comes from fans and the media, and the internal pressures faced by the athlete increase. He is isolated, often becomes introverted, has a sense of guilt, and must continue to work to win through all this pressure.

Most of us will never have the champion's combination of attributes, but the dedicated competitor will work to develop them and put to best use those attributes he does have. Winning psychology is the ultimate source for the strength, determination, concentration, and ability to cleverly perform tactical moves during competition.

Starting Line Tactics

Racing tactics begin by studying the competition and the type of race. For typical interval, single-start races, take a look at the starting order to know who will be skiing around you during the race. Know who you can expect to pass and prepare yourself to be passed by others. Determine how you will deal with these situations. Keep cool if your plans don't materialize. If you'd estimated that another racer would catch you about 5 km into the race, don't get psyched out if he catches you at 2 km—he might be having a super race and you shouldn't give up but should try to ski with him.

In mass or dual starts, evaluate your goals and abilities in deciding how assertive you want to be at the starting line. If you figure you'll run a marathon in four hours, there's no sense starting out as fast as the guys who will finish in 2½ hours. Most marathon courses are relatively easy the first 3–4 km and then have a good climb about the 5–6 km point. If you start out too fast for your conditioning level and are already in an oxygen debt at 2 km, you'll definitely be in trouble for the remaining 48 km. Ski within your ability. This holds

The racers just keep coming during the mass start of the American Birkebeiner at Telemark, Wisconsin. In a mass start event, try to avoid entanglements with other skiers. Falling down, like the guy behind the skier with bib number 466, can really be a problem.

true for dual starts. If you're starting with a guy of superior ability, don't ruin your race by trying to keep up with him. Run your own race.

On the other hand, if your goals and abilities are high, go for it from the start signal. In studies done at the 1979 Pre-Olympics, the sports medicine people found they could come close to predicting the finish order after the first kilometer of the race. If a skier was 5 seconds behind the leader at 1 km, he'd wind up about 75 seconds behind after 15 km.

If you hang back in a mass start to conserve energy, forget it. Everyone else will be charging out of the start, and you'll waste more energy trying to pass them later than you will pushing up to your level of ability from the start. The best strategy for a mass start race is to stay uninvolved and away from the herd. Ski hard and aggressively at the start signal and free yourself from the masses as soon as possible.

Dual and triple starts are often greeted with groans by competitors, but I think they are exciting and a great way to enhance your racing expertise. The important thing to remember is to be cool and run your own race. Don't arrive at the start without a plan of attack. Will you take the lead or let the other skier take it and shadow him? You'll likely be starting with someone of comparable ability, but you must determine if you are confident enough to take the lead. Don't wait until you are in the race to decide how to deal with your costarter or you'll end up running his race rather than your own.

Be aware of the track situation over the first half kilometer in a dual start race. Be aggressive out of the start and know the tracks; the 10 or 15 seconds you gain might make the difference at the finish line.

Dual starts present interesting tactical situations. Experience gained in dual starts will increase your competitive expertise much more rapidly than single starts. In the long run they will make you a much more confident and cool competitor under pressure because you'll know how to control your own race.

Psychological Games and Tactical Ploys

There are many tricks and psychological games played in cross-country racing. When I've discussed these with racers and race observers, there's often been a bad reaction and doubt about the ethical validity of these tactics. However, competition is not a tea party. Realistically, it is a battle involving psychological warfare along with technical and physical skill. The victor is tough, focused on his goal, and willing to do everything within the rules to get to the finish line faster than anyone else. I don't necessarily advocate all the tactics to

This is a typical dual start. John Sacket, left, knew he could start three seconds ahead of the go signal because of electric timing, so he is charging out ahead of Tim Caldwell during the 1980 U.S. National 50 km.

be presented here, but I feel it's important to inform the racer of the types of things he may encounter, particularly in international competition.

Psych games begin before the race starts. One racer will tease another about his equipment, his wax, or a difficult section on the course. It might not be a conscious effort by the joker, but the effect is to plant a seed of doubt in the other racer's head. The racer, if he lets this banter get to him, will begin to doubt himself and feel that he or his equipment won't be equal to the task ahead.

It can get worse out on the course. Let's take an example of two skiers—I'm the aggressor and you're susceptible to psych games. It's a mass start race and we're near each other at the start line. I'm confident and make some seemingly harmless gibes about your wax. The gun is fired and we take off. Angling for a better position, I ski across your skis. You get mad and chase after me, catching up in the woods.

I let you pass me on an uphill and jump in the tracks right behind you. I follow you, letting you expend the most energy as the leader and getting you increasingly nervous. It's much easier to ski behind someone, particularly if the pace is satisfactory, so I sit back there and cool it.

Eventually I start clicking your heels—I let my skis run up on the ends of yours. You ask if I want by and I apologize for the clicking and say no. A while later, I start clicking your heels again, apologize, and refuse to pass. You're getting irritated; your concentration on your race is weakening. If you get mad enough, you might take a whack at me with your ski pole—I've seen this happen a number of times in competition.

On the next downhill, I hop in the other track and blast by you, letting you know that my skis are faster. You catch me on the uphill and I hop back in behind you, again letting you pull me along. The finish line is approaching and I prepare my final move. Near the bottom of a downhill, I yell for the track. You have to step out of the track, losing momentum, while I flash by, accelerating. I pull further away on the next uphill and charge to the finish, leaving you far behind.

You blew it because you lost control of yourself and let me destroy your concentration and dictate your race. You fell for the pressure I exerted and were unable to ski your own race. You should have ignored me, picked a good spot to shake me, or tried some of your own tricks on me.

There are all sorts of tactical ploys the racer will pick up the more he's involved in competition. It's simply a part of the game. You're bound to be involved with other racers on the course, and you must learn how to control yourself and your race, handle tense situations, and make the right decisions without wasting either mental or physical energy. Plus, you must concentrate on every detail of the race for anywhere from 15 minutes to 6 hours.

If someone is following on your heels, one way to get rid of him is to continually switch tracks. He'll have to follow you back and forth from track to track, which will hamper his concentration and confuse him enough so you'll likely be able to lose him on the next opportunity. Another trick is to blow him away mentally by charging every uphill. A guy did this to me in the Birkebeiner. I had much better skis, but after watching him double pole up every gradual hill for 25–30 km, he psyched me out with his strength. He took the fight out of me, and I eventually gave up trying to chase him.

When you're planning to pass someone, pick your spot with care. Evaluate the condition of the track, the other skier's ability, and upcoming difficult sections of the course. You don't want to get caught passing someone of marginal ability on a hairy corner or he could take you out with a fall. Plan ahead when tracking and know the course. Remember, you must call for the track loudly and clearly.

Part of knowing the course is being aware of the condition of each track. When were they reset? Is one track faster than the other? Does one track suffer from marginal snow? Look for the track that will give you the best ride. Don't assume you have to herringbone up a hill. If you have a feel for your wax, you should know if you can run up it. Don't let some track-setting machine or the skiers in front of you determine your tactics. Continually evaluate the conditions and be thinking all the time. Don't wind up at the finish line back in the pack because you failed to attempt something out on the course. Be willing to try new and daring moves. You're trying to gain a fifth of a second here and another fifth there, which will add up by the time you reach the finish. The little tactical moves will make the difference.

Another tip: pay attention to spectators and coaches along the course. They will often provide you with bits of useful information that you can evaluate and use to your advantage. And remember, the tactical ploys related here are only a handful of the hundreds of tactical moves made in competition. The more you race, the more you'll learn about being a tactically smart competitor.

Marathon Tactics

A few special tips are in order for marathon racing. Importantly, be ready to go long before the scheduled start. Often the press of the crowd in back or some overanxious racers in the front will cause the masses to take off before the official start time. With thousands of people involved, there's just no way for the officials to control a false start. Be ready.

Many racers assume that because of the distances involved in marathons continual concentration is not important. I'm convinced you have to concentrate more in a marathon than in a shorter race because the minute you get mentally sloppy you'll be technically sloppy, thereby wasting energy.

During the first four or five kilometers, ski carefully to avoid entanglement with other skiers. Make good moves, seek clear tracks, assert yourself now and then, and pick your way clear of the crowds. During a marathon I work on my transitions carefully because any unnecessary loss of momentum will hurt. When I'm carrying speed into an uphill, I am careful to make a good change-up to keep my momentum. At the top of the downhill, I get into a tuck immediately. Being lazy about getting into a tuck will kill you by the end of the race because losing 40–50 feet of glide on every downhill will add up to over 50–60 km. Be alert and concentrate on getting all the velocity and momentum out of each move.

Keep an overview of the whole race in mind. Don't burn yourself out over the first half trying to get away from the crowd and find yourself exhausted with 25 km to go. Pay attention to your body signs and save energy for that final 10 km, which is where the race actually occurs. A race either comes apart or together for an athlete during the final stretch. If you plan your race right, you can pass more people at the end of the race than you did during the first 20–40 km. But don't cruise to the final stretch—if you get to the last few kilometers and still have a lot of energy left, you've run a bad race.

For many skiers, especially first-time marathoners, the race is simply survival, covering the distance. I don't want to sound like an alarmist, but the potential for disaster in a marathon must be considered. As a marathoner runs out of energy, he becomes very susceptible to the cold. This can reach a point where he loses his bearings, wanders off the trail, and lies down where he can't be found. Therefore, it's important to take advantage of all the services built into good marathons. There should be feed stations every 6–10 km. Don't pass up any feed station. There are also first aid stations and equipment repair stations where you can rewax and repair or replace a broken ski, boot, binding, or pole. Be aware of these services and you've no need to be concerned. Yours isn't a solo effort against the course and the elements because there are people at stations all along the way, all day long, who are there to help you finish.

If you do feel like you're going under, you should know where the next first aid station is from studying the course map ahead of time. Stop, eat some food, climb in a sleeping bag for 10–15 minutes to get your body heat generated. Change to dry clothes if possible. If you feel up to it, finish the race.

One thing a lot of international skiers do in distance races is change to a dry hat during the race. The body's major loss of heat (and energy) is through the head. You won't believe how much better you feel when you change to a dry hat midway on the course.

Unless it's serious, you needn't give up when you feel you're going under. Grab something to eat and plod along. In 1980 at the Birkebeiner, I went under at about 42 km. I struggled along for 5 km and then, probably because of a feed, my body made a comeback. I felt good again and charged on to the finish. Don't get feeling so sorry for yourself when you go under that you ignore a comeback and don't take advantage of it. Watch your body signs throughout the race.

Feeding

In any race of 30 km or more, the race organizers are required to have two feeding stations along the course. Longer races will often have more stations, and the smart athlete will augment this by carrying his own food in a fanny pack or having a coach or someone out on the course with some.

I always carry my own feed in a long race and have found that a small baby bottle works well. In case I happen to miss a feed or feel that my body needs something extra, I'm prepared.

Don't pass by a single feeding station unless you're carrying two or three feeds of your own. I take every bit of food I get my hands on in a race, and the time spent is well worth it. If you pass a station in hopes of gaining time on the next guy, forget it. You'll pay for it later when he has the energy to pass you and you're hitting the wall.

Carrying your own feed in a distance event can pay big dividends and may save the race for you. Here I'm drinking out of a small baby bottle on a gradual downhill. The bottle is kept in the fanny pack.

A long race doesn't really begin until the final 10 km. Everything you do to get yourself to that last leg in good shape is to your benefit. Take all the feeds you're offered. Don't refuse feeds from another team's coach, unless you're nervous about the contents. Everything you do until the final leg should be geared to having enough energy so you can actually race through the last 10 km.

Much has been written and said about what is the best feed. There are a lot of good drinks available. A word or two of caution about caffeine: caffeine sometimes causes arrhythmic heartbeats. Sports medicine experts won't test an athlete with an arrhythmic heartbeat from caffeine, so no one should go out and test themselves in a marathon using caffeine as a feed. Check with a doctor or physiologist before you use caffeine.

In addition to feeding with an electrolyte replacement drink, I've found a bit of solid food really helps relieve the sensation of starvation out on the course. Try a donut or some other easily digestible solid to augment your liquid feeds.

Sprint Race Tactics

For women, sprints are 5-km races and 5-km legs in relays. For men, anything under 30 km is considered a sprint, including 10-km relay legs and 15-km races. However, just as the 400-m run in track is now considered a sprint rather than a middle-distance event, the 30 km at the international level is becoming more of a sprint event. The tactical effort has changed as racers' conditioning has improved so that a 30 km is often an all-out charge the entire distance.

Because of the immediate effort required in sprints and relays, the prerace warmup is particularly important. Timing is critical; the racer should have only 5–8 minutes to recover and prepare before he's out on the course racing full bore. At any major race, you'll see competitors in the starting gate with their uniforms pretty well soaked from working up a good sweat in warming up. Stretch and do some hard, fast skiing just before your start time.

In sprints, there is simply no time to make the slightest error. You must have the course completely memorized and know exactly where you want to be and how you want to take each section. Momentum is vital, and a hesitation will cost several places in the results. A fall in a women's 5 km is a disaster, especially on the international level. Even if it only takes 10–12 seconds to get up and going, you could lose 5–15 places in the results just from this error.

In sprints, concentration shouldn't be a problem because of the relatively short time involved in covering the course. You simply must be aware and alert every second and take advantage of every situation to gain those fractions of a second that will gain you a better finish.

Relay Tactics

Not only are relays the most exciting races to watch in cross-country skiing, but they are a real event for the competitor. When a racer puts on a bib for a relay, somehow he becomes a different person. Perhaps it's pride in the nation, division, or area the team represents or simply the fact that two or three other people are depending on him for the team effort. Whatever the reason, the relay racer becomes an animal, particularly in international racing. There is no love lost between competitors, and the boundaries of the rules are overstepped more often than not.

With poles and skis kicking up the snow, racers charge from the start at the 1978 Putney Relays. Be ready to fight for position.

This is the straddle relay tag being executed by Tim Caldwell and Doug Peterson, foreground, during the international meet at Val Gardena, Italy, in 1977. Caldwell is giving Peterson a good shove to get him underway. Note the vintage one-piece knicker suits.

The starts are, other than mass marathon starts, the wildest happening in ski competition. With the number of false starts, you'd think a ski relay was a 100-yard dash. In the 1977 men's relay at the Pre-World Championships in Lahti, Finland, the officials made the mistake of having both the scoreboard and the starter announce the countdown for the start. The scoreboard got ahead of the official starter, and when the starter got to "go" the racers were long gone. The racers had covered almost a kilometer before they were stopped.

In vying for position, the racers will resort to almost anything. They'll cut people off, ski over tips, ride up on the backs of skis, knock people down or off the track, and stab at them with poles. It's incredible.

The last major meet before the 1976 Olympics was at Reit im Winkl, West Germany. Thirty teams started the relay and by the final leg, 23 teams were bunched together—12 skiers in one track and 11 in the other, skiing tips-to-tails. I yelled at the three U.S. skiers in the pack that the race would come down to a final sprint over the last kilometer or two, which is what happened. Within about 400 meters of the finish, an Austrian tried to pass an Italian near where I was standing. The Austrian screamed and yelled for the track two or three times, but the Italian wouldn't budge. The Austrian got so frustrated that he stabbed his ski pole into the Italian's rear end; he didn't just tap the guy, but sunk it in. Nonetheless, the Italian continued to refuse to give up the track. A protest was lodged after the race, and the Italian team was disqualified. I never did hear how long it took his fanny to heal.

This sort of tactic isn't limited to men, nor is it new. In reviewing films of the women's relay at the 1964 Olympics, I saw one woman whack another on the side of her head with a ski pole when the latter failed to relinquish the track quickly enough.

Regarding tagging, the FIS rule states that one's hand must touch some part of his teammate's body, not his equipment, within the tag zone for a legal tag. There are two basic methods for tagging. The finishing skier will ski up to the side of his teammate and touch him while he is beginning to get underway. A method used successfully by the U.S. team is to ski behind the person to be tagged with your skis outside of his. Instead of simply tagging him, you give him a big shove to enhance his momentum through the tag zone. This method takes a bit of practice to avoid mixups, but it's perfectly legal.

Wax Problems

There isn't a ski racer who hasn't gotten into a race only to discover he's missed the wax. Just keep in mind that when you've got bad wax, it's likely that you're not alone. Everyone in the race is facing the same difficult conditions. Don't give up. Stop and rewax, knock the ice off your skis, or do whatever it takes to get going again. You'll find out at the finish line that 90% of the other skiers were having the same problems.

I remember the North American 15-km Championship back in 1975. Waxing was nearly impossible. During the race, which involved a fairly strong field of Europeans, a couple of the U.S. guys considered quitting. Bill Koch was one because he had to stop and rewax and then stopped again, took his skis off, and knocked them against a tree to get rid of the ice. He continued on and finished second. He was totally amazed with his result until he realized that all the other racers, Europeans included, were having the same problems.

One trick to remember is that you don't have to stay in the tracks. Track-setting equipment usually leaves the snow between and beside the tracks as hard or harder than the snow in the tracks. After being skied, tracks can be mushy or glazed and your wax might not work as well as you planned, so ski between the tracks or on the edge of the packed area and your otherwise marginal wax may work fine.

DEALING WITH TRAVEL

Travel is a fact of life for the ski racer. The sooner you accept having to move around from race to race, the better off you'll be—and the better your results will be. Compared with Europeans, Americans seem to get unnecessarily upset about traveling. If you plan your trips well, are organized and prepared to adjust, you'll be ready to race with no ill effects of being on the road. Simply accept the minor hassles and inconveniences of being away from home and adjust to new situations without losing stride and your focus on the point of the trip, racing.

Planning and Packing

As a competitor, you should be aware of your race schedule for the season well in advance. Get an early start on mapping out an itinerary for each trip, making reservations, and accumulating the materials and gear you'll need to take along.

If your trip involves a plane flight, book space well in advance. This will avoid a last-minute panic and is likely to save you money. Talk to a travel agent to find out the discount fares, excursion rates, and breaks for booking 30–60 days in advance. On an international flight, buying your ticket well in advance can save you a couple hundred dollars. If you're going with a team or can organize a group, the fare is also likely to be less.

Get hotel reservations in advance as well. Race sites get booked up quickly, and the earlier you make a reservation the more likely you'll find a place you like, close to the race and within your budget.

Don't forget to send in your entry form for the competition. Get a phone number for the race organizer so you'll be able to call ahead to find out the logistics of the event. The money spent on the telephone will make your travel and organization that much easier. Ask about things like places to eat, starting times, waxing facilities, location of the race, and any changes from the announced schedule.

For international travel, you'll need a passport. Get this before the season starts whether you're certain of a trip to Europe or not. It takes two or three weeks to get one, so you want to be ready if a trip abroad comes along. If you've already got a passport, make certain it won't expire during the season. Passports are good for five years. If you will be traveling behind the Iron Curtain or to any politically sensitive areas, you'll need a visa for each country. Without them you'll either waste a lot of time at the border or be refused entry entirely. It's best to get them in advance.

For international competitions, it's wise to obtain an international racing license from the U.S. Ski Team. This gives you the seal of approval from your national federation to compete in foreign events and will give you an additional identification to satisfy race organizers. Not all events will require such a license, but it's best to be prepared. You don't need one for World Loppet League events, for example, but while you're in Europe you may decide to enter another race that does require a license.

Take plenty of money with you—perhaps a bit more than you think you'll need, especially if you're traveling where you won't be able to cash checks. A credit card is good insurance for unexpected expenses. Travelers checks are insurance against theft or loss of money. I always feel more comfortable with travelers checks than carrying around a big wad of cash.

When traveling abroad, one of the first things to do when you enter a country is exchange your dollars for the local currency. Do this at the airport or a bank—some official exchange—where you'll get the best rates. Don't get caught without the correct currency or it will cost you. The locals may take your dollars, but not at a fair exchange rate.

Plan carefully when you're packing your bags. Consider the expected social obligations, race banquets, etc., so you'll have appropriate clothes. Don't take anything you aren't certain you'll need; travel light because it's hard enough toting a ski bag and suitcase around without getting bogged down with extraneous stuff you don't use. If you've got too many bags or are over the weight limit, it could cost you money at the airport. When you pack your ski bag, do it carefully to avoid damage to your equipment when bags get thrown around or banged about on top of a car.

When packing your wax kit, keep in mind that it's a $10,000 fine if you get caught with a propane or butane tank on airplanes. If you're going to Europe, propane can be hard to find and heads for the torches fit differently in Europe than in the U.S. Butane is widely available in Europe, so pack an appropriate torch head. When you're traveling with a group, cut down on baggage by consolidating your wax kits into one.

If you're traveling on public transportation, be certain to lock all your bags or at least secure the zippers on your ski bag and the latch on your wax kit. This will help prevent theft of your luggage. Also be certain that your name and address is written clearly and firmly attached to each bag.

When you get to the airport, check your luggage through to the final destination. Be certain the attendant marks the tags legibly so you don't end up at the race site without your gear. Checking your bags through from your local airport might also eliminate over-weight charges. If you travel with a group, let the airlines know you're coming with a great deal of gear and ski bags. Some airlines are pretty restrictive about weight limits, so it's wise to contact them and, hopefully, work out some arrangement so you don't get stuck with a huge overweight charge.

A couple of things to pack would be road maps and good directions to the race site. A converter for electric current is a must if you're traveling abroad because the voltage in Europe is different from that in the U.S. You won't be able to use your iron, tape deck, blow dryer, electric razor, etc., without an adapter.

Adjusting

Don't get uptight about facing a new environment when you travel, particularly to Europe. After you get there you'll soon discover that the language and the color of the money are the only major differences. European cars run on gas and have four wheels, and skiers throughout the world put on their racing uniforms one leg at a time. Language is less and less a problem in Europe than it was in the 1960s when I first went over. If you do take up a language, learn German because it is the language of ski competition.

The big concern for skiers taking long trips from the States to Europe or to the East coast from Alaska is adjusting to the time change. When I traveled with the U.S. team, we figured that it took about a day of recuperation for each hour of time change. It's a lot easier, for some reason, to travel from east to west and the adjustment isn't as difficult. But it simply takes time to get your body into the local schedule of sleeping and eating.

We tried all sorts of methods and tricks when I traveled to Europe with the U.S. team. With good planning, regaining your rhythm and balance to a new time zone can be less painful. Five or six days before a long trip, start adjusting your eating and sleeping habits slowly toward the time zone of the race site. Go to bed later, get up later, eat your meals later. Eat a good meal before you board the plane and sleep during the entire flight. Try to get some empty seats around you (which is increasingly difficult) so you can be comfort-able. Don't eat on the plane or watch the movie. Just sleep. Some of the skiers on the U.S. team take mild sleeping pills for long plane trips.

Upon arrival at your destination, immediately assume the rhythm of the time zone. Eat when it's meal time and don't go to bed until it's bedtime. This latter step might be a bit tough, but it's the best way to get rapidly acclimated. Take a walk or a light jog and relax, but don't take a nap. When the local bedtime does roll around, you might have trouble getting to sleep after the tension and excitement of the trip, or you might wake up in the middle of the night because your body's clock hasn't adjusted yet. Read or do something to relax. I don't want to recommend them, but a lot of skiers use sleeping pills because this first night's adjustment is crucial. Don't take them the night before a race, though.

The next day should be a bit better. You can train and get ready for the first race. If you have a good workout, you might take a short 15- or 20-minute nap. As time goes on and your body clock is adjusted to the time zone, you can increase the length of your naps. After two or three days, you should be pretty well adjusted, back into your regular training routine, and sleeping and eating on schedule.

The Suitcase Mentality

The more serious you get about racing, the more time you'll spend away from home, living out of a suitcase for long periods, staying in strange beds, and depending on restaurants for food. Accept it, get into it, be flexible in dealing with whatever hassles come up, and learn to enjoy yourself. But don't lose sight of your purpose; keep your mind in focus on racing.

There's no sense sitting around feeling sorry for yourself or complaining about different cultures, different foods, and different lifestyles. Get rid of psychological barriers and appreciate the experience.

Lots of people view the life on the national team as pretty glamorous. The skiers are traveling all over the world and seeing sights and meeting people that most folks only dream about. In fact, this is a very inaccurate picture of life on the team. The scope of the serious racer's world is limited—it has to be. He is spending so much time training, racing, and traveling that he only has time to rest in between. His excursions to museums, operas, and other sightseeing places are few and far between. International racers spend most of their free time resting in a controlled situation so they are ready to race and train. Besides, after two or three trips to Europe, the excitement seems to wane for the serious racer. He gets into a regimen of sleep, eat, train, rest, race, travel.

Life off skis for the elite racer can actually become boring. He's stuck in obscure places for long training camps and often has a lot of time on his hands between races. It's important in these types of situations that you learn how to relax and keep occupied. Don't lie around in bed, sleeping out of sync with the clock. The smart athlete will get involved with light activities to pass the time.

Much of your off-ski time will be spent working on your equipment. Otherwise, the individual can get involved in a variety of activities suited to his taste while on the road. Take advantage of your situation and get to know the area you're visiting. Short sightseeing trips are a good break. A lot of skiers are amateur photographers. Some keep travel diaries and combine them with their photos for slide shows when they get back home. Read the local newspaper and watch TV; even if you don't know the language you'll be able to follow the names, particularly in sports. A number of countries carry old American TV programs, and U.S. movies are frequently shown in local theaters. Find a hobby you can take with you that doesn't fill up your suitcase. Read books. Play backgammon, chess, or cards. Listen to music. Just don't let your mind stagnate while away from home for long periods. Keep active and know how to relax so you can focus your main energy on competition.

SPECIAL CONCERNS OF THE RACER

In addition to all the other aspects of cross-country skiing that occupy your time and mental energy during the racing season, you must be aware of other special concerns that will affect your success. You have to control your diet so your body will be ready for competition. You must take care to rest and recover from training and racing properly. You must understand the affects of training and racing at altitude.

Diet and Weight Control

Most sports medicine experts and physiologists agree that no special diet is necessary for the North American athlete. We are fortunate to live in a society where good food is plentiful and where a balanced diet will provide the athlete with the necessary nutrients to satisfy his bodily needs. The main concern for women is controlling their weight; for men it is ingesting enough calories.

Men in a strenuous training program normally use up as many calories as they consume. Top male skiers ingest 5,000–7,000 calories daily, yet their bodies are only 6%–10% fat, compared with the national male average of 15 % body fat. A nutrition expert told the men on the U.S. team that it didn't really matter what they ate because they eat so much they are bound to get all the vitamins, minerals, and nutrients they need.

On the other hand, the average female racer's body composition should be 13%–18% fat. The national average for women is 25%. Because of this fat content, women skiers shouldn't consume more than 3,000–3,500 calories a day. The intake for men and women will, of course, be lower for skiers not on a heavy training program.

Low body fat is part of reaching optimum conditioning levels. Admittedly, it's difficult for the athlete to limit eating, particularly when so many other things are sacrificed to be successful as a skier. Most women skiers simply have to control their weight. This means counting calories.

If you need to lose weight, the best advice is to see a doctor for a good diet. If you need to lose 10 or 15 pounds, don't try to take it off fast if you're in a training program. An ideal program would reduce about two pounds a week. More pounds off in a week and you'll be removing muscle tissue at the same time as you reduce your body fat, which is obviously not in your best interest. Taking off weight is often a slow or impossible process for someone in training because fat is often translated into muscle and muscle weighs more than fat. The way your clothing fits is often a better indicator of loss of fat than your weight because your body tightens during a conditioning program. Physiologists use devices known as fat calipers to determine the percentage of fat in one's body. Calipers are the best way to determine if your weight control program is working.

Athletes should stick to balanced diets of good food. Special diets usually end up causing problems for the skier. Not only is it possible that they don't supply enough necessary nutrients, but it's hard to follow them when traveling. If a skier is in Czechoslovakia and he can't get his special vegetarian meal, he'll be in trouble when forced to change his diet.

Before training or racing, most physiologists advise athletes to work on an empty stomach or one well on the way to emptying. Food in the stomach can cause cramps during strenuous exercise because oxygen is being pumped to the working muscles and not to the stomach muscles. Be aware of your individual digestion time and plan ahead before a race or a workout so your food is fairly well digested. Three hours is an average digestive period. Before racing, avoid foods that take a long time to digest such as proteins. And don't be fooled by that old wives' tale about eating a candy bar or honey just before a race—it can actually be harmful.

Carbo Loading. Carbohydrates are one of the prime sources for glycogen, the muscle fuel. Therefore, carbohydrates are particularly important to athletes involved in distance and endurance events. Carbo loading, as it's called among athletes, is a program designed to load the muscles with glycogen.

A few words of caution. Don't try carbo loading without reading what the experts say about it. It's definitely a controversial program and can be dangerous. The theory behind carbo loading is that the muscles can be trained to store more glycogen by depleting their supply of it frequently. Frequency seems to be the key. If the program is followed too often (more than three times a ski season), carbo loading can cause serious, even fatal, kidney damage. Also, most experts agree that carbo loading has only a minimal effect in races lasting 30 minutes or less.

The following method of carbo loading is that used most often by U.S. skiers. Six days before a marathon, the athlete takes a very hard workout that depletes the glycogen stores in the muscles. Some skiers work out hard two days in a row for a double depletion effect. For the rest of the week preceding the race, the skier packs in the carbos and trains easily. If his normal diet is one-third meat, one-third vegetables, and one-third carbohydrates, the athlete will alter his diet to three-fifths carbos and one-fifth each of vegetables and meat (sticking to light meats such as chicken and fish). Carbos include foods like spaghetti, bread, potatoes, starches, and rich desserts. Some carbo loading plans call for the athlete to limit his carbo loading for three days after the strenuous exercise, then load up.

There are other, less drastic methods to build up carbohydrates than carbo loading. Many distance athletes don't like loading for several reasons, including the fact that too much time is spent in easy training. Athletes in serious training deplete naturally in training anyway. Many skiers simply eat more carbos during the two days before a race.

Rest and Recovery

Rest and recovery are among the athlete's major concerns during the hectic racing season. I've seen all too many skiers go under mid-season because they haven't taken proper care of themselves. Don't throw away the season and all the time and effort you've put in preparing for it by ignoring your body's need for rest.

The best clue that you're tired comes from monitoring your resting pulse rate each day. If your pulse is elevated for two or three days, take a day off and rest. A well-planned break is certainly better than four or five days wasted being sick.

Many beginning racers don't understand that rest must become a part of their daily regimen as their training and racing loads increase. The amount of energy required to work out two or three hours a day must be compensated by a nap or mid-day rest period and a good night's sleep. This goes on day after day after day: train, rest, train, sleep, race, rest, train, sleep. It's a fact of the racer's life and there are no two ways about it.

Your training log, your coach, and your pulse will tell you when you're tired psychologically or tired physiologically. Adjust your program, take a break, get some rest before you get sick. Plan rest periods into your month, and you'll end up with a stable program.

As a rule of thumb, U.S. Ski Team members try to spend one hour in bed for ever hour out on the course, particularly after a race. Be organized after competition so you can recover. Drink replacement fluids at a medium temperature immediately after a race. Change to dry clothing and ski a few kilometers to warm down. While you are skiing, think about the race and how you performed. Then take a shower and a nap. Get up and eat a light meal. Take a walk. Eat some more light foods. Do some stretching. Go to bed.

Don't get into the reward syndrome after completing a race. Many skiers think it's award time, so they overeat, overdrink, and underrest. Recovery from a race is just like working into racing—you have to go slow and easy. Your body can't tolerate huge meals right away; eat four or five light meals the day after a big race rather than three heavy meals. Get plenty of rest and sleep. Stretch those muscles so they'll be ready to perform for you again. Watch your pulse rate and train easily until you feel ready to go again.

Remember that the guy who finishes 900th in a marathon or citizen race may have expended as much energy as the winner. Both of them need to take care of themselves. When you're fatigued and cold, your resistance is way down. Getting sick is a real setback, so take care of yourself. It's fun to enjoy the camaraderie, the spirit at the finish line and at the awards ceremony, but it's more important to change your clothes, replenish fluids, warm down, and rest.

Racing and Training at Altitude

For every bad story you may have heard about skiing at high altitudes, I've heard a good one. I approve of training at altitude. We used altitude wisely and successfully in preparation for the 1976 Olympics, and the Europeans have grown increasingly enamored with altitude training in readying for important competition. The Finns, Russians, Swedes, East Germans, and West Germans all spent two or three weeks at high altitude before coming to Lake Placid for the 1980 Olympics. Based on these teams' results, they must be on to something.

Athletes, particularly in track circles, hear a great deal about blood doping. It's alleged that some runners have about a pint of blood taken out of them five or six weeks before a major competition. A few days before they want to perform at their maximum, they are given a transfusion of their own blood. The purpose is to increase the volume of the blood and thereby the hemoglobin in the system. Hemoglobin gives the blood its ability to carry oxygen to the muscle cell.

Training at altitude is natural blood doping because it increases the amount of hemoglobin in the bloodstream, thus enhancing oxygen uptake capacity. Because there is less oxygen in the air at higher elevations, your body is forced to adjust. The first sign is that you breathe faster when training at altitude. The next effect is an increase in the amount of hemoglobin in the blood, which improves the body's maximum oxygen uptake ability.

As an example, Doug Peterson's oxygen uptake improved dramatically in the fall of 1979 after training in Europe on glaciers at 8,000 feet and above. Dr. Bob Arnot of the U.S. team's sports medicine group tested Doug before he left for Europe and found his oxygen uptake was 85 ml/kg. When Doug returned from a month of training at altitude, Arnot tested him again and Doug scored a high rate of 93 ml/kg. After another five weeks, in which Doug was training intensely at low altitude, his oxygen uptake level was 88 ml/kg.

Under his closely monitored program, Peterson improved his workload capacity through training at altitude, as demonstrated by the lasting improvement in his oxygen uptake maximum. He gained the benefits of blood doping by natural means and was able to increase his workload because of his improved ability to take in and efficiently use oxygen.

Training and racing at altitude must be done with a carefully controlled program to obtain the benefits. Be smart and give your body time to adjust. During the first two or three days at altitude, adjust by reducing the volume and intensity of your training. The most important thing is to get plenty of rest because it will take your body more time to rebuild its depleted reserves. As your body adjusts, you can gradually increase your pace and your volume, but watch your body signs, particularly your pulse rate, before making increases. If you have any kind of conditioning base, your body will be fully acclimatized to the altitude after a week or 10 days, or perhaps less.

One piece of advice from the physiologists: don't train at altitudes above 9,000 feet. At this elevation, you have to greatly reduce your volume and intensity and it's likely that any benefits will be negated by fatigue and the length of recovery time. Extended sessions at altitudes below 9,000 feet can have the same effect.

A couple of weeks of altitude training should be followed with a good dose of interval work at low elevation to gain the full and lasting benefits from the oxygen uptake increase. The athlete needs to readjust his tempo when returning to low altitude, and this is best done through intensity training. Further, full recovery from altitude training requires a reduction in the volume of training, so endurance workouts should be reduced. The blood doping effect of altitude training will be continued and the conditioning level will be improved by intensity work at low elevation.

Racing at altitude creates even more controversy and debate than altitude training. Some folks were so adamant about it in 1980 that the Central Division cross-country skiers weren't allowed to compete in the U.S. Junior National Championships at Devil's Thumb, Colorado. This was an unfortunate overreaction that cost the athletes their well-deserved opportunity to race in their major competition of the season.

I'm not saying that athletes who live at altitude don't have an advantage over low-landers when racing at high elevations. But this advantage can be balanced out if the lowlanders are given the opportunity of a week or 10 days to adjust to altitude. There certainly have been many instances when well-conditioned racers have arrived at altitude and competed successfully after only two or three days of adjustment.

When racing at altitude, be open minded and don't believe all the wild stories about the problems you face. Experience altitude and its effects for yourself. Be cool about it and don't panic. Talk to others about how they've made the necessary adjustments and draw your own conclusions.

On race day, it is more important than ever to warm up before the event when you're at altitude. Prepare your body for the effort so it will be ready and aware of the demands. The next consideration is to work yourself into the race. Don't blast out of the start and put yourself under with an oxygen debt from which you can't recover. Hold back a bit and ease into the race over the first kilometer or so. After the race, be certain to get plenty of rest.

Results from junior national competition at altitude have convinced me that the advantages of racers who live at elevation are actually minimal. They can't ski any faster than the lowlander who is in control of himself, has had at least a couple of days to adjust, and runs a smart race. I've seen too many cases of lowlanders pulling off excellent races at altitude to be concerned about competing up there.

Adjusting to altitude is an individual matter. The more highly conditioned athlete will adjust faster. Skiers have an advantage because they are using their full body, so adjustment comes more rapidly. The machines we've got standing on skis now are so efficient and well conditioned that it doesn't take them more than two or three days to adjust and be ready to train at maximum levels to gain the benefits of altitude training.

Put all your training efforts from May to April and from one year to the next to maximum use by being professional in your approach to competition. Be organized, prepared both mentally and physically, and attentive to all those details that divide the hacker from the successful racer. Plan your racing season intelligently. Stay in small ponds until you're a big fish; move into increasingly stiff competition only when you can be fairly successful. Have a goal for each race and treat each realistically—you can't win them all, which doesn't mean you shouldn't try nor be devastated when you don't.

Have a race strategy and carry it through. Memorize the course and ready your equipment. Importantly, ready your mind so you enter the race with a positive attitude that carries you through the stress and problems encountered on the course. The goal in a 10-km race is to reach the 10-km finish line totally spent, having skied well and hard. Don't reach the 9-km point exhausted or have another kilometer of effort left in you at the finish. Learn to balance on the fine line between pushing too hard and not hard enough.

Again, be professional. The strategy, tactics, concerns, and suggestions I've presented in this chapter should be plugged into your winter program. When the season comes, get out there and race—go for it with the professional touches that will make the difference between being an average racer and a racer who reaches his competitive potential.

7

WAXING

The Final Link

After the hundreds of hours and thousands of kilometers of training and preparation, a racer's success often boils down to selecting the correct canister or tube of wax on race day. Waxing is the final link between the racer and the snow; the final link to success in competition. Waxing requires only a fractional amount of the skier's time, but choosing the wrong wax can spell disaster for the competitor. Although races have been won on marginal wax, bad wax is an added burden the skier must work to avoid. No amount of preparation and training can fully compensate for slow skis and no kick during a race.

Waxing fiberglass skis is hard work, requiring a great deal more knowledge and practice than was needed for waxing wooden racing skis. Fortunately, modern equipment and waxes have had an immeasurable effect in producing faster skiers and sounding the death knell for wood skis and pine tar, which no longer have a place in serious skiing.

I've been waxing skis for about 30 years. It's never been easy, but it's always been something I enjoy because waxing is such a great challenge. The advent of fiberglass skis in 1974 has made the waxer's job more complicated than ever, but it's also more satisfying because the waxes developed for Alpine skiing and the modern kicker waxes mean the waxer can do a better job of creating the most efficient ski for every condition.

This chapter is designed to explain all the intricacies of today's waxing. With the correct information and a proper evaluation of the variables involved, modern waxing will provide the best kick and the best glide to keep the racer one stride ahead.

TYPES OF SKIS

Many people fail to wax correctly because they do not understand their skis. Time and again, racers will blame a poor result on bad wax when they've actually selected the wrong skis, not the wrong wax, for the conditions.

There are several types of fiberglass racing skis, each designed for specific snow conditions. The design is based on factors including the humidity and temperature of the snow, the condition of the snow crystals, the age of the snow, how the tracks are prepared and maintained, and the type of waxes to be used. Each type of ski requires certain waxes or wax combinations that will complement the snow conditions. Powder skis, for example, will not work successfully in granular snow conditions because the kicker wax wears too quickly.

The serious racer should have three types of skis: a soft powder, a hard powder, and a granular snow pair. Although limited in use, many racers also travel with a pair of waxless skis.

Soft powder skis are designed for use when the snow temperature is between −9° and −1° C (15°–30° F). The ski is very flexible, or soft, in order to maximize the contact between the kicker wax and the soft snow. Most soft powder skis have a single camber or flex pattern.

Hard powder skis are used in snow temperatures between −18° and −9° C (0°−15° F) when the tracks are hard packed. The ski is slightly double cambered and is not as flexible as the soft powder ski. In these conditions, a stiffer ski is needed to avoid constant contact between the kicker wax and the snow, which causes loss of wax. Also, the stiffer ski is faster in cold conditions because the kicker wax is off the snow during the glide phase. Hard powder skis may also be used in some skare and klister conditions to keep the kicker wax off the snow while gliding.

Granular snow skis, or klister skis, have a true double camber construction with a stiff flex pattern designed for use when the snow is icy and around −18° C (above 0° F). The stiffness of this type of ski minimizes the contact between the kicker wax and the snow, enhancing speed in these conditions. Granular snow skis are also used in klister conditions (0° C when the snow is wet and contains free water), skare conditions (−8° C and below when the snow is harsh and icy), and in heavy binder conditions (when the snow is abrasive).

Waxless skis are an option like another tube of wax in a wax kit. They work in difficult conditions when the temperature hovers around the freezing mark. Although waxless skis had been used successfully just three times in international competition through the 1979 season, they will be an increasing factor as ski manufacturers continue to improve the no-wax base patterns. In testing, mohair bases lose their effectiveness after about 12 kilometers. However, the various milled patterns are getting better and better each year.

PREPARING NEW SKIS

Once you have selected your three pairs of skis, you will need to prepare the bases. The bases must be smooth, receptive to wax, and able to retain it.

Most bases on cross-country racing skis are made of a synthetic known as P-Tex 2000, which has a micropore surface that contains thousands of microscopic pores designed to hold wax. Prepping the base fills the pores with wax, opens pathways into the pores for successive waxing, and determines how the wax is released while skiing. (The friction of the snow on the base of the ski continually pulls wax from the micropore base in the glide areas.)

Bases on most racing skis come from the factories covered with tiny, hair-like filaments known as P-Tex ruff. The ruff increases the base's surface area, thereby exposing more pores to receive the initial coats of wax before the ruff is removed. Some ski companies are now smooth-grinding the bases of their skis at the factory, eliminating the first steps of ski prepping. Only the final stages of sanding or scraping and waxing are needed.

The base on a typical ski. The hairy texture is P-Tex ruff, which must be removed in the prepping process. Some ski companies remove the P-Tex ruff at the factory, but these skis are not race ready. They require either scraping or sanding.

There are currently two techniques in vogue for preparing new bases: scraping and sanding. The first step for any new ski is to clean the base of any dirt with a commercial ski cleaner available from wax companies.

Scraping

The scraping method of base preparation begins with an application of hot Alpine wax over the entire bottom of the ski. Prepping is one of the few times Alpine wax is applied to the camber pocket, or kicker wax zone, of race skis. Using an iron at low heat, spend 3–4 minutes working the wax into the base of one ski. The heat encourages the wax to penetrate the micropores. Some racers also use hair dryers to blow warm air on the ski in an additional effort to ensure wax penetration. A ski warm to the touch on the top surface of the tip and tail sections is a good indicator that the wax is penetrating into the base. Add more wax as it works in. Be certain to keep the iron moving to avoid overheating the base because it is possible to bubble the P-Tex or cause it to separate from the ski if the heat is excessive.

After hot waxing one ski 3–4 minutes, spend an equal amount of time on the other ski. Hot waxing is a slow process, requiring continual ironing and several applications of wax to each ski. When the wax has been thoroughly worked into each ski, let the skis sit for a time to continue the wax penetration. Ideally, the skis should be left in a warm room overnight. Synthetic skis love indirect heat!

Now the skis are ready to be scraped. Spend a little extra money on a quality metal scraper that will hold a good 90° edge. Always keep the edge of the scraper square by using a mill bastard file. If treated well, a good metal scraper will last a racing career.

In scraping the ski base, work in good light with the ski held firmly in a vice or on a ski bench. Always scrape from tip to tail to establish a molecular alignment corresponding to the movement of the skis on snow. Apply thumb pressure to the center of the scraper to make certain it conforms to the base. Properly handled, the scraper will also "true up" the ski bottom so it is square and flat. With long, smooth strokes, firmly remove the penetration layer of wax and the P-Tex ruff.

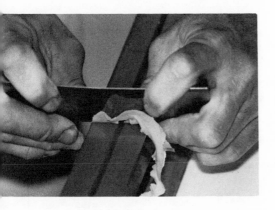

Working from tip to tail, a metal scraper removes the P-Tex ruff and wax and squares the base.

This ski has been prepped. The glide zone (upper portion) is waxed while the camber pocket is ready to receive kicker wax. Note the lines in the groove. These are created when the groove is routed in at the factory and must be smoothed out in the prepping process.

The skis are now ready to receive more wax. After several applications with an iron, remove the wax. This time, use a plastic scraper. (Continued use of the metal scraper can damage the base and alter the squared surface of the ski bottom.) The waxing and scraping continues until the bases are in mid-season form. When the base is properly prepared, it has a shiny appearance.

The final step is to remove the Alpine wax from the camber pocket. Scrape the zone with a metal scraper, then clean the pocket three or four times with wax remover and a rag. Use the remover liberally and be certain the rag or cloth is clean, especially for the final application. The camber pocket will take on a whitish tinge when all the Alpine wax has been removed.

This procedure is the ideal method for scraping new skis. Most people assume the time-consuming process is necessary to develop a fast racing base. However, on many occasions racers have prepped a new pair of skis the night before a successful competition. It's possible to do a good job of prepping a ski in a few hours.

Sanding

Sanding is the most recent technique developed for prepping the bases of new skis. Again, the first step is to clean the base. Obtain several grades of high quality sandpaper, such as Bear Adalox or Tri-M-Ite, which may be used dry or wet on plastic, wood, and metal. Begin with a #100-grit sandpaper wrapped around a rigid, square block. Using long strokes, sand each ski by working from tip to tail. To sand the groove, cover a wooden dowel or a rounded edge of the wooden block with sandpaper. Next, sand the base and groove with #120 sandpaper. The goal of this sanding is to remove the P-Tex ruff and to work a true, or squared, surface into the base by sanding away any irregularities.

From this point in the sanding process, each type of ski is treated a bit differently because each requires a varying degree of smoothness to complement the snow conditions in which each ski will be used.

Follow the specifications in the accompanying chart. If you have only one pair of skis, prep them for snow conditions most typical of the area where you ski.

CHART 12
Sanding Gradients

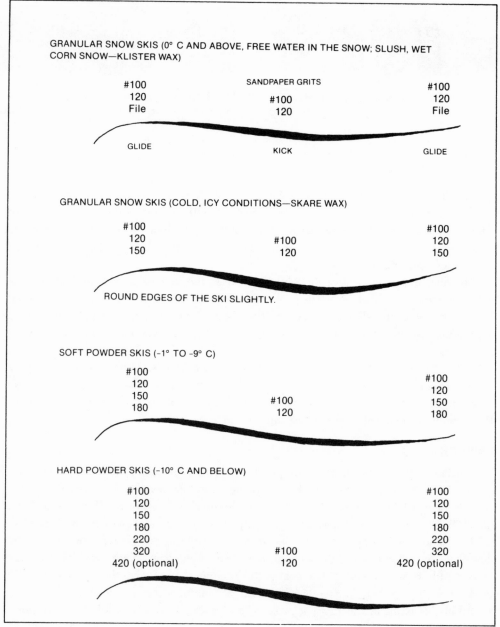

GRANULAR SNOW SKIS (0° C AND ABOVE, FREE WATER IN THE SNOW; SLUSH, WET CORN SNOW—KLISTER WAX)

#100	SANDPAPER GRITS	#100
120	#100	120
File	120	File

GLIDE   KICK   GLIDE

GRANULAR SNOW SKIS (COLD, ICY CONDITIONS—SKARE WAX)

#100		#100
120	#100	120
150	120	150

ROUND EDGES OF THE SKI SLIGHTLY.

SOFT POWDER SKIS (-1° TO -9° C)

#100		#100
120		120
150	#100	150
180	120	180

HARD POWDER SKIS (-10° C AND BELOW)

#100		#100
120		120
150		150
180		180
220		220
320	#100	320
420 (optional)	120	420 (optional)

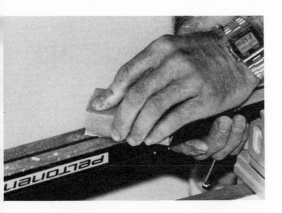

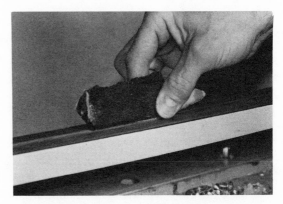

With the ski held firmly in a vise, the base is sanded to remove P-Tex ruff and square the base. Wrap sandpaper around a square, firm block and sand with long, firm strokes.

Prepping the groove with sandpaper. Although some skiers disagree, I believe the groove must be prepped and waxed with the rest of the ski because it is in contact with the snow in both the glide zones and camber pocket. The groove and texture variations must be smoothed.

Granular snow skis are sanded or filed, depending on the type of snow. In very wet conditions, the skis will be filed. Also note that the camber pocket receives a different treatment than the glide zones. Don't forget to sand the grooves with each gradient of sandpaper.

Once the sanding stage is completed, flush each ski with water. This is an important step because the residue of grit created during the sanding process must be removed.

A second step in removing grit is to melt a surface layer of wax onto the base. Do not iron the wax into the base; you're trying to remove the grit, not drive it into the base. Remove the cooled wax and grit with a sharp plastic scraper. Repeat the process until there is no grit residue in the scrapings.

Next, work penetration layers of hot Alpine wax into the glide zones of the base with numerous applications. Scrape the glide zones until shiny. Alpine wax need not be applied to the camber pocket at this stage. In fact, some skiers prep the camber pocket with penetration layers of kicker wax at this point in sanding or after removing the Alpine wax in the scraping process. Select a kicker based on the snow conditions the type of ski is most likely to confront.

Prep Wax Selection

Waxing experts and the wax and ski companies recommend prepping new bases with a soft, red Alpine wax to best penetrate the micropores. I suggest you prep with a wax that will be more compatible with the specific conditions for which each type of ski has been designed. For example, because of the flex characteristics, temperature range, etc., of hard powder skis, they will be waxed with blue Alpine wax 75%–80% of the time. Therefore, it is logical to prep this type of ski with Holmenkol, Falline, or Rex blue Alpine wax, not a red, which is at the other end of the wax spectrum.

Prepping this way gives each type of ski its own personality so it is ready to match the conditions in which it will be most often used. This method avoids mixing incompatible waxes. Although red penetrates more easily, other waxes will do the same job if a bit more time and effort are spent working them in with an iron.

A Note on Prepping Waxless Skis. The glide zones of waxless skis must be prepped and waxed in the same fashion as waxable skis. The same principles apply. Keep in mind that waxless skis will often be used in warm conditions, so wire brushing or filing the glide zones is often in order.

MODERN WAXES

Despite the dramatic changes in cross-country skis since 1974, it's incredible that so many people remain in the waxing Dark Ages. If you race on modern skis, you should use modern wax. The old-fashioned brands (Ex-elit, Vauhti, Ostbye, Bratlie, Stjarnglid, Haka, Jack Rabbit) have not been chemically updated for effective use on synthetic skis. The modern waxes have been developed specifically for the new ski bases. Skiers are simply asking for trouble if they continue to use the old waxes.

Rex, Toko, Swix, Falline, Holmenkol, and Rode are the leaders in the development of modern Alpine and kicking waxes for cross-country skis. These brands incorporate synthetics, resins, and refined oils in their waxes, making the waxes stable, durable, and waterproof. They also have the best characteristics for compatible bonding to the bases of fiberglass skis.

Some of the wax companies also offer separate waxes for the glide zones in addition to Alpine wax. Stay away from these gliders. The components used in glide waxes make them more durable but slower than Alpine waxes because they are not specifically related to temperature. Tests with the U.S. Ski Team proved that Alpine waxes have sufficient durability if applied properly to penetrate the base. They will last 50–70 km in normal conditions.

All the modern brands have the same color codes for kicker waxes based on their temperature suitability. The color coding is consistent for all the brands for all types of kicker waxes—klister, skare, and hard kicker waxes. This means that if Swix blue is selected for the kicker on race day and a skier doesn't have Swix in his wax kit, he can safely substitute a Rex blue kicker.

The number of waxes in each brand line varies somewhat. For example, Holmenkol doesn't have an extra blue and Rex doesn't have a yellow klister. So, there will be times when a racer has to move into a different brand of wax to cover the existing conditions. This is particularly true for Alpine waxes because no one brand has waxes efficient in every temperature range.

Because waxes are developed for conditions in a specific country, blue waxes in one line may, for example, be a little softer than those of a brand developed in another area. Racers need not get terribly concerned about this variation because it is slight—perhaps a difference of one or two degrees centigrade. Having kick won't be the problem, so go with the faster wax.

However, as we move into the 1980s, the companies are broadening their lines to meet all conditions. Waxes are growing increasingly specific for each condition. Currently, for example, the ranges for purple and extra blue overlap each other. Eventually, there will be a new wax developed that will specifically fit the conditions between purple and extra blue. The idea of more waxes seems, at first, to add complexity to the already difficult job of wax selection. However, the availability of more specific waxes will actually make wax selection less complicated. More waxes will reduce the need for mixing waxes as the companies isolate wax hardness.

In addition to developing more specific waxes, some waxes are developed for certain race situations. Special red was developed by Swix for conditions at Lahti, Finland, during the 1978 World Championships. (Of course, the wax was available only to the Norwegian team during the meet.)

SELECTING THE CORRECT RACE WAXES

There are no secrets to waxing. Waxing correctly simply requires hard work. You hustle around, dig out all the bits of objective criteria, plug them into the mini-computer that sits on top of your shoulders, evaluate the information, and come up with the right wax.

In selecting waxes, be objective and flexible. Don't get locked into one brand and ignore the others. Don't let anyone tell you you can't try something new. Keep thinking all the time and don't get backed into corners with preconceived notions of what will work. Many experts remember all the wax combinations they have ever used and try to reapply them. My advice is to treat each race day as a new day for waxing and work with only those conditions in mind.

The goal of waxing is to develop the most efficient ski possible. As a coach and racer, I know how important it is to have the fastest, best kicking pair of skis in the race. To achieve this goal, the waxer must be concerned with the following variables in selecting both Alpine and kicker waxes: snow and atmospheric conditions, course profile, racer's technique, and the type of ski selected for the conditions.

Snow and Atmospheric Conditions

The prime variables to consider on race day are the snow and the weather. These provide the most objective wax selection criteria. Pay attention to the local and national weather reports to be aware of forecasted trends and weather changes.

Temperature. Temperature is the most important waxing criteria and the one 99% of waxers would choose if they had only one selection criteria to pick a wax.

Establish both the air and snow temperatures. (Most racers and coaches work in centigrade.) Keep in mind that snow temperature lags behind air temperature about one or two hours. If the snow is signifiantly colder than the air early on race day, it is safe to assume it will warm up to the air temperature by race time. The reverse is also true—if the snow temperature is considerably warmer than the air, you can assume the snow will cool down to the air temperature. Wax toward the air temperature. If the air temperature is above freezing and has been for a few hours, you needn't bother to check the snow temperature. The snow will be 0° C no matter how high the air temperature rises.

Humidity. Humidity is almost as valuable in wax selection as temperature but is often ignored. If you don't have a hygroscope, the weather report will tell you the relative humidity (the percentage of moisture in the air).

As a rule of thumb, use warmer wax in high humidity and colder wax in low humidity. The humidity is frequently low at high elevations. For example, if it's −5° C at Telemark, Wisconsin (elevation 1,500 feet), and the snow called for a special red or purple, the same temperatures at 9,000 feet in the Rocky Mountains would likely call for a green or special green simply due to the low humidity.

Snow Age. The age of the snow must be considered in selecting wax. New snow crystals have sharp points and a higher moisture content, so a harder wax is appropriate. Older snow is drier and has more rounded crystals, so a softer wax is in order. For example, based on humidity and temperature, you may have selected an Alpine wax combination of red and blue. If the snow has a sharp crystalline structure, add a white paraffin to the red-blue combination. The paraffin hardens the combination, which, in turn, halts the drag effect of the sharp points digging into a softer wax.

Trail Grooming. No matter what the age of the snow, how it has been groomed will affect the performance of the wax. What grooming equipment is used to set the tracks? How much have the tracks been skied? When were the tracks set?

Snow crystal configuration can be drastically modified when groomed with the modern track-setting equipment. Well-tracked and maintained snow is to the waxer's advantage because snow conditions throughout the course will be faster and more consistent. The crystals in groomed snow are more rounded and more tightly packed.

How the snow is groomed may not appear to be vital, but during the 30-km race at the 1976 Olympics it certainly was. The organizing committee had assured us the tracks would be reset the night before the race. On race day, as U.S. team member Ron Yeager skied out to set up a feeding station, he radioed us in the waxing hut to report that the tracks had not been reset and were, therefore, icier than we had anticipated. We had been debating whether to add a binder to the kick zone. Yeager's information convinced us a binder was necessary. Bill Koch went out and won his silver metal with the binder on.

Course Profiles

Organizers of most major races in the U.S. and all European events have course profiles available to competitors and coaches. Get one and study it as part of your wax selection procedure and race preparation. Even if you ski the course before the race, the profile is useful in waxing and planning your support.

Flatter courses, such as the Lake Placid Olympic trails, will allow you to wax a faster ski; you won't need as much kick, so you can wax for glide. On the other hand, a more undulating course, such as the World Cup trail at Telemark, will require a better climbing ski. In this case, consider waxing thicker, softer, and longer in the camber pocket.

Technique

Your technique will influence wax selection. Also, final adjustments in applying the kicker wax are determined by an individual skier's ability and technique.

Once the wax is on, however, the technique you use will be a function of the way the wax works. If the waxing job is less than perfect, the skier must adjust his technique to make the best of his wax job. After the race had started in the 1980 Eastern Championships, I realized that my kicker was too long for the conditions. I adjusted my technique so that my weight was further back than normal. This adjustment gave me a better glide because I wasn't putting as much pressure on the kicker zone as I skied.

The racer often finds himself in conditions requiring a technique modification because it's unlikely snow conditions will be uniform throughout the course. He has to ski differently when he hits a patch of snow exposed to the sun than he skis in the woods.

Choosing Skis

After every race, there is always talk about how this coach or that racer missed the wax. However, the ski is "missed" as often as the wax. The racer must carefully consider all the options in selecting the type of ski to be used on race day. Be flexible in selecting skis; don't go with a soft powder if the snow crystals tell you a granular ski will be more efficient.

Wax Selection Guidelines

Following are three charts that I devised as guidelines for selecting Alpine waxes, hard waxes, and skare/klister waxes. The charts are simply guidelines—basic parameters for wax selection. With all the variables to consider when choosing a wax or wax combination, exceptions to the rules of the chart are always possible. When using the charts, don't ignore the other variables involved in wax selection.

Alpine Wax Selection Chart. Five companies currently produce Alpine wax suitable for use on the glide zones of fiberglass cross-country racing skis: Swix, Toko, Holmenkol, Falline, and Rex. Chart 13 isolates the temperature range in which each brand is useful.

The Alpine chart isolates only the temperature ranges of each brand and does not include color ranges within each brand. Each brand of Alpine wax has its own color coding system, and each company provides its own color breakdown in charts that come with the wax. When the waxer has established the temperature range for the day, he selects a brand line(s) appropriate to the temperature. To choose the appropriate wax within each brand, the waxer must use the selection charts provided by each company because the coding system is not consistent throughout the five brands.

The skier should stock his wax kit with brands of wax most suited to the conditions in his area. Because of the prevailing temperature, humidity, and snow conditions of the Northwest, a Seattle skier will rely mostly on Swix and Toko. Someone in Wisconsin would most often use Holmenkol, Falline, or Rex. If the skier travels, he needs to expand the number of brand lines in his wax kit. I always travel with Holmenkol, because it is a mid-range wax. I also carry waxes on each side of the Holmenkol range—a warmer brand and a colder brand—to cover the other ranges I'm likely to encounter. I keep each company's wax chart taped to the top of my wax kit for easy reference.

There is a great deal of overlap in the ranges of the Alpine waxes. Testing and evaluation of other selection criteria come to play in determining the best wax on race day.

Kicker Wax Selection Charts. The two charts for kicker waxes are used with the six brands of modern kicker waxes: Toko, Swix, Falline, Rode, Rex, and Holmenkol. These waxes—including hard waxes, klisters, and skares—are color coded, and the coding is consistent in all the brands. The charts I've devised are based on temperature but are broken down between hard waxes and klister/skares, with each chart further divided based on the condition of the snow.

On the charts, each color of wax has an optimum and an extreme temperature range for the snow condition indicated. The optimum range is the temperature zone where the color of wax is most likely to be used alone. As the temperature moves to the extreme range of each color, the wax is more likely to be used in combination with another color. In other words, don't jump to the next color of wax when the optimum temperature for one color is exceeded; the wax may still be the best kicker or it may be best if used in combination with another color.

CHART 13
Alpine Waxes (Glide Zone)

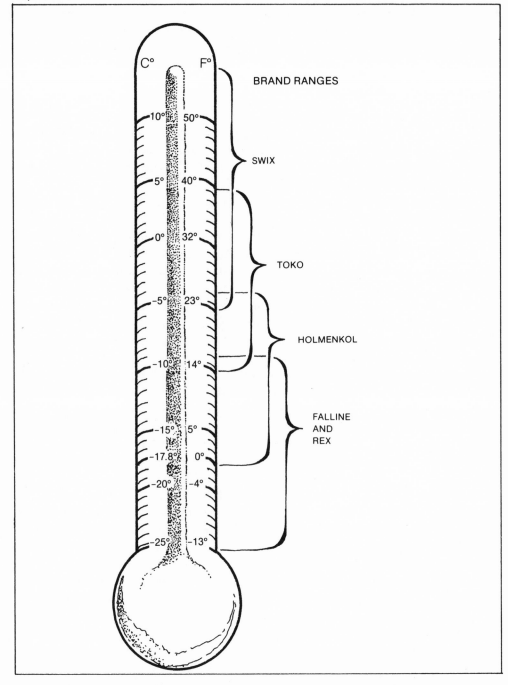

CHART 14
Hard Waxes

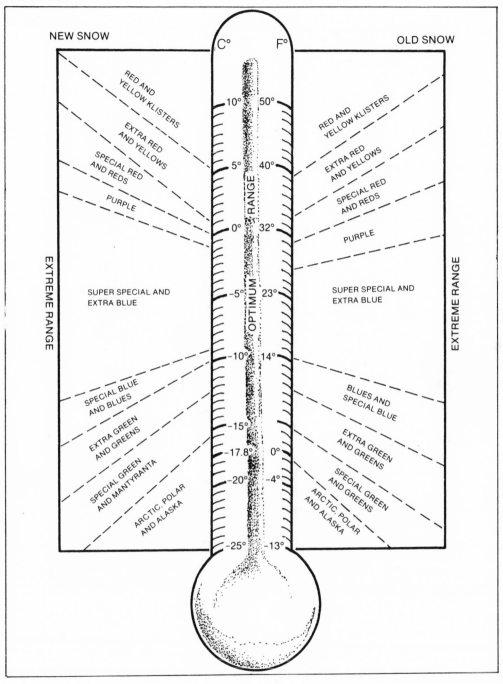

NEW SNOW

OLD SNOW

C° F°

RED AND
YELLOW KLISTERS

10° 50°

RED AND
YELLOW KLISTERS

EXTRA RED
AND YELLOWS

5° 40°

EXTRA RED
AND YELLOWS

SPECIAL RED
AND REDS

SPECIAL RED
AND REDS

PURPLE

0° 32°

OPTIMUM RANGE

PURPLE

EXTREME RANGE

SUPER SPECIAL AND
EXTRA BLUE

−5° 23°

SUPER SPECIAL AND
EXTRA BLUE

EXTREME RANGE

−10° 14°

SPECIAL BLUE
AND BLUES

BLUES AND
SPECIAL BLUE

EXTRA GREEN
AND GREENS

−15°

EXTRA GREEN
AND GREENS

SPECIAL GREEN
AND MANTYRANTA

−17.8° 0°

−20° −4°

SPECIAL GREEN
AND GREENS

ARCTIC, POLAR
AND ALASKA

ARCTIC, POLAR
AND ALASKA

−25° −13°

CHART 15
Skares and Klisters

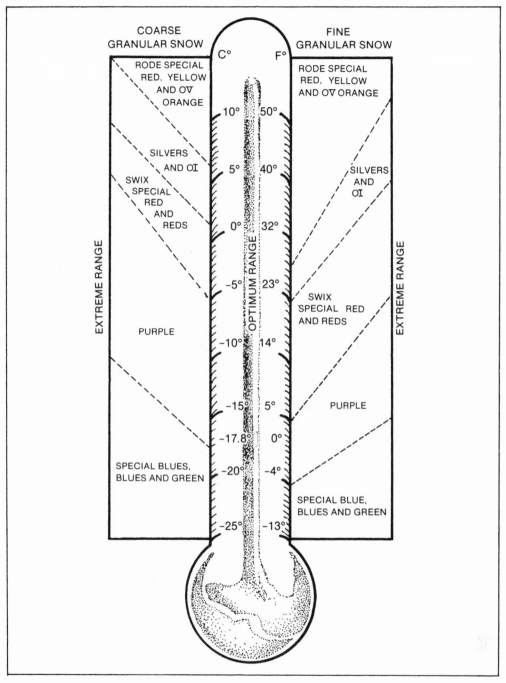

COARSE
GRANULAR SNOW

FINE
GRANULAR SNOW

C°   F°

RODE SPECIAL
RED, YELLOW
AND OV ORANGE

RODE SPECIAL
RED, YELLOW
AND OV ORANGE

SILVERS
AND OI

SWIX
SPECIAL
RED
AND
REDS

SILVERS
AND
OI

SWIX
SPECIAL RED
AND REDS

EXTREME RANGE

EXTREME RANGE

OPTIMUM RANGE

PURPLE

PURPLE

10°   50°
5°   40°
0°   32°
-5°   23°
-10°   14°
-15°   5°
-17.8°   0°
-20°   -4°
-25°   -13°

SPECIAL BLUES,
BLUES AND GREEN

SPECIAL BLUE,
BLUES AND GREEN

As an example, assume we have new snow and temperatures around the freezing range. From Chart 14 we see that extra blue hard wax would likely be used alone as the kicker in its optimum range between −3° and −8° C. Extra blue has an extreme range of −12° to 4° C. Therefore, if the temperature is 3° C, the best wax might be a combination of extra blue and purple. As it gets a bit warmer, reds might also be added and perhaps even a yellow. The waxer has to evaluate all the variables involved. If it's 3° C in Colorado, extra blue alone might be the best kicker because low humidity makes the snow act colder than the actual temperature.

Moving to the klister/skare chart, the waxes from purple up through red, yellow, and orange are considered klisters. Skares are the special blues, blues, and greens. The chart is divided by snow granulation. Fine granular snow is most likely to occur in the West because of low humidity. The chart calls for softer waxes at colder temperatures with fine-grained snow because the fine snow crystals require a soft wax to grab and provide kick.

The klister/skare chart (Chart 15) is read the same way as the hard wax chart. For example, as the temperature moves below −10° C in coarse snow, purple klister might be used over a layer of special blue skare. In fine-grained snow at −5° C, you might have a base of special blue with a combination of purple and a special red or red on top.

Skares might further be used in a thin layer as a binder under klisters to prevent softer waxes from rolling over the edges of the ski. I think it's a mistake to use skare as a binder with hard waxes, though. If you're on the proper ski and the temperature is cold, it's best to go with a hard wax binder under a hard wax—it's always faster. Hard wax binders are used to aid wear and the bonding of the hard wax to the skis in granular conditions.

The use of hard wax binders and klisters and skares as binders depends on the snow granulation. If the temperature is around freezing and the tracks are glazing, you might use a red klister as a binder or cushion and then refer to the hard wax chart, which would indicate a purple, a red, or a special red hard wax, or a combination of the three. You have to test the possible waxes and combinations and use your experience in deciding whether to go to a hard wax or stick with a straight klister.

Testing Waxes

Time and matched pairs of skis are the prime elements in successful wax testing. The more time you have for testing, the more likely you'll come up with the best wax. By using several matched pairs of skis, the variables in testing are reduced and it is possible to be more objective.

Based on the wax selection criteria, you have selected a few combinations of Alpine wax to be tested. Apply each wax or wax combination the full length of one pair of test skis and scrape. Number the skis and write each combination on a piece of paper. This helps you be objective.

Before you head out to the course, select the kicker waxes you want to test and put them in a fanny pack, along with corks, scrapers, and a rag or Fiberlene for cleaning the skis. The fanny pack will save time and trips back to the wax hut. Klisters and skares may mean return trips, unless you have a pack large enough to hold extra klisters and skares, plus a brush and a torch.

Initial wax testing should be done on a gentle hill with a flat outrun away from the start area. This situation provides ideal testing because it best approximates the conditions of the diagonal stride and the glide speed occurring most frequently when racing. All Alpine waxes will be fairly equal on steep downhills; the outrun will demonstrate which wax is actually the best. Don't expect one wax combination to be markedly better than the next; there will only be a marginal difference.

However, this marginal difference may be vital during a race. The U.S. Ski Team biomechanical study determined that a racer takes an average of 1.6 strides per second. In a 15-km race, assume the skier diagonal strides the entire distance and finishes in 45 minutes. This means he will take 4,320 strides during the race. If his Alpine wax gives him a glide that is two inches longer per stride than his opponent, the skier will have a 220-meter (720-foot) advantage over the opponent at the finish line.

To test Alpine wax, stand upright and still and glide down the gentle slope and out onto the flat. Mark the point where the skis stop gliding. Repeat this test on each pair of skis 3–5 times, marking the stopping points and standing upright in the same position each test. This process should narrow the best Alpine wax to what is on two pairs of skis. It's possible that one pair will obviously be the best. If the wax on two pairs of skis is very close in the glide test, test them on a much steeper hill. This should eliminate one wax and determine the best gliding wax for the day.

After settling on the best Alpine wax, remove the wax from the camber pocket with a metal scraper. Apply one combination of kicker wax to each test ski (a different wax on each single ski). Be consistent in the placement and amount of wax applied. Return to the gentle hill and repeat the Alpine wax test. This time, concern yourself with the end of the glide and how each ski compares with the other in a pair. The minute differences between kickers are best indicated at the end of a glide; the slower skis will have the best kick most of the time. As a check, test the waxes for kick as you ski to the top of the hill. Test each pair of skis a couple of times, then mix the best ski from each pair to compare them.

When you have narrowed the best kicker wax, test by climbing a hill of some magnitude. Climb once with poles and once without them. This final test should determine the best kicker wax combination. Remember, you are looking for the fastest ski with a good kick.

If there is time before heading back to wax the race skis, check the temperature again to see if any change is indicated. Check the tracks now that people have skied them. Are they getting soft or are they glazing? With skis waxed with the selected combinations, ski some of the course, particularly the highest sections of the course as a final test to ensure that the correct wax has been selected.

Keep in mind that it is possible to test waxes before race day. Relieve race-day pressure by testing wax during training sessions the week preceding the competition. These early tests may not come up with the right wax combination, but, unless the weather changes drastically, the tests will at least narrow the combinations of Alpine and kicker wax to be tested on race day.

Although I stated that there are no secrets to selecting the right wax, this does not imply that waxing is simple. Waxing takes a great deal of thought, study, time, experience, and work. Even then, picking the best wax can be difficult.

The best day of my career as a waxer, thus far, was about a month before the 1976 Olympics during the meet at Reit im Winkl, West Germany. All the American men were seeded toward the front for the 15-km race. The tracks were glazed and the temperature hovered around the freezing point. We decided to use a kicker combination of Rex red klister and red hard wax mixed with Rex OI. The course was two laps around a 7.5-km loop. When our guys came around the first lap, the U.S. coaches knew they were doing well, but they were ignored by the other international coaches and no one used our skiers for interval timing. By the middle of the second lap, we began to hear all this swearing and screaming out on the course as the other coaches realized the U.S. team was creaming the top stars. Led by Koch in third, the U.S. wound up with five guys in the top 10. Everyone began talking about the Americans' "secret" wax.

There are good days and bad days waxing. Sometimes you hit it just right, but other times you are out to lunch no matter how hard you work at it. Then it's up to the racer to make the best of a marginal situation.

WAX APPLICATION

Selecting the correct wax for race day is only half the battle. Proper application of that wax is equally important for success on the tracks. Wax application, like everything else in cross-country skiing, requires practice and knowledge of how to use the tools and equipment available.

Application of wax to fiberglass skis depends on indirect heat. Heat causes the wax to penetrate and bond to the micropore surface of P-Tex bases. Thus, waxing should be done in a heated room. If this is impossible, I would resort to waxing in a car with the heater on. Warm bases are most receptive to wax.

Use an electric iron with a thermostat to control the heat. It's a good idea to pack a long extension cord in your wax kit so you'll have access to electricity. Waxing irons heated with a torch should be used only if electricity is unavailable. There is no way to control the temperature of waxing irons, and direct heat from torches or from overheated irons may damage skis and alter wax characteristics. Skis can only withstand indirect heat, and an electric iron is the best way to provide indirect heat.

Before applying wax, scrape the skis. The kicking zone must be bare of wax, so apply wax remover with a clean cloth. Also be certain your iron, brushes, scrapers, and other tools are clean. Miscellaneous old wax, dirt, and grit can easily end up in your wax, which will definitely not help you ski faster.

A hand iron heated with a torch should be used only if electricity is unavailable for an electric iron. Waxing with a hand iron is a last resort but is better than no heat in applying both Alpine and kicker waxes.

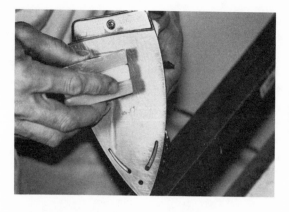

When dipping a combination of Alpine wax onto the base, hold the wax high on the iron so it mixes before reaching the ski. This method is used for combinations of up to three or four waxes. Be certain the iron is clean.

Alpine Wax Application

The method used to apply Alpine wax is dependent on the number of waxes in the combination. If a single wax is used, drip the wax onto the glide zones by holding the stick of wax against an iron set at 130°–140° F. If the wax smokes, your iron is too hot. After the wax has cooled a bit, iron it into the base using much the same motion you would use to iron clothing. Keep the iron moving to prevent scorching the wax or damaging the base. Drip on more wax as the ski accepts the initial penetration layer. Alternate ironing the tip and tail of each ski for about two minutes, then work on the other ski. Repeat the process three or four times.

The drip method may also be used for wax combinations of one:one (one blue and one red wax, for example) or two:one (two blues and one red). Be careful to hold the wax evenly against the midsection of the iron to ensure even melting. Then iron in the wax three or four times.

When using multiple combinations of Alpine wax, melt the waxes in a saucepan. An example of multiple combination would be three parts blue, one part red, and two parts yellow. A small camping stove heated by a propane or butane tank works well to melt the wax. The wax is applied to the ski with a one-inch brush and then worked into the ski with an iron. Melting wax in a pan can save both time and wax, even when using a single wax, when a number of skis are being prepared for a team of racers. On the other hand, I've seen individual skiers take a bar of Alpine wax, rub it on their skies, then iron it in as a way to save on wax.

Preparing Alpine Wax

After ironing the Alpine wax into the base, the skis are ready for the final preparation stage—working the wax into the best thickness and texture for the conditions. Four methods are available to the waxer, depending on the conditions: scraping, shaving, wire brushing, and/or filing. The first step is to determine the amount of wax that would remain on the ski. The two determinants are temperature and the condition of the snow. Generally, more wax is left on the ski in warmer temperatures to reduce friction and help overcome the suction created between the ski and the wet snow. Conversely, cold temperatures usually call for the removal of excess wax in order to eliminate drag.

However, the age and crystalline structure of the snow must also be considered. If it is

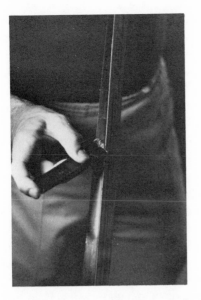

The first step in removing Alpine wax is scraping the sidewalls. Excess wax on the sidewalls will mean a slower ski.

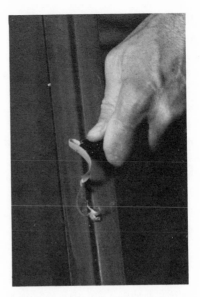

The second step in removing Alpine wax is scraping excess wax from the groove. Work from tip to tail.

In cold temperatures when most of the Alpine wax is to be removed, scrape the wax off by pushing a plastic scraper along the base, working from tip to tail.

−9° C but the snow is old and rounded, it is better to leave on more wax. On the other hand, if it is −9° C and the snow is new, excess wax should be removed because the snow crystals will have sharp points that will dig into excess wax and cause drag.

Scraping. In cold conditions (−13° C and below), scraping is used to remove as much Alpine wax as possible, unless the snow crystals are old and rounded. First, take a small plastic scraper and remove wax that has dripped off the base onto the sidewalls of the skis. Then use the rounded edge of a plastic scraper to remove wax in the grooves. Take a broad plastic (never metal) scraper to remove the wax from the base. Push the wax off with the scraper, working from tip to tail for molecular alignment.

When the Alpine wax has been scraped off and the kicker wax applied, put the skis outside to cool. Then scrape the glide zones once more with a plastic scraper to remove wax that might be compressed out of the micropores as they cool and contract.

Shaving. Shaving is the method of removing a limited amount of Alpine wax when the temperatures are above −13° C or when the snow crystals are rounded or old. This method leaves more wax on the skis than does the scraping method. First, remove the wax on the sidewalls, then remove some of the wax in the groove by gently pulling on the small, rounded scraper. To prepare the base, gently pull on the wax with a plastic scraper, working from tip to tail. This process evens out the ironing job but leaves a layer of wax on the ski.

Wire Brushing. In wet snow conditions when more Alpine wax is needed on the ski, use a wire brush on the glide zones (never on the kicker zones). This process breaks the suction created between the water in the snow and the base while skiing. This suction effect may be compared to what happens when a layer of water exists between two sheets of glass. To avoid the suction, use a stiff wire brush and take two or three firm strokes down the glide areas, working from tip to tail.

Filing. The technique of filing mini-grooves into the glide zones was developed by Fischer and was, for a time, kept secret. Filing works well to break the suction created while skiing in extremely wet snow conditions when there is free water in the snow.

Before applying Alpine wax, run the edge of a file down the glide zones. Hold the file firmly with both hands, use your fingers against the sidewalls for a brace or guide, and pull the file away from the tip toward the tail. Press firmly on the ski to develop a striated texture on the base. The striations should be increased in size as the amount of free water

With several firm strokes, the glide zones are striated with a wire brush to avoid suction in moist snow.

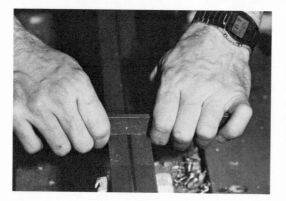

In extremely wet conditions, the glide zone is filed to reduce the suction between the snow and ski. Filing is used when the moisture content of the snow is such that water drips when a handful of snow is squeezed. The file creates striations in the base. Using your index fingers as a guide along the edge of the ski, press firmly, and work from tip to tail.

in the snow increases. Therefore, have a couple of variously graded mill bastard files in your wax kit. The base of the ski will be filed into striations much like those on a phonograph record. The tiny grooves may be removed later with a metal scraper or sandpaper. After filing, apply the hot Alpine wax; then shave and wire brush the glide zones. This process has a double effect in breaking suction; when the outer layers of wax wear off, there are striations in the base.

Hard Kicker Wax Application

Kicker waxes are broken down into two categories: hard waxes and klister/skares. Each type of kicker requires its own method of application. The goal in applying wax to the camber pocket is the same as in Alpine wax application—getting the wax to penetrate the micropores of the base.

Hard waxes are the easiest of the kicker waxes to apply and are used most frequently. Many waxing specialists, particularly Scandinavians, insist that hard waxes should be applied in several very thin layers. This isn't necessary. The Japanese proved in the early 1970s that it makes no difference whether the hard waxes are applied in one thick layer or in several thin layers. Layering hard kickers is a waste of time, unless conditions require using combinations of wax.

Ironing. To apply kicker wax, I prefer using an electric iron unless no electricity is available. The first step is to be certain both the iron and the camber pocket are clean and free of wax. Then rub the required thickness of the hard wax onto the camber pocket and work it in with an iron. Remember, the kicker should never extend behind the heel plate; in fact, I don't think it should extend behind the arch of your foot to ensure that you're riding on Alpine wax and not kicker wax on downhills. More kicker wax may be applied as needed after the skis have cooled. Additional coats may be ironed in, while the final coat should be corked into the base.

Ragging. Ragging is a method of kicker wax application that is used when there is no electricity source for an iron. Fold a soft cloth or piece of Fiberlene into a rectangle a bit narrower than half the width of the ski and long enough to obtain a brushing action. Apply the wax, then follow a torch up and down the camber pocket with the cloth, using a light painting motion. Perfecting this technique requires a bit of practice. When enough wax has been applied, let the skis cool and work the wax in with a cork. If a rag is unavailable, it is possible to work the wax in with a brush or a cork and a torch.

With a torch to heat the wax and base, follow the flame down the camber pocket to smooth kicker waxes. This process is known as ragging.

A torch may be used on the penetration layer of kicker waxes to ensure that the wax bonds to the base. The torch may also be used to glaze a harder wax over a softer wax by passing it quickly back and forth over the kicker zone.

Adjusting Kickers. After allowing the skis to cool from the wax application, ski on them for at least a kilometer (except in wet conditions) before making any adjustments to the kicker.

I have a three-letter code for adjusting kicker waxes: TLS. If your kicker is not working, the first adjustment is to make it thicker. If it still doesn't work, make the kicker longer. If that doesn't work, add a softer wax. Remember—Thicker, Longer, Softer. TLS.

If you lengthen the kicker area, be certain to feather the wax on the front end—decrease the thickness of kicker toward the glide zone. This is particularly important if the wax extends beyond the camber pocket. If a softer wax is needed, return to the original, shorter length of the kicker. Should the wax become too thick, scrape it off and start over. Thick wax will tend to ice up in warm conditions and will drag in most conditions. Remember, a long kicker—one beyond the camber pocket— will drastically affect the glide capabilities of the ski, particularly in the diagonal stride.

If you are uncertain exactly where the camber pocket ends, put on an extra-long kicker wax then go out and ski. Progressively cut back the kicker by two inches with a metal scraper. Ski, cut back the kicker, and ski again until you have no kick. Reverse the process (add two inches of wax) until a balance between good kick and good glide is found. This should define the camber pocket.

Klister/Skare Application

Klisters and skares are used in conditions when the snow has melted and refrozen. Klisters are effective in wet, granular, refrozen snow, and skares are used when the snow is very harsh and frozen. Because these conditions occur infrequently in many sections of the ski world, many skiers have little experience in the selection and application of klisters and skares.

There are three main factors to consider when applying skares and klisters. Be certain to smooth them well to prevent icing. When combining more than one, mix them well. Clean the sidewalls before putting the skis out to cool to prevent the skis from becoming slow or grabby.

Ironing. Ironing in klisters and skares works best when only a single wax is used or when using skare for a base wax. Apply the klister/skare in long streaks on each side of the groove; globbing the wax on prevents an even coat. Then iron the wax into the ski.

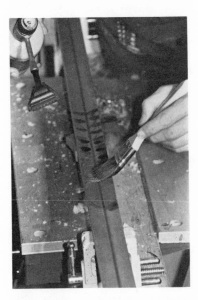

When using a combination of klisters, apply them in diagonal strips. Heat them moderately with a torch and brush the klisters in using a circular motion to mix the different waxes. Then smooth the waxes.

Brushing. Apply the wax to the ski in long lines when using one wax or in short, diagonal lines when using more than one klister/skare. Take a 1- or 1½-inch paintbrush and follow a torch up and down the ski. Using a painting motion, smooth the wax, much as is done in the ragging method. If more than one wax is being used, swirl the waxes with the brush before smoothing to ensure a thorough mix.

Painting. Paint on klisters and skares when there are a large number of skis to be waxed and you plan to use more than one wax. Warm the tubes and then empty them into a saucepan. Mix the waxes thoroughly as they heat. Paint the waxes on the ski with a brush, much like Alpine wax is painted on the glide zones.

WAXING TIPS

Waxing well is a function of experience and experiments. After more than 30 years of skiing, I have learned a few tricks about waxing. Following are a few tips and suggestions that should make the difficult job of waxing a bit easier.

Alpine Waxes

■ The latest thing in Alpine waxing is to mix brands. This technique works best using waxes from the same temperature range. An example would be to mix one part Falline blue with two parts of Holmenkol blue.

■ Never polish Alpine wax with a cork because it makes the wax too smooth, increasing the suction with the snow.

■ Hot waxing is a never-ending process. Your skis should always be carrying wax—for travel, summer storage, always. The wax protects the bases, keeps them clean, and prevents them from oxidizing.

■ Be certain to keep Alpine waxes clean. Don't let dust and dirt from your wax kit end up on the bases of your skis via wax.

Kicker Waxes

■ Many waxers don't think it's necessary to prep and wax grooves, especially in the camber pocket. I would suggest they look at some ski tracks; the groove is in obvious contact with the snow, so it must be waxed and prepped like the rest of the base.

■ In cleaning kickers from skis after a race, use a plastic scraper to remove the majority of the wax. Finish the job with wax remover. Use a torch only if all else fails. By the way, dry-cleaning fluid (known as Perc) available at any dry cleaners works well to clean skis and is much cheaper than the wax removers available from the wax companies.

■ Avoid using your hands to rub in waxes because the grease from them will cut the wax. I'd only use my hands if I were out in the woods and didn't have a cork or rag along.

■ If you don't let skis cool after waxing, they will be slippery or icy. Remember, synthetic skis take longer to cool than the old wooden skis.

■ I am a synthetic cork supporter. The synthetic corks require much less elbow grease and do a better job of smoothing wax. You need three open-celled corks in your wax kit: one for soft kickers, one for hard kickers, and one for klisters and skares.

■ Binder wax is used under extremely harsh conditions to bond the kicker waxes to the ski and improve their wear. Binders are now used much more frequently by racers with fiberglass skis. In harsh conditions, a binder and hard wax combination is faster than a skare and hard wax mix. Stick with a stiffer pair of skis to avoid wear. Any of the application methods are acceptable for bonding the binder to the ski, although ironing is the most effective method. Apply binders only in thin or medium-thick layers. If the binder is hard and rubs on spottily, hold it directly in a flame for a few seconds and then apply it with long strokes. In applying the kicker wax over the binder, use heat to bond the two. You may want to pass the kicker wax through the flame. The final coat of kicker may be applied outside. Polish with a cork, being careful not to rub too hard and pull up the binder.

■ Skiers should be aware of how to wax for man-made snow. Machine-made snow is very slow when it is first laid down due to the amounts of air and moisture in it. Once it has been farmed, manicured, and tracks have been set, it becomes very hard and is likely to be abrasive because it is actually ice. A binder will often be necessary when the temperature is below 32° F. Above that, man-made snow calls for klister/skares sooner than natural snow. The one thing to watch for is that the machine-made snow changes characteristics very fast as the temperature changes.

■ If you are racing in marginal conditions or over 30 km, wear a fanny pack with extra waxes and a scraper and small cork so you can rewax if necessary. Even if you have coaches out on the course with extra wax, they aren't likely to be in the right place at the right time. Snow changes quickly, but if you carry a fanny pack, you'll be able to make the change immediately.

■ When first developing waxing skills, don't limit yourself to one brand of wax, as many people advise. Work with at least two brands so you learn faster and, importantly, have a basis for comparison of each brand's glide and kick efficiency.

■ Without the option of changing wax, the skier has the option of changing his technique during the race if he has blown the wax or wax application. Technique is a function of wax application; you have to adjust your technique to the wax you've applied. For example, if your kicker is too long for the conditions, start double poling on those flats where you otherwise would be gliding.

■ If you lose a lot of kicker wax while racing, switch skis. Wax wears on the inside edge first, so the 15 seconds it may take to switch skis from one foot to the other will give you kick that may save minutes off your race time.

■ In wet conditions, stay off your racing skis until the last possible moment. Trust the wax job and warm up on test skis. The water and dirt the wax picks up will cost time, particularly in the first kilometers.

■ When using klister/skare waxes, keep your skis moving. Don't stand still or the chance of the kicker icing is increased. Also be aware that it is easy to pick up paper and dirt in the start area.

■ If you need to make final adjustments to your skare/klister kicker when out on the course or in the start area, warm the tubes of wax up by placing them in your armpits for easier application.

■ Be aware of snow crystal size in selecting klisters and skares, particularly in spring conditions. Temperature may indicate a blue skare, but crystal size may call for a red klister. A mix of the two is necessary.

■ Remember to be especially careful cleaning your skis after using skares and klisters. Remove all the wax.

■ When using silver klisters, remember that Rode silvers are for kick, Rex are for glide, and Swix is in between. Be careful with Rex and Swix silver klisters because both contain aluminum powder, which can overpower other waxes in a combination. Mix them well during application.

■ In warm conditions, use a coat of hard skare under the warm klisters to keep them from sliding over the edges and into the grooves of your skis.

■ In variable klister/skare conditions when the snow changes from wet to frozen, layer the klister under the skare rather than mixing them. The skare is faster through the wet snow and the kick will come from the cushion effect of the klister underneath. In order to layer the skare, cool the klister down before adding the skare layer.

■ Rode Chola is supposed to be a binder for klisters and skares, but Rode special blue, Rex blue, and Swix green are all more effective.

■ I often break the old rule about only applying a softer wax on top of a hard one. Try putting a couple of coats of a softer wax under the selected kicker wax. For example, put a coat or two of Rode blue under a Rode green kicker. To improve the bond between the two waxes, hold the harder wax in a flame to soften it, then crayon it over the softer wax. This technique puts a cushioning effect into the kicker. The grip is improved because the soft wax acts like a cushion. Also, in longer races as the harder wax wears off, the softer wax will grip as the temperature climbs and you tire.

■ Try mixing extra blue waxes with other colors. The result is blellow (extra blue and yellow), bled (extra blue and red), and burple (extra blue and purple). These mixes have often been successful. An easier way to achieve much the same result is to use the two-wax systems developed for ski tourers. These "plus-and-minus" systems are wide-range waxes and work well with short kickers. The systems are available from Swix, Rex, and Toko.

■ When planning your kicker for marathons and 30-km races, think backward. The first layer of kicker wax you apply should be planned for the final 10 km of the course, keeping the predicted snow and weather conditions in mind. The second coat of kicker is for the snow on the course 10–20 km from the finish. A distance race will often require three or four different coats of kicker wax and the layers may vary in thickness, depending on the anticipated conditions. You have to be aware of how much time you expect it will take you to finish and what weather and temperature changes are predicted during that time.

■ Watching the weather the two or three days preceding the race will give you a good indication of what will occur on race day. Take advantage of local forecasts as well as national weather trends.

■ When waxing for a race of over 30 km, I'll use binder 90% of the time. The thickness of the binder will vary, depending on the coarseness of the snow the wax will have to withstand.

■ There are times when there is simply nothing to be done to improve your kick. In some new snow, a condition known as snow shear occurs. A longer kick is called for, but the skis will still slip. The wax might be correct and bond well with the snow, but the top layer of snow crystals doesn't bond with the snow crystals underneath. Therefore, the upper snow crystals bond to the wax, but then slip on the crystals below. In snow shear conditions, you simply have to work harder—a good kick wax is nearly impossible so you have to compensate with strong arms and good uphill technique.

The only consistency in waxing cross-country skis is the inconsistency. There are no hard and fast rules to waxing. There are only theories, ambiguities, and variables. Waxing is a day-to-day and, more accurately, an hour-to-hour challenge. The waxer must deal with the weather and utilize the information available. His job is one of continual evaluation. Nothing is concrete. He must take the objective information available and evaluate all the variables to come up with the right wax on race day. Be organized and as objective as possible and a successful wax combination will be selected. Hard work and careful evaluation are the only secrets to successful waxing.

Once the wax is on and the race has started, success is up to the skier. Don't use marginal wax as an excuse for a poor race. It's easy to ski well when waxing conditions aren't a problem. When waxing is difficult, everyone in the race has the same problem. The winners are those who tough it out despite bad wax. Wax may be the final link between the skier and the snow, but the determined racer is the final link in covering the distance one stride ahead.

8

THE CHALLENGE

Be Open Minded and Motivated

Cross-country ski racing is open-ended, individual, and continually evolving. No book can cover the sport all-inclusively through words, pictures, and charts. The skier must absorb the information and then use his imagination, study the philosophies of experts, and be aware of new techniques and theories to determine the best program for him in his quest to reach his potential. While keeping up-to-date on the sport as it evolves, the skier must pay special attention to the various aspects of skiing that remain constant.

The off-season is the time when you find out about your body and its potential. Training for the serious athlete involves a certain amount of overtraining, pushing the body to determine its current limits. This doesn't mean that you go out and bury yourself in exhaustion every training session, but that you are willing to occasionally press yourself to see how your body reacts to maximum effort. You learn most about yourself by overtraining, not undertraining.

One of the weakest parts of the programs of America's elite racers is winter training. Too many racers are unsure of what they should be doing between races to keep in readiness for competition. The goal in the winter is, obviously, success on the race course, but this success won't come without a specific program including a good balance of competition and training. The training must be flexible and planned around the racing schedule, and the athlete must have a good understanding of the type of training necessary between events.

Equipment is perhaps the simplest part of cross-country skiing. The rules are straightforward—obtain the best equipment possible and take care of it. A few minutes spent here and there maintaining equipment will avoid last-minute panics such as running around trying to find a basket for your pole the night before a race when you should be spending your time relaxing and concentrating on that race. If you take care of your equipment, it will take care of you.

Because Americans in general don't compete enough, they have limited racing experience and fail to implement beneficial racing strategy and tactics. Think more about all the seemingly small details of competition that will combine to make your job of covering the race course more successful.

After the hours of training, selection and care of equipment, and planning race strategy and tactics carefully, it's amazing how many racers get out on the course and ski with poor technique. Too little thought and effort is put into technique at all levels by individuals and by the sport as a whole. Fortunately, the recent biomechanical studies have provided us with a concrete base from which we can develop efficient skiing technique.

During racing and training, conversations always seem to begin and end with the subject of waxing. It presents a challenge to examine all the variables and determine the perfect wax for the conditions. However, I like to think that waxing is relatively easy. If you are willing to spend the time and effort and to use your imagination and experiment, you'll find at least an adequate wax.

The ultimate challenge in our sport is to take all its vastly different aspects, from weight lifting to the reverse shoulder, and pull them together so you are able to reach your potential in a particular race, over a particular competitive season, and throughout a racing career. Meeting this challenge involves the ability to recognize our weaknesses, to work hard to determine a better method, and to implement the change into our program. As the philosopher said, know thyself. Look in the mirror with candor and honesty to see who's there. Recognize the missing links in yourself and your program so you build a complete skier through a viable program.

In working with and observing skiers of various abilities over the years, I've identified a common bond among those who have been successful—motivation. The key to their success is their commitment to their sport. They don't require an external source to get them to train and race at their best. Their desire and dedication can overcome their weaknesses and limitations. Provided with a solid program, they move ahead on their own, determined to reach their potential. They are, stride for stride, up with every new aspect of technique, training, equipment, waxing, and racing. This motivation puts them one stride ahead at the finish line.

GLOSSARY

A   **acclimatization** Adapting to varying environmental conditions, such as cold, high altitude, or time zones.

adaptation The changes that will occur in the body due to the specific methods of training.

aerobic In the presence of oxygen.

aerobic threshold The training zone of each individual at which aerobic fitness improves, leading to peripheral circulatory benefits; considered to be 70% of the individual's maximum heart rate.

agility The ability to change direction quickly while maintaining control over the body.

anaerobic In the absence of oxygen.

anaerobic threshold The training zone above which the anaerobic system dominates performance, leading to central circulatory benefits. Considered to be 80% of the individual's maximum heart rate.

B   **balance** The capacity of the body to maintain a state of equilibrium while standing or during motion.

biomechanics The utilization of the science of mechanics to analyze physiological movements.

body composition The relative amounts of fat and lean weight.

C   **calorie** A measure of energy that is the amount of heat required to raise one kilogram of water one degree centigrade.

camber The arc or curve built into skis designed to support the skier's weight while allowing for maximum glide and climb performance.

camber pocket/kicker zone That area of the ski base to be waxed with cross-country kick wax. Includes approximately the middle third of the ski.

carbo loading A process of exhaustive exercise to deplete glycogen in the muscle followed by a three-day diet emphasis on increasing carbohydrate intake.

carbohydrate A basic food stuff, including sugars, starches, and cellulose, that contains only carbon, hydrogen, and oxygen; the primary source of energy.

concentric contraction When the tension or force exerted by the muscle shortens that muscle.

coordination The ability to integrate the action of the body in the most efficient pattern to accomplish a specific movement or series of movements.

cryonetics The use of cold therapy for the treatment of muscular and joint injury or trauma.

D   **dehydration** The condition that results from the excessive loss of body fluids.

duration The length of time of a repetition, set, activity, or workout.

E   **eccentric contraction** Maintaining tension as the muscle lengthens.

endurance The ability to persist in a physical activity and resist fatigue.

energy Capacity or ability to perform work.

extension When the joint angle increases or the parts of the joint move away from each other.

F   **F.I.S.** Federation International de Ski, the international ruling body for skiing.

fartlek (speed play) Swedish term and training method involving the use of different levels of speed during a workout.

fatigue State of decreased physical efficiency resulting from prolonged or excessive exertion.

flexibility The range of motion possible in a joint.

flexion When the joint angle decreases or the parts of the joint move towards each other.

frequency How often a bout of exercise or training takes place.

G   **glide zone** Those zones of the ski base that are treated with Alpine or glider waxes, determined to be about the front third and back third of the ski.

glucose A simple sugar.

glycogen Form in which glucose is stored in the body, found in liver and muscles.

H   **heart monitor** A device, usually worn on the body, to determine heart rates; used to monitor heart rates in training.

heat exhaustion A condition of fatigue caused by prolonged exposure to heat.

heat stroke Overexposure to heat characterized by high body temperature, hot, dry skin, and sometimes delirium or unconsciousness; can be fatal.

hemoglobin Iron molecule found in red blood cells, capable of combining with oxygen.

hyperthermia Increase in body temperature; a potential problem during summer training.

hypothermia Decrease in body temperature; a potential problem during winter training and racing.

I   **imagery** The practice of mentally creating images or pictures.

intensity The rate of exercise; related to maximal oxygen uptake or heart rate.

interval training Method of physical conditioning that alternates periods of activity with periods of rest or active recovery.

isokenetic The contraction of a muscle against a load or resistance that increases while moving.

isometric The contraction of the muscle against a nonmoving resistance.

isotonic The contraction of a muscle against a load or resistance that is constant and moving.

K **kinesthetic sense** The awareness of body parts and positions in relation to the rest of the body.

L **lactic acid** By-product of anaerobic glycolysis.

lever A rigid bar turning about an axis. In physical activity, the bar is the bone, the joint the axis, and the turning or movement is brought about by the muscle.

load The resistance or amount of work required to bring about certain training effects.

M **maximum oxygen uptake (mVO₂)** The power or capacity of the oxygen system. Best single measure of fitness. Evaluated while in an aerobic state.

N **natural intervals** The interval training effect that occurs while running or skiing over undulating terrain. A method of endurance training.

O **orthotics** Devices used to correct alignment, length, and other problems with the legs and feet. Used in the training shoes and ski boots.

overload principle Greater load than normally experienced, used to affect a training effect in the body.

oxygen debt The amount of oxygen consumed during recovery from exercise above that ordinarily consumed at rest in the same period. Created by an anaerobic physical state.

P **parabolic** Concerning the camber line of a ski, this is a smooth curve.

parametric Concerning the camber line of a ski, this has the appearance of a smooth curve but has a definite high point or sharpness at the middle of the camber pocket.

peaking The union of the physiological, psychological, and technical abilities of an athlete that allows him to perform at the highest level of his potential.

plyometrics The lengthening of a muscle (putting it in stretch) before its contractile phase. This encourages a stronger contraction.

power The rate of doing work.

$$\text{Power} = \frac{\text{Force} \times \text{Distance}}{\text{Time}}$$

P-Tex ruff The roughened condition of the P-Tex base of a ski.

pulse rate Frequency of contractions of the heart.

S **self-evaluation testing (SET)** A series of prescribed tests to evaluate a person's level of physical conditioning.

specificity A principle that develops the skills and energy systems to meet the demands of a specific activity.

steady state Where the demands of the exercise are met by the energy system; aerobic state.

strategy The planning and directing of operations for battle. In cross-country, dealing with the variables, logistics, and preparations for competition.

strength The capacity of a muscle to exert force against a resistance in one maximum effort.

stride length The distance a body moves per each cycle of motion.

stride rate The number of times the basic movement cycle is completed in a given time period. Average race pace is 2.2 strides per second for hill running and 1.6 strides per second for diagonal.

T   **tactics** The procedures used to accomplish a specific goal. In racing, those methods (within the rules) that produce the fastest possible time.

tempo training Short training bouts where heart rates and pace are at or above race speed.

total muscle fatigue Principles of Nautilus weight training programs, where you cannot lift the weight another repetition at the completion of the prescribed work load.

V   **velocity** The speed at which the skier moves across the snow. Determined by multiplying stride length by stride rate.

$$\text{Velocity} = \text{Stride length} \times \text{Stride rate}$$

vertical work load The rate (km/hr) times the amount of vertical feet covered divided by the constant 3,281 ft/km in a given training bout or period.

$$\text{VWL} = \frac{\text{KPH} \times \text{Vertical ft}}{3,281 \text{ ft/km}}$$

REFERENCES
AND
SOURCES

REFERENCES

Anderson, B. *Stretching*. (Box 2734) Fullerton, Calif. 92633: 1975.

Barrow, H. M., R. McGee. *A Practical Approach to Measurement in Physical Education*. Philadelphia: Lea & Febiger, 1964.

Clafs, C. E., D. D. Arnheim. *Modern Principles of Athletic Training*. St. Louis: The C. V. Mosby Company, 1969.

Guyton, A. C.: *Text of Medical Physiology*. Philadelphia: W. B. Saunders Co., 1976.

Massey, B. H., et al. *The Kinesiology of Weight Lifting*. Dubuque: William C. Brown Company Publishers, 1959.

Mathews, D. K., E. L. Fox. *The Physiological Basis of Physical Education and Athletics*. Philadelphia: W. B. Saunders Company, 1976.

Mirkin, G., H. Marshall. *The Sportsmedicine Book*. Boston: Little, Brown & Co., 1978.

Page, J., et al.: *U.S. Ski Team Cross-Country Coaches Manual*. Park City, Ut.: U.S. Ski Team, 1978.

Pettersen, L-G., L. Skogsberg, U. Zackrlsson. *Examen Sarbetg Pa Idrottslaralinjen Vid Gymnastik*. Stockholm: Specialarbete Idrottslaralinjen GIH, 1977.

Sharkey, B. J. *Physiology of Fitness*. Champaign, Ill.: Human Kinetics Publishers, 1979.

SOURCES

Edsbyn, 860 Decatur Ave. North, Minneapolis, Minn. 55427. Edsbyn roller skis and poles.

Exel-Silenta, 465 New Boston Park, Woburn, Mass. 01801. Roller ski poles and ferrules.

Exer-Genie, Box 3237, Fullerton, Calif. 92634. Exer-Genie training device.

Reliable Racing Supply, 624 Glen St., Glens Falls, N.Y. 12801. Road Ski roller skis, poles, and overboots.

Sepp Sport, 1805 Monroe St., Madison, Wis. 53711. Roletto roller skis.

United States Ski Association, Box 777, Brattleboro, Vt. 05301. Membership and classification for organized racing.

United States Ski Coaches Association, Box 1747, Park City, Ut. 84060. Training logs, testing and evaluation, films, journals, books, etc.

United States Ski Team, Box 100, Park City, Ut. 84060. International license, national point list, Nordic technical office, national and international racing calendars.

INDEX

INDEX OF
CHARTS AND TABLES